Complexity and the Experience of Leading Organizations

The perspective of complex responsive processes draws on analogies from the complexity sciences, bringing in the essential characteristics of human agents, understood to emerge in social processes of communicative interaction and power relating. The result is a way of thinking about life in organizations that focuses attention on how organizational members cope with the unknown as they perpetually create organizational futures together.

Providing a natural successor to the editors' earlier series *Complexity and Emergence in Organizations*, this series, *Complexity as the Experience of Organizing*, aims to develop this work further by taking very seriously the *experience* of organizational practitioners, and showing how adopting the perspective of complex responsive processes yields deeper insight into practice and so develops that practice.

In this book, all the contributors work as leaders, consultants or managers in organizations. They provide narrative accounts of their actual work, addressing questions such as:

- What does it mean, in actual everyday terms, to lead a large organization?
- How do leaders learn to lead?
- What are the apparent or real contradictions inherent in the experience of leading?

In considering such questions in terms of their daily experience, the contributors (all experienced leaders) explore how the perspective of complex responsive processes assists them to make sense of their experience and so to develop their practice. *Complexity and the Experience of Leading Organizations* offers a different method for making sense of experience in a rapidly changing world by using reflective accounts of ordinary everyday life in organizations rather than idealized accounts. The editors' commentary introduces and contextualizes these experiences as well as drawing out key themes for further research.

Complexity and the Experience of Leading Organizations will be of value to readers from among those academics and business school students and practitioners who are looking for reflective accounts of real life experiences of *leadership* in organizations, rather than further prescriptions of what life in organizations ought to be like.

Professor **Douglas Griffin** is Associate Director of the Complexity and Management Centre at the Business School of the University of Hertfordshire and a supervisor on the Doctor of Management programme run by the Centre. He is also an independent consultant. He is one of the editors of the *Complexity and Emergence in Organizations* series, and the editor of three books in this series.

Ralph Stacey is Director of the Complexity and Management Centre at the Business School of the University of Hertfordshire and Director of the Doctor of Management programme run by the Centre. He is one of the editors of the *Complexity and Emergence in Organizations* series, and the editor of five books in this series.

Complexity and the Experience of Leading Organizations

Edited by
Douglas Griffin and Ralph Stacey

Routledge
Taylor & Francis Group

LONDON AND NEW YORK

First published 2005
by Routledge
2 Park Square, Milton Park, Abingdon, Oxon OX14 4RN

Simultaneously published in the USA and Canada
by Routledge
270 Madison Ave, New York, NY 10016

Routledge is an imprint of the Taylor & Francis Group

© 2005 Douglas Griffin and Ralph Stacey

Typeset in Times by Keystroke, Jacaranda Lodge, Wolverhampton
Printed and bound in Great Britain by TJ International Ltd, Padstow, Cornwall

British Library Cataloguing in Publication Data
A catalogue record for this book is available from the British Library

Library of Congress Cataloging in Publication Data
Complexity and the experience of leading organizations /
    Douglas Griffin and Ralph Stacey [editors].— 1st ed.
        p. cm.
    Includes bibliographical references and index.
    1. Leadership. 2. Management. I. Griffin, Douglas, 1946–
    II. Stacey, Ralph D.
    HD57.7.C65 2005
    658.4′092—dc22   2004026095

ISBN 0–415–36692–5 (hbk)
ISBN 0–415–36693–3 (pbk)

Contents

Contributors

Douglas Griffin is an independent consultant, visiting Professor at the Business School of the University of Hertfordshire, and Associate Director of the Complexity and Management Centre.

Andrew Lee is Director of Human Resources and an Executive Director of UNITE. He trained as an executive coach with the Alexander Corporation. He graduated as Doctor of Management at the University of Hertfordshire in 2003.

Michael Shiel is Director of the Advanced Management Programme at the Irish Management Institute and adjunct faculty member of the Leadership Institute at the University of San Diego, California. He graduated as Doctor of Management at the University of Hertfordshire in 2003.

Ralph Stacey is Professor of Management at the Business School of the University of Hertfordshire and Director of its Complexity and Management Centre. He is also a member of the Institute of Group Analysis.

James Taylor is currently CEO of the University of Louisville Hospital. He graduated as Doctor of Management at the University of Hertfordshire in 2003.

John Tobin is President of the Greater Waterbury Health Network and President/Chief Executive Officer of The Waterbury Hospital. He graduated as Doctor of Management at the University of Hertfordshire in 2003.

Richard Williams was CEO of Westminster Kingsway College, and in July 2004 he left the further education sector to take up a new role as CEO of a charity working with young people and adults across the UK. He has completed the Doctor of Management programme at the University of Hertfordshire.

Series preface

Complexity as the Experience of Organizing

Edited by Ralph Stacey, Douglas Griffin and Patricia Shaw

Complexity as the Experience of Organizing is a sequel to the highly successful series *Complexity and Emergence in Organizations* also edited by the editors of this series. The first series has attracted international attention for its development of the theory of complex responsive processes and its implications for those working in organizations. The perspective of complex responsive processes draws on analogies from the complexity sciences, bringing in the essential characteristics of human agents, namely consciousness and self-consciousness, understood to emerge in social processes of communicative interaction, power relating and evaluative choice. The result is a way of thinking about life in organizations that focuses attention on how organizational members cope with the unknown as they perpetually create organizational futures together. This second series aims to develop that work by taking seriously the experience of organizational practitioners, showing how adopting the perspective of complex responsive processes yields deeper insight into practice and so develops that practice.

Contributors to the volumes in the series work as leaders, consultants or managers in organizations. The contributors provide narrative accounts of their actual work, addressing such questions as: What does it mean, in ordinary everyday terms, to lead a large organization? How do leaders learn to lead? What does it mean, in ordinary everyday terms, to consult managers in an organization? How does the work of the consultant assist managers when the uncertainty is so great that they do not yet know what they are doing? What does executive coaching achieve? What happens in global change programs such as installing competencies, managing diversity and assuring quality? Why do organizations get stuck in repetitive patterns of behavior? What kinds of change may be facilitated? In considering such questions in terms of their daily experience, the contributors explore how the perspective of complex responsive processes assists them in making sense of their experience and so develop their practices.

The books in the series are addressed to organizational practitioners and academics who are looking for a different way of making sense of their own experience in a rapidly changing world. The books will attract readers looking for reflective accounts of ordinary everyday life in organizations rather than idealized accounts or further prescriptions.

Other volumes in the series:

A Complexity Perspective on Researching Organizations
Taking experience seriously
Edited by Ralph Stacey and Douglas Griffin

Experiencing Emergence in Organizations
Local interaction and the emergence of global pattern
Edited by Ralph Stacey

Experiencing Risk, Spontaneity and Improvisation in Organizational Change
Working live
Edited by Patricia Shaw and Ralph Stacey

Complexity and the Experience of Managing in Public Sector Organizations
Edited by Ralph Stacey and Douglas Griffin

1 Introduction: leading in a complex world

Ralph Stacey and Douglas Griffin

- **Mainstream perspectives on leadership**
- **The perspective of complex responsive processes**
- **The properties of complex responsive processes of relating**
- **The consequences of taking a complex responsive processes perspective**
- **The implications for leaders and leadership**
- **The chapters in this book**

Over the period 2000 to 2002, a number of us at the Complexity and Management Centre at the Business School of the University of Hertfordshire published a series of books called *Complexity and Emergence in Organizations* (Stacey *et al.*, 2000; Stacey, 2001; Fonseca, 2001; Griffin, 2002; Streatfield, 2001; Shaw, 2002). These books developed a perspective according to which organizations are understood to be ongoing, iterated processes of cooperative and competitive relating between people. We argued that organizations are not systems but the ongoing patterning of interactions between people. Patterns of human interaction produce further patterns of interaction, not some *thing* outside of the interaction. We called this perspective *complex responsive processes of relating*. One of the volumes (Griffin, 2002) explored what this perspective means when it comes to thinking about leaders and leadership, particularly the ethical implications.

Since 2000, some of the authors in the series, together with other Complexity and Management Centre colleagues in association with the Institute of Group Analysis, have been conducting a research program on organizational change leading to the degrees of Master of Arts by research or Doctor of Management. This is necessarily a part-time program because the core of the research method (see another volume in this series: Stacey and Griffin, 2005) involves students taking their own experience seriously. If patterns of human interaction produce nothing but further patterns of human interaction, in the creation of which we are all participating, then there is no detached way of understanding organizations from the position of the objective observer. Instead, organizations have to be understood in terms of one's own personal experience of participating with others in the co-creation of the patterns of interaction that are the organization. The students' research is, therefore, their narration of current events they are involved in together with their reflections on themes of particular importance emerging in the stories of their own experience of participation with others to create the patterns of interaction that are the organization. The research stance is, then, one of detached involvement.

For some of the students, the central theme in their work has to do with leading and leadership, and how they think about these matters in a way that is provoked by the theory of complex responsive processes. In exploring this theme they also show how thinking differently about what they are doing inevitably involves doing things differently. The purpose of this volume is to bring together some of the work of those who have been concerned with leading. Two chapters are by CEOs of hospitals in the USA, one is by the CEO of a large Further Education College in the UK, another is by the Human Resources Director of a commercial organization, also in the UK, and the final one is by an educator of leaders in Ireland. At the end of this introductory chapter, we give a brief indication of what each of these authors cover and what the central themes of the volume are. We will also be introducing each chapter with an editorial comment. Before doing that, however, we provide a short, and so necessarily compact, summary of what we mean by the theory of complex responsive processes, what it implies about leaders and leadership and how this differs from other traditions of thought about these matters. Further details of these arguments are also set out in Chapter 2, which focuses on the role of the leader emerging in social processes of mutual recognition, and in Chapter 5, which explores how values arise in human interaction and how one might think about the link with leading.

Mainstream perspectives on leadership

The most prevalent way of thinking about organizations today is one in which an organization is understood as a system consisting of individuals who interact with each other to produce it. The organizational system is then understood as interacting with other organizational systems, competing with some to supply goods and services to others as well as to individual consumers, taking in supplies from yet other organizations, and negotiating with regulatory and other government bodies, also understood as systems. In their interaction, these organizational systems create industrial, economic, social and global supra-systems, which then affect them. It is generally thought to be the role of the leaders of an organization to set its direction in the form of vision, purpose, objectives and targets, and then to apply monitoring forms of control to ensure that the vision and so on is realized. It is also generally thought to be the role of an organization's leaders to shape its values or culture, understood to be the deep-seated assumptions governing the behavior of the individual members of an organization. In shaping these values, leaders are exerting a social form of control. One of the most influential writers on leadership and organizations, Schein (1985), says that 'the unique and essential function of leadership is the manipulation of culture' (p. 317).

An equally influential writer, Senge (1990), talks about building a vision as one piece of the 'governing ideas' of the organization, the other pieces being purpose and values, with the three elements together answering to the question of what we believe in. He provides examples of companies who have deliberately constructed values and taught their people in training sessions to act according to those values. The leader forms a personal vision and asks others to follow him or her so that they come to share commitment to that vision, which should flow naturally from genuine enthusiasm for the vision. Leaders must be skilled in building shared visions, and such sharing, which takes a long time to emerge, is the product of ongoing dialogue. Such dialogue is a facilitated conversation in which people suspend their assumptions and listen to each other, thus getting in touch with a common pool of meaning which is said to flow through them. Senge describes leaders as integrators of learning disciplines – they design the governing ideas and the learning process, they act as stewards of the vision through their purpose story and they also assume the role of teachers.

In this way of thinking an organization is treated as a thing, a system, which actually exists outside of the individuals who form it. The leaders play a significant role in designing this system, specifying its purpose and inspiring others to act according to values that will achieve this purpose. The organizational system so created unfolds the purpose and vision ascribed to it by leaders, and for this to happen its individual members must share a commitment to act in a way that does unfold the ascribed vision and purpose. In thinking in this way, we argue, we are covering over the complexity and uncertainty we actually experience in our ordinary everyday experience of life in organizations, and we are positing capacities of foresight in leaders which they do not actually possess. It is for this reason that we have been developing an alternative way of thinking about organizations which has come to be known as a complex responsive processes perspective (Stacey *et al.*, 2000; Stacey, 2001, 2003; Griffin, 2002; Shaw, 2002).

The perspective of complex responsive processes

From the perspective of complex responsive processes, organizations are viewed as patterns of interaction between people that are iterated as the present. Instead of abstracting from the experience of human bodily interaction, which is what we do when we posit that individuals create a system in their interaction, the perspective of complex responsive processes stays with the experience of interaction which produces nothing but further interaction. In other words, one moves from thinking in terms of a spatial metaphor, as one does when one thinks that individuals interact to produce a system outside them at a higher level, to a temporal processes way of thinking, where the temporal processes are those of human relating. Organizations are then understood as processes of human relating, because it is in the simultaneously cooperative–consensual and conflictual–competitive relating between people that everything organizational happens. It is through these ordinary, everyday processes of relating that people in organizations cope with the complexity and uncertainty of organizational life. As they do so, they perpetually construct their future together as the present.

Complex responsive processes of relating may be understood as acts of communication, relations of power, and the interplay between people's choices arising in acts of evaluation.

Acts of communication

It is because human agents are conscious and self-conscious that they are able to cooperate and reach consensus, while at the same time conflicting and competing with each other in the highly sophisticated ways in which they do. Drawing on the work of the American pragmatist George Herbert Mead (1934), one can understand consciousness (that is, mind) as arising in the communicative interaction between human bodies. Humans have evolved central nervous systems such that when one gestures to another, particularly in the form of vocal gesture or language, one evokes in one's own body responses to one's gesture that are similar to those evoked in other bodies. In other words, in their acting, humans take the attitude, the tendency to act, of the other, and it is because they have this capacity that humans can know what they are doing. It immediately follows that consciousness (knowing, mind) is a social process in which meaning emerges in the social act of gesture–response, where the gesture can never be separated from the response. Meaning does not lie in the gesture, the word, alone, but in the gesture taken together with the response to it as one social act.

Furthermore, in communicating with each other as the basis of everything they do, people do not simply take the attitude of the specific others with whom they are relating. Humans have the capacity for generalizing so that when they act they always take up the attitude of what Mead called 'the generalized other'. In other words, they always take the attitude of the group or society to their actions – they are concerned about what others might think of what they do or say. This is often unconscious and it is, of course, a powerful form of social control. According to Mead, self-consciousness is also a social process involving the capacity humans have to take themselves as an object of subjective reflection. This is a *social* process because the subject, 'I', can only ever contemplate itself as an object, 'me', which is one's perception of the attitude of society towards oneself. The 'I' is the often spontaneous and imaginative response of the socially formed individual to the 'me' as the gestures of society to oneself. Self is this emergent 'I–me' dialectic so that each self is socially formed while at the same time interacting selves are forming the social. The social may be understood as a social object. A social object is not an object in the normal sense of a thing that exists in nature but is a tendency on the part of large numbers of people to act in a similar manner in similar situations. The social object is a generalization that exists only when it is made particular in the ordinary local interaction between people. Communication, then, is not simply the sending of a signal to be received by another, but rather complex social, that is, responsive, processes of self-formation in which meaning and the society-wide pattern of the social object emerge.

Relations of power

Drawing on the work of Elias (1939), one understands how the processes of communicative interacting constitute relations of power. For Elias, power is not something which one possesses but is rather a characteristic of all human relating. In order to form, and stay in, a relationship with someone else, one cannot do whatever one wants. As soon as we enter into relationships we constrain and are constrained by others and, of course, we also enable and are enabled by others. Power is this enabling–constraining relationship where the power balance is tilted in favor of some and against others depending on the relative need they have for each other. Elias showed how such power relationships form figurations, or groupings, in which some are included and others are excluded, and where the power balance is tilted in favor of some groupings and against others. These groupings establish powerful feelings of belonging which constitute each individual's 'we' identity. These 'we' identities, derived from the groups to which we belong, are inseparable from each of our 'I' identities. As with Mead, then, we can see that processes of human relating form and are formed by individual and collective identities, which inevitably reflect complex patterns of power relating.

Choices arising in acts of evaluation

In their communicative interacting and power relating, humans are always making choices between one action and another (see Chapter 6 in this volume for a fuller development of this aspect). The choices may be made on the basis of conscious desires and intentions, or unconscious desires and choices, for example, those that are habitual, impulsive, obsessive, compulsive, compelling or inspiring. In other words, human action is always evaluative, sometimes consciously and at other times unconsciously. The criteria for evaluating these choices are values and norms, together constituting ideology.

Norms (morals, the right, the 'ought') are evaluative criteria taking the form of obligatory restrictions which have emerged as generalizations and become habitual in a history of social interaction. We are all socialized to take up the norms of the particular groups and the society to which we belong, and this restricts what we can do as we particularize the generalized norms in our moment-by-moment specific action situations. Elias' work shows in detail how norms constitute major aspects of the personality structures, or identities, of interdependent people.

Values (ethics, the 'good') are individually felt voluntary compulsions to choose one desire, action or norm over another. Values arise in social processes of self-formation (Joas, 2000) – they are fundamental aspects of self, giving meaning to life, opening up opportunities for action. They arise in intense interactive experiences which are seized by the imagination and idealized as some whole to which people then feel strongly committed. Mead (1938) describes these as cult values which need to be functionalized in particular contingent situations, and this inevitably involves conflict.

Together, the voluntary compulsion of value and the obligatory restriction of norms constitute *ideology*. Ideology is the basis on which people choose desires and actions, and it unconsciously sustains power relations by making a particular figuration of power feel natural. We can see, then, that complex responsive processes of human relating form and are formed by values, norms and ideologies as integral aspects of self/identity formation in its simultaneously individual and collective form.

In describing the fundamental aspects of the complex responsive processes of human relating, we have referred on a number of occasions to *patterns* of communicative interaction, *figurations* of power relations, and *generalizations/idealizations* that are *particularized/functionalized* in specific situations. These patterns, figurations, generalizations/ idealizations and particularizations/functionalizations may all be understood as themes, taking both propositional and narrative forms, which emerge and re-emerge in the iteration in each succeeding present of the interactive processes of communication, power and evaluation. These themes organize the experience of being together, and they can be understood, in Mead's terms, as social objects and the imagined wholes of cult values which are taken up by people in their local interaction with each other in specific situations of ordinary, everyday life.

The properties of complex responsive processes of relating

By analogy with complex adaptive systems (Waldrop, 1992; Goodwin, 1994; Kauffman, 1995), the thematic patterning of interaction is understood to be:

- *Complex*. Complexity here refers to a particular dynamic or movement in time that is paradoxically stable and unstable, predictable and unpredictable, known and unknown, certain and uncertain, all at the same time. Complexity and uncertainty are both often used to refer to the situation or environment in which humans must act and this is distinguished from simple or certain environments. Prescriptions for effective action are then related to, held to be contingent upon, the type of environment. However, from the complex responsive processes perspective it is human relating itself which is complex and uncertain in the sense described above. Healthy, creative, ordinarily effective human interaction is then always complex, no matter what the situation. Patterns of human relating that lose this complexity become highly repetitive and rapidly inappropriate for dealing with the fluidity of ordinary, everyday life, taking the form of neurotic and psychotic disorders, bizarre group processes and fascist power structures.
- *Self-organizing and emergent*. Self-organizing means that agents interact with each other on the basis of their own local organizing principles, and it is in such local interaction that widespread coherence emerges without any program, plan or blueprint for that widespread pattern itself. In complex responsive processes terms, then, it is in the myriad local interactions between people that the widespread generalizations such as social objects and cult values emerge. These are particularized in the local interactions between people.
- *Evolving*. The generalizations of social object and cult value are particularized in specific situations, and this inevitably involves choices as to how to particularize them in that specific situation, which inevitably means some form of conflict. The generalizations will never be particularized in exactly the same way and the nonlinear nature of human interaction means that these small differences could be amplified into completely different generalizations. In this way, social objects and cult values evolve.

The consequences of taking a complex responsive processes perspective

We are suggesting, then, that we think about organizations in a way that is close to our ordinary, everyday life in them. We understand organizations to be the widespread patterns of interaction between people, the widespread narrative and propositional themes, which emerge in the myriad local interactions between people, both those between members of an organization and between them and other people. Thinking in this way has two important consequences.

First, no one can step outside of their interaction with others. In mainstream thinking, an organization is viewed as a system at a level above the individuals who form it. It is recognized that this organizational system is affected by patterns of power and economic relations in the wider society and these are normally thought of as forces, over and above the organization and its individual members, which shape local forms of experience. Individuals and the social are posited at different levels and causal powers are ascribed to that social level. In the kinds of process terms we are trying to use, there are no forces over and above individuals. All we have are vast numbers of continually iterated interactions between human bodies and these are local in the sense that each of us can only interact with a limited number of others. It is in the vast number of local (in this specific technical sense) interactions that widespread, global patterns of power and economic relations emerge. The widespread patterns emerge as repetition and potential transformation at the same time. We can then see highly repetitive patterns iterated over long time periods. The general comments we make about such patterns refer to what is emerging rather than to any force over and above those in whose interaction it is emerging. Our general comments on such patterns constitute social objects. In their local interaction people will always be particularizing, taking up in their local interactions, these generalizations, and they may not be aware of doing so. No one can step outside of interaction to design that interaction, and from this perspective it does not make sense to think of leaders as setting directions or designing widespread patterns of interaction which they can then realize. When leaders set directions or formulate organizational designs, they are in effect articulating what Mead means by social objects and cult values. What happens as a result of doing this depends upon how people take up such social objects and cult values in their local interaction with each other.

Second, then, there is no overall program, design, blueprint or plan for the organization as a 'whole'. Designs, programs, blueprints and plans exist only insofar as people are taking them up in their local interactions. Any statements that the most powerful make about organizational designs, visions and values are understood as gestures calling forth responses from many, many people in their local interactions. The most powerful can choose their own gestures but will be unable to choose the responses of others so that the outcome of their gestures will frequently produce surprising outcomes.

The complex responsive processes perspective, therefore, casts considerable doubt on the mainstream understanding of leadership outlined at the start of this chapter. If one thinks of organizations as widespread narrative patterns emerging in local interaction, then it is impossible for leaders to determine values, change cultures or move whole organizations along their own envisioned direction. But how, then, is one to think about the role of leader and the nature of leadership?

The implications for leaders and leadership

From the complex responsive processes perspective:

- The role of leader *emerges*, and is continually iterated, in *social processes of recognition* (Griffin, 2002). In organizations, people work together in groups, and working together means engaging in communicative interaction and power relating in which people are continually choosing what to say and do next, so evoking and provoking responses from each other. These social processes most commonly take the form of ordinary, everyday conversations (Shaw, 2002). As pointed out above, it is this social interaction which forms and is formed by individual selves/collective identities. What emerges, and is continually iterated, is a diversity of selves/identities, where each recognizes and is recognized in their differences. One such difference is that of the role of leader. The role of leader is co-created by all in these processes of recognition. The leader is as much formed by the recognition of the group as he or she forms the group in his or her recognition of the others.
- What is being mutually recognized is the ability of the leader to *articulate emerging themes*, or to deconstruct and so present anew a theme that has become highly repetitive, so as to help the group to

take the next step. Complexity, as defined above, means that as they interact, people are producing further patterns of interaction that are known and unknown at the same time. It is particularly when they deal with the creative, the novel and the uncertain that people find they must act into the unknown. It is in the process of exploring what to do next in such situations that members of a group turn to those who are able to articulate some meaning in what is emerging between them. This is not the same as finding a solution or providing the answer – after all, the leader is acting into the unknown just as much as anyone else. It is, rather, the tentative expression of what may be going on that triggers further exploration by others.

- One recognized as leader will often be identified with what is ideal. There is a *powerful tendency to idealize* leaders where others come to perceive them as embodying idealized values. Norms and values are particular emergent themes organizing the experience of being together – they arise in the process of self-formation (Joas, 2000). The leader does not design them but rather participates in particularly influential ways in the processes of interaction with others in which *values and norms are continually iterated and potentially transformed*. It is the process of idealization that makes the leader particularly influential in this process. However, such idealization brings with it considerable danger in which the leader can easily become a cult leader (Griffin, 2002). Leadership is then essentially about ethics.

- One recognized as leader is likely to be one with an *enhanced capacity for taking the attitude of others*, including the generalized other. It is this capacity that enables one recognized as leader to articulate emerging themes, especially those reflecting the particularization of social objects. What we mean here relates to the capacity for empathy and attunement, as well as emotional awareness and skill. Also involved in this capacity to assume the attitude of others is a particular ability to recognize and articulate the generalizations, the wider social patterns or social objects, which are being particularized in the interaction.

- One recognized as leader will normally be one who *displays greater spontaneity* than others. Here, spontaneity does not mean impulsiveness but rather acting imaginatively, and this involves reflection. Reflection may be understood as a kind of involved detachment. Spontaneity then means the capacity to act in a wider range of ways, taking risks and often surprising oneself and others. Such a capacity must be particularly valuable when it comes to acting into the unknown.

- What is being recognized in the leading–following relationship is a particular *figuration of power* in which the power balance is tilted towards the leader. Power figurations always create collective identities as patterns of inclusion and exclusion, with all the emotions and responses to those emotions that inclusion–exclusion always brings. Leading effectively requires considerable sensitivity to the dynamics of inclusion and exclusion.
- One recognized as leader has a *greater capacity to live with the anxiety* of not knowing and of not being in control. The leader is recognized as one with the courage to carry on interacting creatively despite not knowing.
- It follows from the previous points that one recognized as leader displays an *enhanced capacity to think, feel, reflect and imagine.*

However, in listing the capacities being recognized in the emergence of the role of leader, we are not talking about the attributes of an autonomous individual which that individual has been given, learned or may choose to have. Particular individuals have particular tendencies to act, formed in a life history of acting. However, in any specific situation, such tendencies, the capacities referred to above, are all co-created, they all re-emerge in social interaction, in ongoing social process of self-formation and the recognition by others of that self, while recognizing the selves of others. One cannot identify the attributes of some individual and then conclude that one with the requisite attributes will perform effectively as a leader because how the leader performs will depend just as much on the kind of recognition, the kinds of responses of others. These kinds of recognition are not necessarily all good. We referred above to the tendency to idealize leaders, and this becomes a particularly powerful tendency when people experience high levels of uncertainty and anxiety. The expectations of the idealized leader can very easily become completely unrealistic and, when they are not met, denigration soon replaces idealization. The good and the bad will emerge at the same time. It follows that it is extremely important for leaders to be aware of these usually unconscious group processes, enabling them to resist the idealization and prepare to deal with the denigration. The processes we are referring to easily create neurotic, and even pathological, forms of leadership. In states of great anxiety groups easily become submerged in what Durkheim referred to as group ecstasy, much the same as Bion's notion of groups acting on basic assumption behavior that destroy the capacity for rational work and is related to Mead's notion of cult leadership. The result can often be fascist power structures.

So, what is the practice of effective leadership from the perspective of complex responsive processes? The practice is that of participating skillfully in interaction with others in reflective and imaginative ways, aware of the potentially destructive processes one may be caught up in. It is in this practice that one is recognized as leader, as one who has the capacity to assist the group to continue acting ethically, creatively and courageously into the unknown. This is a very different way of understanding the role of leader to the mainstream perspective in which the leader stands outside the system, designing, manipulating variables and pulling levers in order to stay in control.

The chapters in this book

In Chapter 2, Douglas Griffin outlines the main themes in his book *The Emergence of Leadership* (2002). He explores the relationship between leadership and ethics from two perspectives. First, there is the mainstream perspective based on systems thinking with its systemic notion of self-organization. Then there is the complex responsive processes perspective with its notion of participative self-organization. Many of these themes of this chapter are taken up in subsequent chapters where the authors explore their own experience of leading in organizations.

Chapter 3, by Richard Williams, who was at the time of writing Head of the Westminster Kingsway Further Education College in the UK, explores his experience of how his subordinates perceive and respond to him. He recounts his discovery that his subordinates fear him and explores how he might make sense of this. A key theme in this chapter is the emotional involvement of the leader and his subordinates with each other.

In Chapter 4, by John Tobin, CEO of Waterbury Hospital in the USA, provides a detailed account of some of his ordinary, everyday interactions with his colleagues at the hospital. He reflects upon what leading has come to mean to him and how this has led him to change some of the ways he interacts with his colleagues. He explains how he has come to understand leading as a social process in which the leader engages with others in a manner that is both detached and involved at the same time. He also explores the fluid nature of leading, showing how it is not simply located in the one recognized as leader but shifts back and forth to others in social processes of mutual recognition.

Chapter 5 is by Ralph Stacey who develops a complex responsive perspective on the emergence of norms, values and ideology in organizations. From this perspective values arise in social processes of self-formation and self-transcendence and so cannot be designed by leaders.

In Chapter 6, James Taylor, CEO of the University of Louisville Hospital in the USA, explores his experience of interacting with others as leader. His focus is on the detail of interaction in the living present and he indicates how this focus changes what he does as a leader. He explains how he has come to understand leadership as a cult value.

Chapter 7 is by Andrew Lee, Human Resources Director of Unite plc in the UK. He reflects upon his previous experience as an executive coach to leaders in other organizations. He outlines the mainstream literature on executive coaching and its origins in humanistic psychology with its emphasis on unlocking the individual's unrealized potential. He describes how he has developed a very different understanding of executive coaching from the perspective of complex responsive processes. This leads him to move away from the objective, distanced stance of the coach in one-to-one coaching to a much more involved stance in which the coach and client are together participating in a relationship characterized by power differentials and processes of inclusion and exclusion. He understands change to arise in the shifts of patterns of power relations, which are also shifts in identity. He then reflects on his own experience as a leader in his current organization and explores how his role as leader has much similarity to the coaching relationship. He describes how he has come to understand what he is doing in a different way and how this moves him to do what he does differently.

Finally, in Chapter 8, Michael Shiel explores the experience of educating and developing leaders. Moving from the notion of leader as one with particular personal attributes enabling him or her to determine direction and design values to a notion of leader as emerging in social processes of recognition has significant implications for how leaders may be educated and developed. Michael Shiel shows how his practice as educator of leaders has altered with his change of perspective.

Each chapter points to an idea of leadership that differs from those we most commonly encounter in the organizational literature. They move away from the future focused ideas of leaders having visions, from the notion of leaders as those who define values, in fact from the notion of the leader as hero. Instead they focus on leaders as participants in the process of human relating in the present, reflecting on and making sense with others of how they are responding and what that means. They all show how thinking in complex responsive processes terms leads to a different way of acting. This is not a view of leaders instrumentally using tools and techniques, but of leaders who are present in interaction. Key themes running through all the chapters have to do with social processes of mutual recognition, involvement and detachment. The chapters by those who explore their experience of leadership and educating leaders focus on the micro-interaction of leaders and others in their ordinary everyday work together in the living present.

However, it should be borne in mind that all the chapters are concerned with experience. It is all too easy to slip into thinking that by emphasizing ordinary human relating in the present, helping others to make sense of what is going on and so on, we are talking about something which is fundamentally good. This is not the stance we take. The human relating that we are trying to understand produces evil just as easily as good. In fact what is evil and good is negotiated in the same processes of human relating. People who are particularly skilled in empathizing with others as leaders could quite easily use such leadership skills to manipulate and brainwash those with whom they are interacting.

References

Elias, N. (1939) *The Civilizing Process*, Oxford: Blackwell.

Fonseca, J. (2002) *Complexity and Innovation in Organizations*, London: Routledge.

Goodwin, B. (1994) *How the Leopard Changed its Spots*, London: Weidenfeld & Nicolson.

Griffin, D. (2002) *The Emergence of Leadership: Linking self-organization and ethics*, London: Routledge.

Joas, H. (2000) *The Genesis of Values*, Cambridge: Polity Press.

Kauffman, S. A. (1995) *At Home in the Universe*, New York: Oxford University Press.

Mead, G. H. (1934) *Mind, Self and Society*, Chicago, IL: Chicago University Press.

Mead, G. H. (1938) *The Philosophy of the Act*, Chicago, IL: Chicago University Press.

Schein, E. H. (1985) *Organizational Culture and Leadership*, San Francisco, CA: Jossey-Bass.

Senge, P. M. (1990) *The Fifth Discipline: The Art and Practice of the Learning Organization*, New York: Doubleday.

Shaw, P. (2002) *Changing Conversations in Organizations: A complexity approach to change*, London: Routledge.

Stacey, R. (2001) *Complex Responsive Processes in Organizations: Learning and knowledge creation*, London: Routledge.

Stacey, R. (2003) *Strategic Management and Organizational Dynamics: The Challenge of Complexity* (4th edn), London: Pearson Education.

Stacey, R. and Griffin, D. (eds) (2005) *A Complexity Perspective on Researching Organizations: Taking experience seriously*, London: Routledge.

Stacey, R., Griffin, D. and Shaw, P. (2000) *Complexity and Management: Fad or radical challenge to systems thinking?*, London: Routledge.

Streatfield, P. (2001) *The Paradox of Control in Organizations*, London: Routledge.

Waldrop, M. M. (1992) *Complexity: The Emerging Science at the Edge of Chaos*, Englewood Cliffs, NJ: Simon & Schuster.

2 Leadership and the role of conflict in processes of mutual recognition: the emergence of ethics

Douglas Griffin

The link between the theory of self-organization developed by Ilya Prigogine and management theories of leadership is by no means immediately self-evident. Prigogine (in Prigogine and Stengers, 1984, 1997) himself points to the enormous consequences for rethinking communication as the core of understanding social interaction. This is especially relevant to theories of leadership which would seem at first to be in complete opposition to self-organization. What is needed is a paradigm of emergence for the social sciences which does not directly depend on the success of theories developed in the sciences of complexity following the work of Prigogine and others. In the following, the concept of life-process, as developed in the work of the pragmatist George Herbert Mead (1934, 1936, 1938, 1968), is suggested as a link between the natural and the social sciences in moving towards such an understanding of self-organization. The role of leader emerges in social interaction in the iteration of ongoing purposes and processes of mutual recognition. Contrary to the conclusions of leadership theories developed on the basis of systemic theory, including cybernetics and autopoiesis (e.g. Senge, 1990; Schein, 1992; Wheatley, 1992; Hampden-Turner, 1994), leadership is viewed in terms of the incompleteness of organizations and societies, constructing the future within the constraints of the past as the negotiation of conflict in the present. Leadership is not seen as thought before – or apart from – action, but rather as dealing with the unknown and the emergence of genuine novelty. Such a theory of leadership is a restatement for our own contemporary times of the tradition of ethics begun by Aristotle, and it provides an important perspective on globalization which has emerged as the key ethical issue of this age.

Globalization: beyond the boredom and abstract idealization of ethical debate

Globalization has emerged as the issue of our times. It has become a focus, an umbrella for a number of major issues, around which the heart of the matter which we call ethics has come alive for us in its full intensity. Ethics and moral philosophy are always at risk of being collapsed into either prescriptive do's and don'ts exemplified, for instance, by the seminars run by consultancies in companies on various topics of ethical norms, or into the hopeless idealization of the indeterminate values and visions of abstract 'leaders'. When ethics comes alive, the sense of paradox, which is at its very core, becomes a lived experience. This is the paradox of stability and change which makes us aware of the evolution and the emerging incompleteness of society.

The Nobel Prize-winning chemist, Ilya Prigogine (1984), formulated a new view of self-organization, one that accepts rather than eliminates paradox, when he talked about order emerging from disorder in far from equilibrium conditions. The notion of order and disorder present *at the same time*, as a paradox, challenges what has become one of the main pillars of Western scientific thinking concerning causality and time. We notice this dominant way of thinking about cause and time, with its taken-for-granted elimination of paradox, when we ask such questions as:

- How is it that organizations stay the same in order to get work done and also change in order to surprise the competition?
- Are we actively forming the organizations we work in, or are we being formed by these organizations?
- Are organizations simple or are they complex?

What we spontaneously tend to do is to argue that in each instance organizations are both. They both change and they stay the same. They are both forming us (as cultures) and we are forming them (planned structuring and re-engineering). They are both simple (explicit procedures) and complex (unstructured networks). Notice that in each answer we find the connectives 'both . . . and'. We have a taken-for-granted ability not to sense that the questions we are asking could be taken as paradoxical (see Griffin, 2002). However, in Prigogine's new questioning of self-organization we find the expression 'at the same time'. What is now being challenged in the natural sciences by such thinkers as Prigogine, therefore, is precisely *the validity of the elimination of paradox*. Prigogine draws attention to a notion of self-organization, which is by its very nature paradoxical. He talks about the presence of order and disorder *at the same time* in far from equilibrium conditions. Taking this perspective we would answer the questions posed above in a very different way. We would say that organizations stay the same and change at the same time, that we form them while being formed by them at the same time, that they are simple and complex at the same time. The challenge being presented by thinkers like Prigogine, therefore, is to explore just what paradoxical answers like these might mean when it comes to making sense of our experience of life in organizations, both for us today at the level of corporations and for national states interacting globally. What view would we take of ethics? What would this mean for the way we think about leaders?

The emergence of the issue of globalization in our times is not at all dissimilar to the emergence of the concept of 'polis' in Athens at the time Aristotle wrote his *Nicomachean Ethics*. It was in essence an attempt to renegotiate the understanding of citizenship in Athens, so that Aristotle, who had not been born there, would be able to remain as head of a household. He lost his 'case', but in doing so established this very alive tradition of arguing for change, which paradoxically is only possible on the basis of stability. The polis, and the very nature of politics, emerged at the edge of the known-unknown, the incomplete, which is for us today the issue of globalization.

Ethics is a matter of everyday life, the life-processes which are the focus of sociology and management theory. After the significant advances in the understanding of the concept of life and life-processes in biology as the theories of first and second order cybernetics and autopoiesis, we today face the challenge of differentiating the concept of life, life-world and life-processes as a way of thinking emerging independently of natural sciences, in spite of the strong resonances and legitimate analogies.

Towards a paradigm of life-process independent of the natural sciences

There are then two fundamentally different ways of thinking about life-process in organizations. The first of these ways of thinking, systemic self-organization, is derived from the paradigm of life-process which has emerged in the natural sciences. Paradox is eliminated by positing dualisms and then examining first one side of the dualism, followed by the other, in an alternating serial manner. Following this thought procedure, humans understand nature in terms of autonomous systemic wholes, hypothesized to unfold a pattern already enfolded in them in an 'as if' manner (see Kant, 1987 (1790)). Human beings could also, quite separately, understand their own actions in terms of the goals they set themselves as autonomous individuals and the judgments they make as to the ethics of their actions. In making such judgements they formulate hypothetical imperatives and test actions against them, so discovering the nature of universal categorical imperatives. The procedure is the same, whether understanding nature or human action, and it is that of the objectively observing scientist.

This kind of approach is reflected in most modern theories of management and organization. In particular, this approach is evident in modern systems thinking as reflected in the currently much discussed theories of the learning organization and autopoiesis, whereby the organization is viewed as a living system. An organization is understood as an autonomous whole. It is reified, and intention is ascribed to it by autonomous individuals who manipulate it. This way of thinking immediately leads to a very particular view of leading and leadership. The action of leading is located in autonomous individuals, the leaders, who become the objective observers of organizations as whole systems and the formulators of visions and values which provide the leadership according to which such systems are to unfold their future. Leadership, now split off from leaders, is located in the system. Closely connected to the question of leadership is the question of ethics. Basically, ethics becomes a matter of individuals abandoning their selfishness and submitting to the harmonious whole of organizational culture. Participation is understood as participating in a greater whole. When writers draw on the complexity sciences from the perspective of systemic self-organization, they do not introduce any radical challenge to systems thinking, the learning organization or organizations as living systems. Indeed, they simply reinforce all of these perspectives.

A significant weakness in this whole way of thinking is the manner in which it abstracts and distracts from our ordinary everyday experience of interacting with each other in the present. Such abstraction distracts our attention from our own responsibility for what we are doing and what happens to us in organizations. It leaves us feeling that we are simply victims of the system. An alternative way of thinking is participative self-organization, where participation does not mean participating in a larger whole, but rather participating in the direct interaction between human bodies. Instead of positing an autonomous individual, human beings are seen as knowing what they know about nature and about themselves through the same process, the social process of interacting with each other. Indeed they *become themselves in the process*. This perspective of participative self-organization forms a theory of organizations as complex responsive processes of relating.

Central to this theory is a notion of time that is different to that implicit in systemic self-organization (see Griffin, 2002). In systemic self-organization, the implicit notion of time is linear. This may be seen in the prescription for leaders to form a vision of the future to guide the direction of the organization. Implicitly here, the past is factually given because it has already happened and the future is ahead, waiting to be unfolded. In the perspective of participative self-organization, the present itself has a time structure. The past is not simply factually given because it is reconstructed in the present as the basis of the action to be taken in the present. The past is what we re-member. The future is also in the present in the form of anticipation and expectation. It too forms the basis of action in the present. Furthermore, what we are anticipating affects what we remember, and what we remember affects what we expect, in a circular fashion, all in the present as the basis of our acting. In this way, the movement of the living present is experience, having a circular time structure that arises simply because human beings have the capacity to know what they are doing. This notion of the present differs from another way of focusing on the present, which is described as liberation from worrying about the past and from feeling anxious about the future by ignoring both. The result is a view of the present in which autonomous individuals encapsulate themselves. This also stands in stark contrast to the dominant view in the organizational world where the future is split off and exclusively focused on in the form of vision, simple rules, values and plans, so *distracting attention from the present* and reducing the future to simple aspects that may be manipulated to determine the present. The notion of the present as participative is one in which the future, as expectation and anticipation, is in the detail of actual interactions taking place now, as is the past as reconstructions in this process of memory. There is no dismissing the past or the future, nor is there any distraction of attention from the present of what we are doing together.

This shift in one's way of thinking leads to different understandings of leadership and ethics. The action of leading is no longer split off from the nature of leadership. Leaders emerge in the interaction between people as the act of recognizing and being recognized. Ethics becomes a matter of our accountability to each other in our daily relating to each other. What is ethical emerges as themes that organize our experience of being together. The distinction between systemic and participative self-organization is thus fundamental to the whole argument for a concept of life-process as an independent paradigm of sociology and management theory.

Life-process in nature: the perspective of systemic self-organization

Over two hundred years ago, The German philosopher Kant developed the concept of 'systems' according to which he viewed organisms in nature as autonomous self-organizing wholes. Despite his strictures against thinking of human action in systems terms, organizational theorists over the past fifty years or more have done just that and the notion of an organization or a culture as a reified autonomous whole continues to underlie dominant thinking today. The move to understanding organizations as 'learning systems', 'living systems' and even 'complex systems' is fundamentally a reaffirmation of Kant's concern for the autonomy of systems. Autonomy here means unity and wholeness, and it is thought that this wholeness can be uncovered and instrumentalized by organizational leaders, just as scientists can supposedly discover and manipulate the wholeness of nature.

Kant's method of looking at a system 'as if' it were following the laws of a given hypothesis was taken up by mathematicians and became a theory of modeling. The success of such modeling led to the reification of the systems models, that is, to the taken-for-granted understanding that they were things, and the 'as if' regulative idea came to be understood as the system's 'intention'. It came to be believed that in reality a system is actually governed by some regulative idea, such as a vision, and the 'as if', hypothetical nature of Kant's thought slipped into the background. In this way of thinking it is still very common to understand an organization in reified terms as having an intention, as following a vision or acting according to values. It is the leader who is thought to be able to manipulate and change the 'intention' of the organization according to his or her own goals, purposes, vision and values. Or some democratic grouping of individuals is empowered to formulate the vision and the values for the organizational system. Leaders are thought of as autonomous individuals observing the system and the system is also understood as an autonomous self-organizing whole. This is referred to as paradoxical, but in a very particular and limited sense.

The reason why beliefs of the kind mentioned above are seen to be paradoxical flows from the way in which the two kinds of autonomous wholes, individuals and systems, are thought about. They are understood in a serial manner over time, 'first . . . then'. This is actually thinking that eliminates the kind of paradox Prigogine has spoken of. However, this very way of eliminating paradox is what many organization theorists are now calling paradox. It is claimed that culture, for example, is paradoxical because culture *both* acts on individuals *and* individuals decide what the culture should be (e.g. Schein, 1992; Hampden-Turner, 1994; Pascale, 1999; Lewin and Birute, 2000). What Prigogine is proposing in his concept of self-organization is not about serial or alternating perspectives. It is the notion that individuals form culture while being formed by culture at the same time, implying emergent, evolutionary change acting into the unknown. This simultaneity and its corollary of emergence and uncertainty is not recognized when it is held that individuals can change the culture and apply it to others, so reducing culture to an instrument which leaders can use in the service of their own goals and strategies.

A 'reductionist' concept of paradox leads to an ethics whereby individuals are required to submit themselves to the visions and values revealed to them by their leaders, or democratically chosen by them as empowered individuals. Participation then becomes submission to a harmonious whole variously described as shared values, common purpose, common pool of meaning, transpersonal processes, group mind, collective intelligence, simple rules and so on. The ethical choice is that of voluntary submission to a larger, harmonious whole. This way of thinking about ethics and leadership has many consequences. The freedom to choose actions and explore their ethical implications is located primarily in the leader, when in the role of system designer, while the other members of an organization are required to conform to the emerging leadership of the whole as indeed must the leader in the role of steward and teacher (e.g. Senge, 1990) .

Furthermore, systems thinking provides no explanation of novelty within its own framework. Since the systemic whole is unfolding the given vision of the leader as regulations and practices there is no novelty in the operation of the system. Nor is there any explanation of how the leader comes to design the system or form the vision imposed on the system. Positing a harmonious whole removes diversity and conflict. Since diverse persons, by definition, are not submitting to the whole and so not losing their individuality, there is bound to be conflict, but this is either ignored or condemned. Theories of the learning organizations and living organizations, as well as most applications of complexity theory to organizations, ignore diversity and conflict and their role in generating novelty.

By setting up a whole outside of the experience of interaction between people, a whole to which they are required to voluntarily submit if their behavior is to be judged ethical, this way of thinking distances us from our actual experience and makes it feel natural to blame something outside of our actual interaction for what happens to us. It encourages the belief that we are victims of a system, on the one hand, and allows us to escape from feeling responsible for our own actions, on the other. In other words, it alienates us. We come to feel that our actions are insignificant parts of some greater whole and that there is nothing much we can do about it, especially when management becomes a matter of changing *whole* organizations.

An ethics based on autonomy, of the individual or of a systemic whole, is an ethics based on universal moral principles, which do not depend upon social or natural contingencies. They do not reflect the present context in which people are interacting with their particular life circumstances, aspirations and motivations. This is an idealized view of ethics in which autonomous leaders exercise their freedom independently of the contingencies of nature and society.

Life-process in social interaction: the perspective of participative self-organization

Organizations are not things at all, let alone living things, but rather they are processes of communication and joint action. Communication and joint action are life-processes but not alive in the sense of the biological paradigm of life. It is the human bodies communicating and interacting that are alive. This immediately focuses attention on the communicative interaction between the living human bodies that are an organization. This is the basis of the alterative perspective of participative self-organization as the process sustaining and potentially transforming identity directly in participating in ordinary interactions between people. Participation is that of the embodied human beings with each other rather than the modernist concept of the autonomous individual. Experience cannot be understood in terms of the individual alone but in terms of a world in which the individual plays an active part. Individuals come to an understanding of themselves in the continuity of their action, in the world in which they play an active part, and this is a social self-organizing process. Knowing and knowing selves are social processes. Drawing on the analogy provided by the complexity sciences, interaction of this kind has the intrinsic capacity to form patterns and, when the interaction is between diverse human beings, those patterns may be genuinely novel so that the world becomes a different world through the amplification of difference. Human beings collectively change the world in their acting and, at the same time, this changing world changes them. Novelty is not necessarily some major change, but it is necessarily unpredictable. In other words, novelty is that which is not simply determined by the past. This is a point of major significance in thinking about organizations. Most people nowadays seem to think that it is necessary to manage novelty by first formulating values and simple rules that create the 'right conditions' in which people will act to produce novel outcomes. However, since novelty is unpredictable, it is impossible to specify in advance any rules, simple or complicated, that will lead to the kind of future novelty anyone may have decided upon in advance.

The move to the perspective of participative self-organization is a complete contradiction of systemic self-organization, and as a theory of action it has implications for understanding leadership. Leaders emerge in the interaction between people as an act of recognition. Effective leaders tend to be those who have, in the course of their lives, developed more spontaneity and ability to deal with the ongoing purpose and task of interaction. Leaders are individuals who have enhanced capacities for taking the attitudes of the other members of the group. On the basis of this they spontaneously take risks and enhance communication within and between groups. Improvisation and vision are thus not simply located in individuals, but are rather emergent processes of recognizing and being recognized.

Leaders act and leadership is action. This immediately means that a theory of leadership is also a theory of ethics. Ethical values emerge in interaction as a reflection of the emergence of leaders. Large-scale organizational and cultural events emerge in everyday social interaction through participation in local events. Values are sustained and passed on in this ordinary social interaction, as themes that pattern our actions in terms of local interaction.

Cult values and the potential failure of ethics

Values that seem to transcend this local interaction do not do so in any real sense, but in an ideal sense which can only become real in the functional reality of the present. Experience is interaction and it is *the present*. The ethics of reason and idealism to be found in those who take the perspective of systemic self-organization, with its appeals to universals and wholes, has failed to prevent the atrocities of instrumentalized, large-scale genocide and the incremental destruction of the planet.

Taking a participative self-organization perspective leads to a 'minimal' or everyday ethics as opposed to the edification implied in the 'greater' ethics of idealized universals. We find such an ethics in the smallest detail of our everyday lives, especially in language. It is in the fascination with the idealized whole as cult values (see Mead, 1968), and people's simple identification of themselves as parts of it, that ethics fails. This happens because there is no questioning of the whole as such, only the instrumentalizing and optimizing of 'selves' as parts in service of the whole. Local interaction is then alienated from a genuine present because it is in the service of a whole that is not part of the experience of the present. To retain the emphasis on sustaining the whole, one must impose a preconceived meaning on local interaction. This in turn results in understanding the present in a detached way because it has, in a very real sense, been predetermined.

The perspective of participative self-organization as life-process moves away from the autonomous individual but neither denies individual freedom nor posits the existence of a transcendent whole. Instead it retains the radical notion of paradox as individual responsibility in social processes. Cult values are then seen as the heritage of our past which we functionalize as the present, in constructing our future. This necessarily means working with difference and conflict. It is important, for instance, that the head of a hospital articulate the cult value that 'we are all here to provide the best possible care of every patient'. But in every action taken conflict will emerge based on the past experience of all those participating: what strength of dosage, how many times a day and so on, negotiating the use of resources and the needs of the patients – as actions moving into the future.

Ethics and leadership

Leadership, as a theory of ethics, is thus concerned with action in the present constructing the future, and this means that it has to do with 'who' is acting into the future, the matter of identity. The underlying concern has to do with persons, and the notion of person combines two opposite aspects, namely changeability and stability. This combination of transformation and continuity is at the core of what identity is about and therefore at the core of what ethics and leadership are about.

The modernist theory of ethics assumes that we are autonomous individuals, each of whom is capable of making rational decisions based on reflection apart from and before action itself, weighing the consequences of the outcomes and deciding whether or not to proceed. In other words, it is assumed that people 'have' experience and are also able to detach themselves from it in order to manipulate and change it through thinking. Ethical leaders are those who are able to understand the consequences of their actions better than others or have proven themselves worthy of imitation because of the way they keep to the contract. Others, therefore, voluntarily agree to follow them and tend to be lumped together as followers.

The perspective of participative self-organization as life-process moves away from thinking about ethics and leadership entirely in terms of stability. One can avoid thinking in terms of ethical universals as 'fixed realities' against which human conduct is to be judged, apart from and before action with meaning known in advance. Instead one can view ethics as the interpretation of action to be found in the action itself, in the ongoing recognition of the meanings of actions that could not have been known in advance. Motives then do not arise from antecedently given ends but in the recognition of the end as it arises in action. The moral interpretation of our experience is then found within the experience itself as new points of view that emerge in the conflictual interaction in which the future is perpetually being created. This view of ethics avoids simply idealizing in a cult manner and focuses on how idealizations are functionalized in the everyday conflicts in which we are always negotiating the future on the basis of the past. It avoids detaching from the everyday present of social interaction and instrumentalizing ideologies that go unnoticed and unchallenged.

The role of cult leader

As groups evolve and develop a past they begin to recognize various members in roles, one of which is leader. The 'mask', the role, of leader emerges in the concrete, everyday processes of recognizing, and those participating are continuously creating and re-creating the meaning of the leadership themes in the local interaction in which they are involved. One could understand the 'mask' of the leader as the idealization of leader, the cult leader, whereas the role refers to the functionalizing of the ideals in the everyday conflicts of interaction. The idealized cult leader role is functionalized in the appointment process but, once appointed, there is a strong tendency for this move from idealization to functionalization to be reversed as the newly appointed leader is idealized by the group. The leader then becomes a cult leader, that is, leader of a group of people directly enacting idealized values, cult values, which they are subtly pressured to conform to. This creates a problem for subsequent leadership appointments. It is especially difficult to succeed a charismatic leader who has led a cult of his or her own personality, and the easiest way of dealing with this is to attempt to establish another cult.

The emergence of participative leadership

Leadership themes emerge in the ongoing process of group interaction in which personal and collective identities are iterated and potentially transformed. Leadership themes emerge over time and have virtually unlimited meanings for a group. Groups tend to recognize the leader role in those who have acquired a greater spontaneity, a greater ability to deal with the unknown as it emerges from the known context. But the complexity also has to do with embodied human beings with strong emotional themes, which have emerged in their past and constitute the enabling constraints that are the structures of their participation in the present. Themes of leadership become enacted and these may include mother, genius, grandfather, college football coach, ruthless princess, perpetrator of domestic violence, shepherd, iron lady, czar and so on and on. As the size of a group grows, the number and complexity of these simultaneous patterns also increases, making it impossible to manipulate them. These themes greatly affect power-enacted structures and they are themselves greatly influenced by the structures that are co-created.

Idealized leader roles distract attention from the functionalization of roles and values emerging in everyday interaction. All other roles are also lumped together as 'followers', giving a highly simplistic view of interaction, while reducing differentiation and thus meaning. This way of thinking masks conflict and disenfranchises the negotiation of power.

I would propose another way of thinking about ethics and leadership. This focuses attention on everyday interaction between people in their local situation whose participation is their present. It is in these interactions that ethical interaction emerges and it is also therefore in this interaction that roles emerge, including the roles of leaders. Leadership emerges in the mutual processes of recognizing among those who have agreed that they have work to do. Motivation emerges in the *political*, in negotiating the conflicts which emerge in achieving this.

References

Aristotle. *Nicomachean Ethics*.

Griffin, D. (2002) *The Emergence of Leadership: Linking self-organization and ethics*, London: Routledge.

Hampden-Turner, C. (1994) *Corporate Culture*, London: Piatkus.

Kant, I. (1987) *Critique of Judgement*, trans. W. S. Pluhar, Indianapolis: Hackett (first published 1790).

Kant, I. (1956) *Gesamtwerke*, Wiesbaden: Insel Verlag.

Lewin, R. and Birute, R. (2000) *The Soul at Work*, London: Orion Business Books.

Mead, G. H. (1934) *Mind, Self and Society*, Chicago, IL: University of Chicago Press (1970).

Mead, G. H. (1936) *Movements of Thought in the Nineteenth Century*, Chicago: University of Chicago Press (1972).

Mead, G. H. (1938) *The Philosophy of the Act*, Chicago, IL: University of Chicago Press (1967).

Mead, G. H. (1968) *Essays on Social Philosophy*, ed. J. W. Petras, New York: Teachers College Press.

Pascale, R. T. (1999) 'Surfing the edge of chaos', *Sloan Management Review* 40, 3: 83–95.

Prigogine, I. (1997) *The End of Certainty*, New York: The Free Press.

Prigogine, I. and Stengers, I. (1984) *Order Out of Chaos: Man's New Dialogue with Nature*, New York: Bantam Books.

Schein, E. H. (1992) *Organizational Culture and Leadership* (2nd edn), San Francisco, CA: Jossey-Bass.

Senge, P. (1990) *The Fifth Discipline: The Art and Practice of the Learning Organization*, New York: Doubleday.

Wheatley, M. J. (1992) *Leadership and the New Science: Learning about Organization from an Orderly Universe*, San Francisco, CA: Berrett-Koehler.

Editors' introduction
to Chapter 3

At the time of writing this chapter, Richard Williams was CEO at the Westminster Kingsway Further Education College in the United Kingdom. The college had just been subjected to an inspection by Ofsted, the government body charged with the quality of education delivery by the schools and further education sectors. The outcome for the college was mixed in that the quality of management received a good report while the quality of teaching was judged to be inadequate, requiring a program of improvement. If the college were to fail to achieve the required improvement then action would be taken against the college and its management. It is against this background that Williams explores his role as leader in relationship to other managers in the college. He tells us about his encounter with these managers at a leadership development program to which they had been sent. He was invited to this event by the facilitators who wanted him to talk about the strategic plan and his vision for the college. The facilitators met him and primed him for his appearance by telling him that his managers felt disempowered and afraid of him.

Williams describes his feelings on hearing this, against the background of his feelings about public sector policy on quality inspections and the manipulative use of shame to get members of public sector institutions to comply with centrally determined targets and quality monitoring procedures. What he is pointing to is how being told that others are afraid of him immediately raises feelings of concern and anxiety and how this creates the potential for the kind of 'involved', emotional thinking that John Tobin explores in Chapter 4 of this volume. We can see from his story how Williams remains aware of his emotional reaction but holds it in tension with what Tobin, drawing on Elias, describes as detached thinking. This tension between involvement and detachment is transformed as the detached involvement which Tobin holds to be a central aspect of the act of effective leading.

What Williams is doing in this chapter, therefore, is exploring the emotional patterning of the power relationships between a leader and his or her subordinates, paying particular attention to the impact of local and national contexts on such patterning. In making sense of this experience he was drawn at first to a psychoanalytic perspective. From this perspective one would understand the experience in terms of the regression of the group, due to feelings of anxiety, to defensive states of dependency and aggression. However, he finds this intrapsychic perspective unsatisfactory and moves to a much more social perspective from which he understands the behavior of the group in terms of power relations rather than regression. He locates this in the wider context of power relations between the college for which they work and the bodies carrying out the government's centralized control and judgement of further education institutions. He argues that the technologies of power, elaborated as social objects, form a powerful instrument of control reflected in power figurations which people tend to reify. He draws attention to the effects on people of the public naming and shaming which the government uses as an instrument of control and the ethical dilemmas this creates for people in leadership positions. He identifies the emotional and ethical tensions between implementing the national policy and dealing with the people who report to him. It is the highly performative aspects of government policy which create the anxiety people feel and then locate in him as leader. It is this, rather then regression, which explains the way his managers treated him at the workshop. A key issue in the feelings people have towards him is his inevitable remoteness as a leader. This remoteness, or absence, creates the need for the kind of fantasies people spin about him.

Williams points to how mainstream views of leadership constitute a constraining and oppressive social object because leaders are supposed to know what is happening, where they are going and so be in control, making any expression of vulnerability impossible. It is this heroic view of leadership which encourages people to believe that they need the leader to do things they cannot do and at the same time find the leader fearful and destructive as a judging, punishing figure.

He argues that the dominant discourse of improvement in the UK public sector has reduced all purpose to performance, so establishing an oppressive cult of performance. This creates particular ethical dilemmas for one whose educational values are at odds with such a cult but who nevertheless finds that, as leader, he must conform to, and administer, the performance requirements set by central government. For example, it will be his responsibility to remove people who do not meet centrally set performance standards from the organization. Here he is pointing to the centrality of power relations and ethics in the act of leading (see Chapter 2 by Griffin in this volume) and the struggle he has with how to relate to those he has responsibility for leading. He suggests that his ambivalence about what he is doing in conforming to public sector policy has a destabilizing effect on his relations with peers and those he leads. He links this to the matter of identity and how the policies of control threaten identities and so raise anxiety levels.

The chapter provides some explanation of how and why senior managers at the college have come to regard their leader as a fearful power figure which has become magnified to an extraordinary degree of unreality. He links this fantasy that people have created about him to both his presence amongst them but even more to his absence. Here, we believe, he is pointing to a general tendency in organizations of any size. Inevitably the leader is a distant, even solitary figure, and since people lack much direct contact they fill the meaning vacuum with exaggerated fantasies representing idealization or denigration, easily flipping from one to the other. Williams refers to how all involved are enacting roles of powerfulness-powerlessness, inclusion-exclusion and dependency. The chapter also points to how dynamics of blame, dependency and denigration arise as a response to the kind of threat to collective identity created by the poor performance report.

3 Leadership, power and problems of relating in processes of organizational change

Richard Williams

- Threats to identity, shame and fear
- The senior management workshop
- Appreciative inquiry
- The 'fear' issue
- Sense-making
- Conclusion

This chapter arose from an experience I shared with a small group of senior managers from the further education college at which I am the CEO. They were participating in a leadership and management development program and my contribution to this program was to be an input on the institution's strategic plan priorities and to talk with the group further about my 'vision' for the future. This previously agreed agenda was never enacted. My experience of this session was intensely emotional. What emerged instead in my work with the group was a conversation that involved all of us in drawing out a great many fantasies, fears, feelings of anger and anxiety about the context in which we are working together and our relationships. Central to this process was a conversation about me, my leadership role, their power (or their perceived/alleged lack of it) and their relations with both their own line managers as well as with those they manage. In this experience I was reminded of the singular and singleton status of the leader in a group.

In the early stages of my reflection upon this experience I placed great reliance on Morris Nitsun's *anti-group* thesis to explain the group processes I observed and in which I felt myself to be a participant.

Nitsun ascribes the idea of the *anti-group* to processes whereby powerful and reactionary forces take hold of groups, particularly those faced with great pressures to change in significant ways, leading to the possibility of the abandonment of the group's project, the destruction of the group itself or, potentially, its creative transformation (Nitsun 1996). I have found the *anti-group* explanation to be increasingly unsatisfactory for the following reasons.

First, Nitsun's thesis is rooted in a tradition of psychodynamic analysis which treats the individual as a self formed separately from group processes of interaction. This perspective has the tendency to locate causality in either the individual or the group and by implication to treat the group as being of itself a meta-personality whose behavioral characteristics may be identified and analyzed *as if* it were a singularity. Here the social context acts as a trigger mechanism for the release of individual or group pathologies that in some way are rooted back to archaic traits of the human psyche. Nitsun's example of the influence of changes in the National Health Service upon the emergence of *anti-group* responses in health service 'sensitivity' groups is an example of this approach (Nitsun 1996, pp. 91–101).

Second, Nitsun's work relies heavily on notions of projection, introjection and projective identification to explain the emotional responses of individuals to each other. Increasingly these concepts appear to me to be based upon a metaphysical understanding of human interaction in which individuals are assumed to be able to exchange psychic contents with each other in a way that takes no account of the biologic nature of the human form and therefore of the relationships existing between bodily interaction, feeling, emotion and consciousness explored by writers such as Damasio (1994, 2000) and Solms and Turnbull (2002).

An alternative perspective, informed by the idea of complex responsive processes, situates the idea of self in a social context as being *formed by* and *forming*, at the same time, patterns of social interaction out of which individual emotional responses emerge. In this explanation it is interaction, the cycle of gesture and response between individuals occurring within the temporal structure of the living present, which is the context within which causality is located. Human interaction is therefore the context in which the self is formed (Stacey *et al.* 2000, pp. 35–36). In this perspective causality shifts from being found within individuals or groups (i.e. the responsibility of) to the wider social contextual circumstances that form and are formed by their interactions.

In working with these themes, I have found that the perspective which is used for explanation has profound consequences for thinking about action. In psychodynamic perspectives, for example, lines of thinking develop that follow an *if-then* logic that is familiar to systems thinking. That is to say, there is a cause-and-effect relationship between behavior and context that is predictable. I found too that in working from this perspective I was drawn to locating the responsibility for my emotional reactions with other group members. In this sense my experience was of being the object of their projections. This is a theme that is common in much psychodynamic literature concerning the relationship between the leader and the group. Alternatively I felt drawn to blaming myself. In this scenario, the group's reaction to me was the product of feelings that I was responsible for creating, an output resulting from my pathological, anxiety-creating input. This tendency to locate responsibility with the personality traits of the leader resonates too with much of the leadership and management theory that is mainstream today and which builds on personality archetypes, often drawn from Jungian psychology, to construct development models for leaders and leadership roles (Stacey 2003, pp. 129–156; Hay Group 2002).

By contrast I have found that working with the idea of complex responsive processes has drawn me to thinking about the way in which our perspectives of reality and our emotional world of experience are both *formed by* and *forming* the social context and the character of human interaction in a perpetual process of construction and reconstruction. I have become interested too in what social convention, in general, and processes of organizational power relating, in particular, enable us to reveal about our feelings for and emotional responses to each other. I am attempting to understand some of the emotional processes at work in groups within organizations by using a specific institutional case study as material for reflection. Specifically, I am exploring the relationship between the leader, the group and the emotional responses that emerge as the felt experiences of participants in this nexus of interactions.

Threats to identity, shame and fear

Currently, I experience a sense of uncertainty about how to go about doing my job. I came into senior leadership positions in education with a sense of purpose that was strongly rooted in my experiences of teaching and of working with students. As I progressed through the promotional ladder my practice became informed by the themes of modernization that have swept through the whole of the public sector in the UK. Now I find myself working in a context that both challenges and compromises fundamentally the principles that drew me to the work I do.

Policy at the macro level is determined in a way that now encompasses the design of service structures to ensure its delivery. This is manifest in frequent and highly complex centrally driven restructuring initiatives, the centralization of control over resource allocation and decision-making and the emergence of new regulatory bodies whose sole function is audit and compliance across the system. In this context the perception of perverse institutional behavior is translated into the failure of individuals. Heads of institutions are now caught up in a burgeoning process of bureaucratic controls designed to limit their scope for local decision-making only to those that are consistent with the design intentions of their political masters (Fink 2001).

Threat, shame and fear have also become dominant tools informing the management disciplines that have been implemented across the public sector. I object to these developments. At the same time, as the head of a major institution, I am implicated in the wider management processes which rely upon such tools. This is a paradoxical position and one which makes me feel unclear about how to frame my professional practice in ways that are relevant and effective to the organization for which I have responsibility and which make sense to me in ways I feel to be authentic and ethical.

I was once much more comfortable with implementing the changes that accompany the modernization process. I was comfortable too with being seen as a high-performing principal able to implement change in line with this agenda. Now, seven years on in my experience of being a CEO, my early naivety has gone. The early optimistic influence of writers such as Senge on my thinking has evaporated. I no longer believe that individuals realize vision. I do not have faith in the bigger vision that is the agenda of our time. I sense that my feelings of discomfort with this agenda and my sense of its ultimate pointlessness, allied to the impact on my behaviors of my experience on the Doctor of Management program at the University of Hertfordshire, may have had something of a destabilizing effect on my relations with peers, my immediate team and those whom they line manage. I am aware that a wider awareness among others of changes in my interests, attitudes and behaviors has evoked a response that has been both positive and negative.

In May 2002, eighteen months after its formation from the merger
of two other large and relatively underperforming institutions, Ofsted
(Office for Standards in Education) inspected the new college. The
college was judged to be 'inadequate'. The process of inspection was
painful for everyone in the institution. The inspection report was highly
critical of the teaching in a number of departments, and this challenged
profoundly the self-image and certainties of many staff. This was
especially the case for those who had long-service histories and who
in a range of contexts had been most resistant to the imposition of new
working practices, targets and performance standards. The leadership
and management of the college were judged in the same process to be
satisfactory. For myself and my team, this outcome was of considerable
political importance but across the institution it evoked strong feelings
of being blamed and shamed. These feelings were accompanied at the
same time by many other strong reactions: for example, that those
deemed by their peers to have been underperforming were being called
finally to account.

Institutions have to respond to inspections with action plans intended
to address areas of 'weakness'. For an 'inadequate' institution this is a
particularly challenging process since there are multiple agencies that
police the process of 'improvement'. In our case I faced great pressure
from some sections of my board to 'deal with' the teaching staff
associated with areas of work judged to be underperforming and to 'root
out' those who were responsible. Although I refused to do this, I found
myself adopting positions in public in which I was uncompromising in
terms of not tolerating what had been judged as unacceptable professional
practice (a 'we' identity aligned with a threatening authority) and at the
same time supportive of individuals in their attempts to work within
the wider context of their job roles (a 'we' identity aligned with
colleagues facing a threatening authority).

Norbert Elias wrote extensively about the issue of 'we' identity in his
study of relationships in a small urban industrial community. Elias'
theory was that groups form identities in order to manage processes of
power relations within which individuals experience the phenomenon
of established and outsider relationships (Elias and Scotson 1994).
The formation of insider/outsider, them/us, we/they relations is now
endemic across the public sector and has emerged as a powerful feature
of the process of distancing policy-makers from service providers as
one group set targets for the other group to 'deliver'. Increasingly my
experience is of trying to hold a problematical *at the same time* position

of paradoxical responses of being a fully aligned risk-managing agent re-enacting and/or reiterating the wider power dynamic at work in the sector generally and questioning, in practice, the implications of this enactment process. I am aware of the extent to which I and others in my peer group (in education and other sectors) engage in a process of self-censorship in the public arena in order to maintain this balance between remaining inside the 'we-identity' of the political mainstream while feeling increasingly concerned about what it takes to sustain such a position.

The senior management workshop

I arrived at the residential program and met the two facilitators (Facilitator-1 and Facilitator-2). Facilitator-2 (F-2) started talking about the group. He was very complimentary about the group and said that they were all talented and committed. A key issue for them, however, was that they felt 'disempowered' in relation to their line managers (that is, the members of my team). In addition, they had talked late into the previous evening about me and their 'fear' of me. Facilitator-1 (F-1) commented that they had also talked about the large group process I had initiated and that they did not like it. In response to a question from myself, F2 offered the view that the 'fear' issue was in some way personal to me and to my relationship with the group. It was not therefore a more general function of my role. The facilitators' view was that I should be careful to be positive about what the group had to say and to welcome their suggestions for change. They felt that it would be a good idea too if I discussed directly the 'fear' issue with the group.

I was not prepared for this interaction. I felt Facilitator-2 was behaving in a way that was quite aggressive towards me. I did not recognize what I understood to be my relationship with the individuals in the group in Facilitator-2's comments. I was aware of myself becoming deeply anxious about the idea of being with the group. I felt as if, in some way, I was going to be exposed during the work group session. I felt too as though I was being both judged and manipulated by Facilitator-1 and Facilitator-2 to ensure that my responses to the group were in some way consistent with their view of what my relationship with the group should be like. This manipulation extended to the way in which I was permitted to enter the workroom. Rather than simply getting up and going into the room, Facilitator-2 explained that it had been agreed that we would wait to be collected by someone from the group. I understood this role-play to signify an intended change in the power relationships that were assumed to exist between the group ('disempowered') and myself ('empowered'). The act of invitation and of being escorted into the room somehow seemed to represent new roles and territories. To enter into these I was to be granted, rather than to assume, permission.

Appreciative inquiry

The session proceeded with C announcing in a comment that was directed particularly to me that individual members of the group were going to make presentations about their work. C said that people would review an aspect of the group's discussions so far in turn and I would be invited to comment at the end of this process. We were into the script and I was to take the role of audience.

The presentation process began. I cannot now recall the detail of what each person said or the sequence in which they made their presentations. The following points do however stand out in my recollection of the proceedings.

The behavior of each individual was in some way breathlessly hyperactive. It turned out that the feedback process which both they and I thought would take a considerable amount of time was over and done with within ten minutes. In fact so quick was this process that when the last person sat down there was something of a stunned silence in the room as everyone looked to me to make the validating (or not) response that Facilitator-2 had primed me to make in his opening remarks. As it happened I resisted the temptation to make a direct response about the content, not knowing what such a response could or should be, but I did respond to the anxiety in the group by saying something in the form of, 'Wow!, and you have only been here twenty-four hours. Can we start again?' In context this had an ice-breaking effect and made everyone laugh. The laughter and the fact that I had provoked it seemed immediately to move us all on. Suddenly I felt in touch with them as a group and as individuals with whom I felt some familiarity away from the centre to which we had all come.

The group had generated a huge volume of physical material as a result of their work together. This material was distributed over three of the walls in the room and on various flipcharts. It communicated a sense of intense and physically frenetic activity. One wall was covered with yellow post-it notes, each of which appeared to contain a key point of reflection or observation. Another wall had large sheets of white paper attached to it. Here the group had summarized the findings of a pre-course activity in which the facilitators had asked them to interview at least four other members of the organization on what they found 'inspirational' about working in the college: this exercise was described formally by Facilitator-2 as an 'Appreciative Enquiry'. On a third wall the group had constructed what appeared to be a huge and quite bewildering collage that spread to the ceiling and in which they had suspended a variety of objects that were connected by threads to the array of materials which had been pinned, glued, stuck, tied and variously appended to the display. The materials had been given to the group in a large cardboard box. As the meeting unfolded and as I reflected upon its proceedings after I had left the centre, the box itself started to assume great significance as a metaphor for other unconscious processes that I felt had taken place in the group.

To receive feedback about this construction, its meaning for the group and the wider organization, we all got out of our seats and stood like spectators at an art gallery around this object as the presenter (E) talked about it. As she reviewed the meaning of each element of the collage (the materials included paper, cloth, modeling clay, wire, CDs, string, pins, hand-drawn signs and symbols and so on) she reached out and used very physical, tactile gestures (touching, smoothing, squeezing) to accompany her verbal explanations. It was clear that the participants felt the importance of this object for them. It seemed clear too from their demeanor that the facilitators felt considerable pride in this object as an outcome of the work of the group.

When we sat down again together and after the moment of laughter had passed, a silence descended upon the group. In that moment I was struck by how much 'play' had emerged between the participants in the period between C announcing their script and the end of the presentations. This I felt was reflected in their skittishness with each other, gestures of personal self-deprecation that referred in a self-referential way to roles they had taken up (or newly discovered) in the short time that they had been together as a group. They seemed unusually solicitous of each others' feelings and aware of the nervousness that each felt in presenting for the group to the power-presence that I seemed to represent for them. Later when we did talk directly about the fear issue, one of them (B) introduced the word 'daddy' to create a sense of the role that they felt I, in some way, represented for them. My affirmation or dismissal of their efforts appeared painfully important to this context and I felt both embarrassment and a sense of shame at the apparent reality of this. I sensed the difficulty that arises for all of us caught up in the dynamics of organizational power to encounter each other with equality of status in our individual engagement with the complexity of our roles. The power differentials that inform our working lives somehow enforce a requirement for us to enact dependency in the presence of an authority figure where in other aspects of our lives we are perfectly able to act authoritatively in our own right, and how we are all caught up in processes that reiterate these relationships up and down the line management structure.

The conversation turned to their concerns regarding their sense of 'disempowerment'. As soon as we started to talk about this it was apparent that the focus of their concerns lay in the line management relationships that now exist between them and their own managers. Here their sense was of being the subject of top-down pressure, one-way communication and endless tasks to be completed, within limited or tight deadlines, with conflicting and different messages also being attached to the communications between them and different managers.

What I observed as being shared in this conversation was a fantasy of organizational life in which most of the pressures of real issues of relating to others had been removed. Issues such as organizational structure, line management, power, responsibility and accountability had all been in some way dissolved. Nobody mentioned the participation of their own line managers, and it appeared that the group had no conception of the possibility of the college requiring a senior team other than their own, now self-organizing, group entity. None of the group appeared to acknowledge how they may have responsibilities both individually and collectively to shape the nature of the interactions that take place within the management group as a whole.

My overwhelming impression of the group in this part of the discussion was that in dealing with the emotional material that had emerged in their time together they had sought refuge in a fantasy from which all the interactions associated with the messiness of the material organizational world had been abstracted. They described a sense of their relationships with others in their organizational life as being wholly 'top down'. In fact they had become so attached to their sense of being at the absolute bottom of a downward chain of command that when invited to reflect upon their responsibilities for the management of others and therefore how they might be perceived in that process, they all floundered, having not factored this into their considerations.

The 'fear' issue

With forty-five minutes to go before the end of the session and sensing that the timing was right both for the group and for me I decided to broach the 'fear' issue. I told the group that I would like them to discuss directly with me their perceptions of what I, through my own behavior, might do specifically to help with the issues that had been raised. An immediate silence descended and everyone looked at the floor. Eventually, conversation started to flow again.

A spoke first. He said that, for his part, he did not find me a 'frightening figure at all'. In fact he found me to be very approachable but he thought that the inspection and its outcomes had put a lot of pressure on everyone and it was known throughout the college that we all had to 'sort things out' or else jobs would be at risk. In A's view the size of the college as it is now constituted and my apparent remoteness from the day-to-day life of the staff created an impression of distance and uncertainty about what I was going to do if the changes that were perceived to be necessary did not happen. A's intervention seemed suddenly to normalize the atmosphere in the room and I, relieved personally by his gesture of solidarity with me, felt more relaxed about carrying on with the discussion.

B has worked with me in a variety of management roles since 1987. B's view was that things were different now in that for the first time I was recognized as having a really strong team around me. These people in turn expected more of others in their roles and it was clear to all of them that they had to take more responsibility for difficult management decisions themselves. Since the merger had taken place I had also become a more remote figure in the college both for all of them and for the staff in general. It was now much more difficult for them to know what I was thinking.

E said that she too found me quite approachable but felt that there were real problems with my visibility around the college. She said that whenever she saw me in meetings either with them as a group or with staff, she always found me to communicate a really strong sense of vision about where we should be going as a college. She went on to say that staff found me 'inspirational' when I talked to them about our work and purpose as an institution. My apparent absence from the day-to-day life of the staff was therefore a real problem for them as managers because no one was now engaged in this communication with staff members.

F referred back to the earlier part of the conversation in which he had talked in quite a theoretical way about empowerment and ownership. He went on to say that he thought it was 'natural' for people to be anxious about the chief executive because in the end this was the person who had to make things happen and to be accountable if they did not. He then went on to talk about football managers who had to achieve results or get sacked.

G spoke about the impact of the merger and the anxieties that this had caused generally. The fact that a number of managers had lost their jobs in the process had added to a general feeling of insecurity. Her view was that she and her peers simply responded to tasks issued by members of my team. This, she felt, diminished their opportunities to contribute in a full managerial capacity.

H's view was that from her perspective the key issue was one of familiarity. She felt that many people were fearful of the new leadership team collectively. The fear issue was therefore not particularly personal to me. She said that staff from the college of which I had not been principal felt me to be very different from what they had been used to in their previous principal. She went on to say that all the new leadership team members were felt by that group of staff (i.e. 50 per cent of the new college) to be 'very different': they expected things to be done and had a determination about them that they had not been used to before.

The group broke up for lunch. I said my goodbyes and left them to continue their work with the facilitators. Their task for the afternoon was to make sense of our discussion of the morning with a view to forming action plans for their return to college.

Sense-making

What emerge from this narrative, I think, are a number of organizing themes that informed our experience of being together. First, the group met in the context of anxieties that had been unresolved in the aftermath of the merger and compounded by the inspection outcome. These related both to the future of the organization and to that of key individuals (of whom I and they were exemplars) working within it. Second, there were anxieties arising from threats to identity for all of us. How were we to understand our new roles in managing in the new larger college? How were we to go on together having been labeled as 'inadequate' by Ofsted? What would I do in response to this? Third, there had been a sharing within the group of aspects of our worlds of emotional experience (fear of me, of the situation, of the future) that had not happened before. Fourth, there was a collective attempt in the script, albeit orchestrated by the facilitators, to experience a process of renegotiation of the power relations between us. Fifth, we struggled to make sense of our fantasies about power. This was both in terms of what I represented to them (validating, judging, deciding) and what they felt they missed (empowerment).

Psychodynamics

Nitsun uses the idea of the *anti-group* to develop Bion's observations about basic assumption behaviors in groups and also to redress what he regards as an over-optimistic view of the therapeutic capability of group analysis. Nitsun attributes this overstated optimism to Foulkes' influence on the group analytic tradition (Nitsun 1996, pp. 32–34).

Bion's approach to groups was psychoanalytic. For Bion, the group is a context that reveals aspects of the individual psyche not otherwise evident in dyadic analytic relationships. The individual in effect arrives in the group as a preformed entity. The group is therefore a situation in which the individual enacts or realizes aspects of self rather than being created as a self as in the thinking of Mead and Elias. Central to Bion's thesis is the idea of the individual and the group in tension. Thus people, argued Bion, are group animals despite needing to find expression in individuality. For Bion the group is therefore an essential context of human experience but one that also holds the inevitable contradictions which arise from conflicting impulses within human experience. This theme (of groups as contexts that are required by the social nature of being but contradicted by desires for individuality) is, I think, of great importance to understanding the particular and determinist perspective in relation to action that a reading of Bion might invite. Bion's approach would lead naturally to the view that groups will always be contexts that will arouse 'regressive' behaviors among group members. This is for the

reason that in Bion's view the tensions immanent within the individual/
group relationship will give rise to the emergence of behaviors that
are based on the archaic conflicts rooted in the origins of social life
(Bion 2001).

In building upon Bion's position, Nitsun identifies behaviors within
groups that are regressive to the point of destruction. Here basic
assumption behaviors become so extreme as to go beyond the boundaries
of what the group can 'contain'. In such an instance, the group falls apart
(often in acrimony) as the defenses represented in the heightened
anti-group behaviors of group members become too powerful for the
group to hold. By contrast, Nitsun also draws attention to the
'transformational' potential of the group – a process that he argues can
release great creativity and focus on the 'group task'. Here Nitsun claims
that a transformational process unfolds within the group, a process which
he characterizes at different times as movement between polarities
(anti-group and work group being the binary poles of what he describes
also as a dialectical process) or as thesis, synthesis and antithesis
((a) anti-group; (b) group in transformation; (c) work group).

> Anti-group and 'pro-group' are the two poles of experience that define
> the development of the group. Within the interplay of the two, the
> group itself is decentred as a static object: it is constantly in movement
> between the opposing modes. The anti-group represents the collapse
> of the dialectic in the direction of destructive processes leading to
> group pathology. The nature of the group pathology will vary in
> relation to the dominant mode of disturbed experience in the group . . .
> this could take the form of fragmentation as part of the a regressive
> response, the empathic gulf created by failures of communication, the
> deadness and despair of the depressive mode, the violence and
> surrender of the aggressive mode, or the combination of several such
> modes in the constellation of group-destructive development.
>
> (Nitsun 1996, p. 204)

Complex responsive processes

In developing an argument for understanding group processes in terms
of complexity theory, and specifically the idea of complex responsive
processes, Stacey draws attention to the dualism within Nitsun's attempts
to locate the *anti-group* within a dialectical process of group dynamics.
Stacey contrasts Nitsun's dialectic that poses the idea of movement
between polarities (which he locates within a Kantian tradition of

thinking) with one drawn from Hegel in which 'the tension of oppositional forces creates a new dynamic in which the opposition remains but with its meaning altered' (Stacey 2003a, p. 296).

Here then is a different possibility for understanding the emergence of destructive forces in groups that focuses attention away from the idea of intra-psychic phenomena and the power of archaic fantasy to the social context and to the sense-making processes of human interaction. Here too the relationship between the individual and the group changes. For both Bion and Nitsun the individual and the group exist at different levels of experience interacting with a social context. Psyche, body and group are split off from each other, interacting as separate entities but sharing, in the group, a common temporal context. Stacey however follows Elias in arguing that the individual and the group are simply different aspects of a single process of human interaction. In this sense, the individual and the group are located in continuous social processes of formation where both regress and progress are constantly possible, where emotion, feeling and meaning emerge socially from the enabling constraints of interaction itself. In this dialectic there are no polarities; only an ongoing emergent process of movement within which relations and meaning are perpetually created and re-created by the participants. Stacey's perspective allows for the abandonment of the idea of dynamics collapsing into polarities but introduces instead the possibility of seeing patterns emerging in processes of relating that enact stuckness, that transform destructively, that engender new creativity. In Elias' words:

> in adopting a wider, dynamic viewpoint . . . the vision of an
> irreducible wall between one human being and all others, between
> inner and outer worlds, evaporates to be replaced by a vision of an
> incessant and irreducible intertwining of individual beings in which
> everything that gives their animal substance the quality of a human
> being, primarily their psychical self-control, their individual character,
> takes on its specific shape in and through relationships to others.
>
> (Elias 2001, p. 32)

Social objects

G. H. Mead elaborated a powerful thesis of social control arising for human beings in relation to the existence, in the field of human perception, of three types of object: *physical objects* present in the natural world, *scientific objects* present in consciousness (but not necessarily present or realizable in the natural world) and *social objects*. Social objects, recognizable in the differentiated patterning of self-similar gestures and responses of associations of human beings, are place-holders for the values, ideologies and attitudes that constitute the raw material for social communication. For Mead, social objects evolve in a manner that is both emergent and, analogically, similar to physical and organic processes of change. Schools, hospitals, churches, factories and so on are all recognizably the same social objects of a century ago. The form of such objects has changed in an emergent way as society has developed new manners, fashions, technologies and working practices. Both the social object and its emergent form are reproduced in the symbolic interaction that occurs between living beings in the course of their own social existence.

Using Mead's perspective it is possible to understand the emergence of the phenomena of mind, self and society as the product of a multiplicity of interactions occurring between individual human bodies. In this process, conversations of gestures involve the interplay of significant symbols in the medium of language, which enable the communication of meaning. Mead's concept of social objects is therefore fundamental to his conceptualization of processes that lead to the construction of meaning in the consciousness of human beings. I want to argue here that Mead's conception of the social object is important for an understanding of the wider situational context (of social, political and cultural influences) which in specific relational conjunctures evokes the emotional responses attributed by Nitsun to the idea of *anti-group* (Mead 1934, 1938, 2002). Events or processes that threaten established identities would constitute such a conjuncture.

Douglas Griffin's work on the emergence of the modern form of organizational leadership contributes further to this understanding (Griffin 2002). Griffin locates the idea of leadership in philosophy, the history of ideas and the ethics of human freedom, and gives meaning to the idea of leadership as a contemporary social object in the Meadian sense. Griffin therefore draws attention to the importance of leadership as a concept that has a contemporary meaning derived from Kantian rationalism. He also draws attention to the importance of systems theory and cybernetics as disciplines of organizational and social management control that reached their high point in the mid-twentieth century. Griffin describes the emergence of a now dominant intellectual formation that views the world in terms of 'parts' and 'wholes', and which therefore splits off the individual from the collective of human experience. Here, managers locate themselves outside of the organizational systems that they exist to 'control'. Here, too, leaders sit at the apex of pyramidal organizational structures apart from the organizational whole that also contains the senior and middle managers and employees for whom they are responsible. The organizational whole (now containing the leader) is in its turn accountable to a board for delivering enhanced shareholder value as in the private corporate sector, or enhanced social value as in the not-for-profit or public sector context.

In drawing attention to the reification of roles (particularly the leadership role) that is central to a systems perspective of organizations, Griffin also explores the implications of this for processes of relating and therefore the wider ethical issues of human freedom. Griffin argues that the dominance of a perspective that reduces individuals, groups and organizations into part/whole relationships is significant for the emergence of organizational forms in which power-holding is both individualized and assumed to be located at the organizational apex. Such a location is accompanied by an equivalent de-powering (or disempowering) of others who occupy lower levels of the organizational hierarchy. These organizational structures facilitate the instrumentalization of power, the deliberate orchestration of its use (expressed in line management structures, employment contracts, appraisal systems and so on). Encoded as norms in the dominant discourse of organizational life, these power structures are also enacted in the self-regulative compliant behaviors of employees.

Affect, performativity and justification

Norbert Elias has drawn attention to the way in which changes in the globalized social context of the late twentieth century continued to iterate with changes in the affective condition of individuals (what he described as the 'affect economy') and which found expression in the intensification of processes of individualization. Elias' concepts of *habitu* (the socially evoked affectual composition of individuals) and *figuration* (the socio-historic character of the net of interdependencies that constitute society) are essential terms that inform an understanding in the present and therefore of being a participant in emergent processes of social formation (Elias 2000, pp. 450–483). As highly dynamic process concepts they draw attention too to the ongoing ways in which the technologies of power are elaborated in the *social objects* of contemporary perception and made concrete in the language structures of everyday conversation:

> individuals have to subordinate their self regulation in speaking to the
> social regulations of their communal language. If they do not, the
> possibility to communicate with each other via a language is brought
> to a standstill.
>
> (Elias 1991, p. 63)

Lyotard and others have identified the emergence of 'performativity'
as the rationale acting as the driving force of postmodern government
policy in relation to education (Lyotard 1979; Ball 2001; Fielding 2001).
In the UK the successful 'delivery' of current education policy is believed
by ministers to underpin aspects of national life as diverse as economic
competitiveness, health, crime, urban regeneration and family policy.
The shift to performative judgements by politicians, policy-makers and
their compliance agencies has in turn led to the emergence of models
of acceptable (and unacceptable) leadership, management, individual
professional conduct and, of course, organizational performance.
Organizational shaming too has become an essential part of the tool-kit
of inspection agencies whose remit and operational processes read like
a script abstracted from Foucault. Public sector inspection regimes
therefore use all the technologies of individualization, scrutiny and
judgement that Foucault identified in his analysis of the emergence
of contemporary forms of socio-political control.

Shotter's work is important here. In his reflections on the idea of the
manager as 'author' or 'scientist' he points out that managers:

> can not just innovate as they please, for the fact is, not just 'anything
> goes' – they cannot be authors of fictions, which bear no relation to
> what the unchosen conditions they face will 'permit', or afford. Their
> authoring must be *justified* or *justifiable*, and for that to be possible,
> it must be 'grounded' or 'rooted' in some way in circumstances others
> share.
>
> (Shotter 1993, p. 149)

The issue of *justification* is central to understanding leader/group
dynamics in organizations, since it points to the way in which the
enactment of power through organizational roles configures relationships
between people. In my view Shotter's use of the idea of *justification* also
draws attention to the ways in which *action* is legitimated through
language meaning. Leaders therefore act legitimately when their behaviors
conform to ways that are described by the word 'leadership'. These
behaviors are in turn validated in a context which is the power relations
that give definition to the word. In Mead's terms this may also be

understood as the social relations that give form to the social object of leadership. To act or to suggest action in ways that are outside of these established norms will therefore create uncertainty, anxiety and great threats to identity for those who might find themselves on the receiving end of leader behaviors which may appear dangerous or simply maverick. I think that Shotter is therefore highlighting the intense pressure which arises from organizational discourse for leaders and followers to behave in ways that conform to normative assumptions. In the public sector normative behavior by a leader would, for example, include the active and energetic embrace of performance management and TQM-type managerial language. Thus for an institutional head to question, for example, the legitimacy of setting SMART targets, or worse to refuse to set SMART targets, as part of an organizational improvement strategy would be an act of rebellion against orthodoxy, the formal agencies and systems of control and common sense itself. Such a gesture would be *unjustifiable* to the extent that it would amount to an act of professional suicide.

Shotter also discusses the ways in which power is used to construct orthodoxy which at its extreme translates into what he, after Bhaktin, describes as 'monologism'. This:

> at its extreme denies the existence outside itself of another consciousness with equal rights and responsibilities, another *I* with equal rights (thou). With a monologic approach (in its extreme or pure form) another person remains wholly and merely an object of consciousness. Monologue is finalized and deaf to the other's response, does not expect it and does not acknowledge it in any decisive force.
>
> (Shotter 1993, p. 62)

I experience daily the requirement to act in ways that are *justifiable* in terms that Shotter describes. I, in my job role, have identity in a socio-political context dominated by performative judgement-making. In my public life I judge and am judged on this basis. The language I use at work is drawn from the monologistic argot that frames countless policy initiatives, statements of targets and improvement initiatives. When I refuse to use this language I know that I am being as clear in my dissent as if I were wearing a badge of political protest. With my peer colleagues I participate also in acts of public self-censorship that collude in and reproduce the power relations which constitute the structures of control across the public sector. I am explicit about my feelings in relation to all of this with only a very few close colleagues.

My experience is that the dominance of performativity in the life of public sector organizations has created among managers intense feelings of fear (of failure) and anxiety about just doing their jobs. Once triggered, these emotions readily flood into the realm of public relationships. The emotional responses labeled as 'regressive' by Bion and further theorized by Nitsun may be understood in this context. In the performative context of the modern public sector, leader and leadership (individualized, visionary, a single locus of ethical and professional accountability) are place-holders for meaning that has acquired cult status of the kind that Mead explored when writing about the significance of religious impulses in social life. Of the idea of cults and their values Mead wrote:

> the cult of a community becomes very concrete, identifies itself with the immediate history and life of the community, and is more conservative than almost any other institution in the community. The cult has a mysterious value, which attaches to it that we cannot fully rationalize and therefore we preserve it in the form, which it always has had, and in its social setting. It tends to fix the character of . . . expression.
>
> (Mead 1934, p. 296)

The world occupied by managers in the public sector is dominated by the performance cult. It is therefore simultaneously monologistic in Shotter's terms (totalitarian in Lyotard's) and densely impregnated with systemic processes of shaming. The responses that Nitsun labels *anti-group* may therefore be shown to emerge in the interplay of gesture and response in a context whose social objects are redolent with power, threat and personal destruction.

The paradox of presence

In my discussion with the group I felt that the 'fear' I represented, as presented by F2, was strongly linked to narrative themes of *presence* and *absence*. I felt that my real or imagined absence was altogether more anxiety-creating for the group than my presence.

The fear of my presence was, I thought, fairly straightforward. In this context I understood myself to exist for the group as a judging, authority figure with the perceived ability to create (by appointing and promoting people such as those present in the room, by validating their work) and destroy (by 'getting rid' of people, by not validating their work efforts, by not valuing them as persons). As a figure in the presence of the group I, like any other CEO in a public or private sector organization, therefore carried the potential for their annihilation. In the narratives of G and H, described above, this potential destructivenes, was not just characteristic of me but had also been seeded in the wider leadership group. Yet as a leader both present to the group and with an aura of potential destructiveness it seemed clear that the group also felt this power to be hugely constructive, protective and important to them. Their 'knowledge' of me (crystallized in their conversations and fantasies of the past thirty-six hours of being together) was that I (not them) could be relied upon to do things to protect them and the institution, which they would and could not contemplate. The actions of the leader, with the power to employ, promote, demote and dismiss, are therefore an important element of processes in which personal identities are both constructed and deconstructed in the organizational context.

The paradox of the co-existence of destructive and creative forces within a single action embodied in a single person or gesture is, I think, a powerful and almost too complex reality for managers in general to both recognize and hold. The wider socio-political context which attaches to leadership the requirement that leaders are one-dimensional makes this ambiguity intolerable. It is in this context, namely the reification of organizational power into the social object of leadership, that I have come to understand the extraordinary degree of fantasy which surrounds the CEO role in organizations. Stereotypes arise in the shadow conversational world of organizations that are allied to these fantasies. Mead's observation about religious attitudes and the emergence of cult values is of relevance here. The cult idea, in this case the potency of the leader, has a mysterious value which is difficult to fully comprehend and rationalize. It is none the less preserved in its form in its social setting. The idea of leadership in its contemporary form, as described by Griffin, has about it this same cult quality in which the individual leader's capacities are idealized (in the expectations of the group) and functionalized (in their ongoing relations with others) (Griffin 2002, p. 195).

The cult of individualized leadership is therefore interlinked with the cult of performance management. Performance management is predicated upon the individualization of responsibility and accountability at every level of the organizational hierarchy. The leader, at the top of the organizational pyramid, is therefore both the primary energizer of this process and the individual point of ultimate accountability. I know from experience that in my job role my actions are articulated in power relations that are consistent with the dominant discourse of public sector performance management. I am aware too of my own vulnerability arising from my exposure to the judgement of others.

The paradox of absence

However, if the idea of *presence* evokes powerful symbolic meaning around the CEO role, the idea of *absence* seems to me to be more intricate and complex in its significance. From an intra-psychic perspective both Bion and Nitsun have emphasized the importance of the perception of an absent leader to the emergence of basic assumption behaviors in groups:

> The *absence* rather than the presence of directive leadership awakens regressive forces in the group. The frustration of the members' wish for explicit leadership unleashes powerful, archaic fantasies concerning the leader and the nature of the group. In attempting to give the group structure and direction, the members resort to the primitive organisation of the basic assumptions. In some respects, these satisfy deeper longings but they erode the capacity of the group to think and to work. . . . I [suggest] that for all their apparent 'groupiness', basic assumption groups are *anti-groups*: their regressive formations undermine group functioning in the sense of coherent interrelatedness.
>
> (Nitsun 1996, p. 109)

In this particular instance, the group referred to my absence in a number of ways, including my reduced visibility in the day-to-day lives of the group itself and their staff since the merger. This made me a more remote figure. Not just physically remote but remote also in a way that seemed to have detached me from the 'feeling' and emotional life of the institution – remote in the sense of having in some way absconded from an earlier more intimate and nurturing set of relationships (referenced by A and G in their narratives). In turn this perceived remoteness appeared to have enhanced the fantasy within the group about my supposed retributive powers. These had also grown exponentially (magnified yet further by the perception of threat to the institution that had emerged as a result of the poor Ofsted inspection outcome).

My absence, too, meant that my power to influence staff members' attitudes to their jobs and to the wider institution had been reduced

(E's fantasy: Who would now take responsibility for communicating 'vision', for being 'inspirational'?). The consequential impact of my absence in other contexts (B's mythology around the 'vacuum' I had left behind after leaving a job earlier in my career) had been brought into the narrative of this group and added further coloration to their feelings towards me. Underneath these observations lay also a further concern that I really might leave the college in this difficult period either by being in some way sacked (F's fantasy about CEOs and football managers) or by getting another job (as I had done before, in B's fantasy).

The experience of absence and remoteness clearly changes the social context of relationships in a significant way. The intimacy of social interaction that is central to processes in which identity is constructed and secured are no longer available. Uncertainty therefore arises in this movement with respect to the ongoing relationship between the leader and others. People once able to rely upon the leader now find themselves exposed to taking on attributes of leadership in relation to others. They find this experience threatening and anxiety-creating, since the processes of formation of identity and self become subject to significant dislocation and reconstruction. Relational patterns start to change right across the organization. I think that the group were giving voice to this experience in our organizational context.

Normative discourse and disclosure

The activities of the group also generated material that related to norms of action and behavior in the social object of leadership. The material displayed by the group therefore represented the publicly permissible conversations of leaders and managers; that is, those areas of discourse that are recognized as having legitimacy within mainstream conventions and as representing what managers should feel good about attending to such as strategy, planning, vision and change. The world of experience that appeared to have risen to the surface for them in their discussions of the preceding thirty-six hours could not be given the same status or treatment, since it is in relation to these more emotional aspects of human relating (i.e. those involving experiences of fear, anxiety, vulnerability) that managers might be most open to feelings of guilt, shame and embarrassment. Such feelings cannot be readily acknowledged or witnessed in a form as tangible as visual displays or other constructions of the group – for the construction itself would make concrete the need for other kinds of discourse and experience to be attended to which in their own way create deep anxiety for group members. Set against the cult of performance management within which the leader is permanently rational and judged by an assumed ability to achieve results, public admissions of other kinds of experience that attest to feelings of vulnerability assume a degree of perversity that will inhibit their expression.

The process of scripting, in the way in which the facilitators and the group sought to manage our interactions, seemed to be designed to eliminate risk, to inhibit the emergence of something 'unexpected', to contain the idea of development or indeed that of novelty. This attempt at orchestration was itself then a gesture of the group that was designed to invoke a response in me which accepted their interpretation of how 'it' would be from now on. I think of the script as an attempt to change the dynamic of the power relations that the group felt to exist between us. I felt that the facilitators had encouraged a kind of behavior within the group that did not acknowledge power relations as a fundamental aspect of organizational roles. Instead, the group had been encouraged to enact a game that would be of no real use to them, or to me in my relations with them, beyond their short stay at the residential centre. This script was therefore, I felt, also an invitation to me to join in this play in order to surrender a contentious and anxiety-creating voice.

Conclusion

Throughout this chapter I have drawn attention to the work of Bion and Nitsun in order to make sense of the experience I have narrated, but both Bion and Nitsun approach the issue of individual and group relations from an intra-psychic perspective. Individuals arrive in the group as formed selves, they exchange (through processes of projection, introjection and projective identification) pre-formed psychic material. They are entities within a bounded whole. This position contrasts greatly with that of Mead and Elias where the self emerges in social interaction. Here the individual and the group, located in a social process, are always being formed in an unbounded nexus of interdependent relationships – the 'network' to which Elias refers in *The Society of Individuals* (Elias 2001, p. 32).

Going further with this in terms of Mead's theories of social interaction, the experience of this conversation was a process of gesture and response out of which meaning emerged. Mead's sense of the dialectical relationship that is the interplay of gesture and response offers a means of understanding the emotional experiences of group participants in ways that are rooted in physical interaction rather than in metaphysical projections and introjections. In Mead's dialectic, gesture by one is meaningful only in terms of the response that is called forth in the other. My interaction with F2 exemplifies this. I had no means of knowing what F2 anticipated in the response that his remarks about fear aroused in me. F2 was certainly not conscious of the thought processes with which I was engaged and have described in the early stages of this project. But in our process of interaction my emotional dispositions in relation to the planned event changed fundamentally from those with which I arrived at the centre. This change in me affected directly my behavior in and with the group throughout the conversation and beyond: hence my current writing. In my interaction with F2, meaning that was not anticipated emerged. Put another way, the intention of the gesture was evident only in the character of the response.

Other aspects of the conversational process may be understood in similar terms. In their gestures and responses prior to my arrival, the group shared their thoughts and fantasies about their roles, our wider working context and me. The *reality* that emerged from this process was manifest in the collage and their collective narrative about our organization. In our ensuing conversation propositions about this *reality* were renegotiated. Alternative hypotheses about the organization emerged and were adopted by all present as new truths with which we would work and go forward together. One example of this was the way in which we discussed and negotiated a different understanding of the status of members of this group relative to their own line managers. My relationship with each member of the group was also altered as a result of the gestures and responses that flowed between us. We acquired new knowledge of how we could be together. This influenced our sense of identities in relation to each other. It affected materially our feelings and behaviors towards each other.

I want to suggest, therefore, that the experience of the conversation I have described may be understood by reference to a social, as against psychodynamic, explanation of a personal emotional world arising in the process of the continuous weaving and reweaving of self (Rorty 1991, p. 93). This is a context within which the individual and the group are simply aspects of one process of interaction.

I also want to argue that these interactions were bounded more by the power relations given by the social context of our meeting (i.e. the centre, the focus on work, the presence of facilitators, our organizational roles) than by tendencies for any of us to regress in ways influenced by archaic psychodynamic forces. From a social constructivist perspective it is vital to understand the contribution of the wider context of power relations to the patterning of the emotional responses of individuals drawn into interaction one with another. The 'good' group-'bad' group juxtapositions that are evident in the work of Nitsun and Bion are incompatible with the process perspective of Elias and Mead. In Mead's writing on conflict and integration in the formation of society he draws attention to the antisocial implications of 'impulses' for self-protection and for self-preservation. He goes on to say however that these same impulses lead to collaborative associations that enhance processes of social protection and of social assistance (Mead 1934, p. 305). Thus within the Meadian dialectic the antisocial and the social coexist in paradoxical relation to each other. Individuals are united by a common social interest:

> and yet, on the other hand are more or less in conflict relative to numerous other interests which they possess only individually, or else share with one another only in small and limited groups. Conflicts among individuals in a highly developed and organized human society are not mere conflicts among their respective primitive impulses but are conflicts among their respective selves or personalities, each with its definite social structure.
>
> (Mead 1934, p. 307)

In this passage, Mead is emphasizing the social dimension of self and personality. This seems to me to offer an alternative way of making sense of my interaction with the group of managers whose residential session I had joined. In Mead's terms any change in the social relation of individuals entails a change in the nature and meaning of self. It is in working with a recognition of this paradox of interdependence that 'leading is no longer split off from the nature of leadership' and within which an ethical approach to leading and managing in organizations may be both recognized and practiced (Griffin 2002, p. 207). Our conversation characterized this process: there was a movement, akin to an ebb and flow, of recognition occurring between us. Fantasies and perceptions were adjusted. I revealed aspects of my experience not otherwise known to the group. They in turn also revealed to me a world of emotional experience of which I was unaware. We experienced our interdependence even if we did not acknowledge this in a formal or explicit way. Selves were, to some extent, recast.

In the process of writing this I have become very aware of my experience of the paradoxical nature of leadership as a process of being and not being in control. Further, I would argue that an act of acknowledging feelings of not being in control, either in verbalization or in gestures that push back the responsibility for knowing and solving, is both essential to a process that enables others to experience their ability to act in the moment but deconstructive of the social object of leadership around which organizational power relations are substantially configured. This deconstruction is fraught with risk. It has the potential to discredit the incumbent leader by creating the appearance of being an outsider in a context where insider relationships are contingent upon the enactment of behaviors that are 'normal' and therefore consistent with commonsense ways of being and doing. Equally, the deconstruction of the idea of knowing and solving on the part of the leader will engender great feelings of anxiety on the part of those for whom the leader is an object of safety and security in a world that is perceived to be turbulent with change and impregnated with threat. It is clear to me however that it is important to find an approach to leading and managing that seeks an ethical basis in emergent processes of communicative action. This means working as an engaged participant in the interactions of those struggling with all these tensions in the living present of their experiences of life in organizations.

References

Ball, S. (2001) 'Performativities and fabrications in the education economy: towards the performative society', in D. Gleeson and C. Husbands, *The Performing School: Managing Teaching and Learning in a Performance Culture*, London: Routledge.

Bion, W. R. (2001) *Experiences in Groups: And Other Papers*, London: Routledge.

Damasio, A. (1994) *Descartes' Error: Emotion, Reason and the Human Brain*, New York: Quill.

Damasio, A. (2000) *The Feeling of What Happens: Body, Emotion and the Making of Consciousness*, London: Vantage.

Deegan, M. (ed.) (2002) *George Herbert Mead: Essays in Social Psychology*, New York: Transaction.

Elias, N. (1991) *The Symbol Theory*, London: Sage.

Elias, N. (2000) *The Civilizing Process*, Oxford: Blackwell.

Elias, N. (2001) *The Society of Individuals*, New York: Continuum.

Elias, N. and Scotson, J. (1994) *The Established and the Outsiders*, London: Sage.

Fielding, M. (2001) 'Target setting, policy pathology and student perspectives: learning to labour in new times', in M. Fielding (ed.) *Taking Education Really Seriously: Four Years' Hard Labour*, London: Routledge.

Fineman, S. (2000) *Emotion in Organisations*, London: Sage.

Fink, D. (2001) 'The two solitudes: policy makers and policy implementers', in M. Fielding (ed.) *Taking Education Really Seriously: Four Years' Hard Labour*, London: Routledge.

Foucault, M. (1991) *Discipline and Punish: The Birth of the Prison*, London: Penguin.

Foucault, M. (1994) *Power: The Essential Works 1954–1984, Vol. 3*, London: Penguin.

Griffin, D. (2002) *The Emergence of Leadership: Linking self-organization and ethics*, London: Routledge.

Hay Group (2002) *Lessons in Leadership*, Hay Group Working Paper.

Hirschhorn, L. and Barnett, C. (eds) (1993) *The Psychodynamics of Organizations*, Philadelphia, PA: Temple University Press.

Lyotard, J. F. (1979) *The Postmodern Condition: A Report on Knowledge*, Manchester: Manchester University Press.

Mead, G. H. (1934) *Mind, Self and Society*, Chicago, IL: University of Chicago.

Mead, G. H. (1938) *The Philosophy of the Act*, Chicago, IL: University of Chicago.

Mead, G. H. (2002) *The Philosophy of the Present*, New York: Prometheus.

Nitsun, M. (1996) *The Anti-group: Destructive Forces in the Group and their Creative Potential*, London: Routledge.

Rorty, R. (1991) 'Inquiry as re-contextualisation: An anti-dualist account of interpretation', in *Objectivity, Relativism and Truth*, Cambridge: Cambridge University Press.

Shotter, J. (1993) *Conversational Realities: Constructing Life Through Language*, London: Sage.

Solms, M. and Turnbull, S. (2002) *The Brain and the Inner World*, London: Karnac.

Stacey, R. (2003a) *Strategic Management and Organisational Dynamics: The Challenge of Complexity*, London: Prentice Hall.

Stacey, R. (2003b) *Complexity and Group Processes: A radically social understanding of individuals*, London: Brunner-Routledge.

Stacey, R., Griffin, D. and Shaw, P. (2000) *Complexity and Management: Fad or radical challenge to systems thinking?*, London: Routledge.

Editors' introduction to Chapter 4

John Tobin, CEO of a hospital in the USA draws attention to an extremely important aspect of the activity of leading which is largely overlooked in the now vast literature on leadership, namely human feelings and emotions. He ascribes this lack of attention to such a basic and pervasive element of human experience to the split in Western thinking between rationality/cognition and emotion. The ideal leader of the organizational literature is one who has emotions so under control that they can be ignored and attention focused on rational action, including the inspiring of followers, which amounts to the intentional and rational manipulation of followers' emotions. Tobin draws on recent brain research to contest this split between rational action and feelings. This research shows that the same areas of the brain are implicated both in emotion and rational action. This means that the ideal leader of the organizational literature is a myth which is impossible to find in actual, practical experience because emotion and rational action cannot be separated.

Tobin points to the relatively small body of organizational literature which does take up the matter of emotion, most notably the writing of Goleman and others on 'emotional intelligence'. However, Tobin argues, this literature perpetuates the split between rational cognition and emotion, and continues to locate emotion in purely individual terms. Goleman treats emotion as a tool that leaders can use in a rational way to be more effective. The emotionally intelligent leader may be trained to be so and to use the tool to create a desired cultural environment and so drive the performance of others. The careful expression of the 'right' emotion by the leader is held to be contagious and to spread throughout the organization. For Goleman, emotional intelligence may be quantified, analyzed and modeled.

In this chapter, Tobin draws on a different tradition of thought, largely the work of Elias and Mead, to present a social perspective on the role of emotion, inseparable from cognition and rational action, in the activity of learning. What he presents is the notion of the leader as a role emerging in social interaction where what is being recognized by others is a developed capacity for detached involvement. Drawing on the work of Elias, Tobin makes a distinction between involved and detached thinking. The scientific method is the prime example of detached thinking, where subjectivity, particularly emotion, is avoided as far as is humanly possible and the stance of the rational, analytical, objective observer is taken. The observer and the observed are held apart as far as is humanly possible. However, before the scientific age, we had no option but to view nature in an involved way. People felt immersed, clearly involved in nature which was believed to be incomprehensible forces acting upon them. Elias called this 'magico-mythic' thinking of a highly emotional kind. While we have come to view nature in a highly detached way which gives us considerable control over it, Elias argued that we have not yet developed models of human interaction, of social processes, which enable us to think about, and control, such social process in the same way that we do with regard to nature. Instead, we think in the involved way characterized by thinking in terms of the social as 'magico-mythical' forces acting upon us. However, the scientific, detached approach to thinking about social and organizational phenomena has been brought to bear and has the effect of covering over the 'magico-mythic' nature of our thinking about organizations. It is 'magico-mythic', involved thinking about organizations, expressed in the language of rational detached thinking, to talk about leaders as special individuals who can harness the forces of culture, human motivation and so on, to move an 'it' called 'the organization' in directions, using tools, that they have rationally chosen.

Tobin counters this confusion of thinking about and leading organizations in an involved way but expressed in a detached way. Involved thinking is highly emotive, impulsive, aroused by anxiety and fear which makes reality testing impossible, so leading to potentially inappropriate action. Detached thinking is controlled, observed, non-impulsive, all in the absence of anxiety and fear. Following Elias, Tobin argues that in social settings it is impossible to think in a purely detached way. In such settings, we frequently do not know what is going on and we often feel anxious. Thinking in organizations, therefore, is always paradoxical: involved and detached at the same time.

Tobin argues that leaders are those who have enhanced capacities for detached involvement but such skills are not confined to them alone. All those engaged in interaction are capable of such thinking and the role of the leader is therefore fluid, and moves between people when they act effectively. Effective leaders assist others to sustain the paradox of detached involvement. He also points to the ordinary everyday experience of detached involvement in the narrative account he gives of a particular incident at his hospital.

He argues against complexity writers who see the complexity sciences as a source for prescriptions to remove hierarchy and control mechanisms. If for nothing else, hierarchy and control mechanism are required to enable us to live with the anxiety of not knowing. He sees leadership as an emerging role and the leader as one who needs to pay attention to the micro detail of interactions with others, particularly the feeling aspects of this.

> The essential notion is that through 'self-distancing', and by bringing our feelings and emotional responses within the scope of our rational thought processes, we are able to experience our emotions in a different way – as an object of our experience. We are better able to control impulsive, habitual behaviors and responses. We can enable better comprehension of the processes in which we are embedded, and thus better cope with the sense of being impelled and constrained by forces we cannot control or even experience directly. We can plan and act in a way that is more likely to produce a desirable outcome. Self-distancing through detached involvement gives us the capacity to become engaged without being overwhelmed.
>
> (p. 78)

4 The role of leader and the paradox of detached involvement

John Tobin

I work as the CEO of a community hospital in a city in the USA with two hospitals – ours and a Catholic hospital of comparable size. Although both hospitals have very loyal constituencies, for as long as I can remember, local business leaders have believed that duplication of programs and services and competition between the hospitals was wasteful and destructive. The pressure to consolidate the two hospitals has become significant in recent years as changes in the US health care system have put both institutions under considerable financial distress. Consolidation of a Catholic with a secular hospital requires the approval of the bishop with jurisdiction in that locality – and such approvals have become increasingly difficult to obtain.

In the late 1990s, trustees from each institution met several times in secret in an attempt to engineer a merger between the two hospitals and to present the bishop with a *fait accompli*. I was made aware of these meetings after they had begun. I was kept informed and allowed to participate indirectly through comments and advice I gave to my own trustees. However, neither hospital's CEO was allowed to participate directly and, to the best of my knowledge, my counterpart at the Catholic hospital was never informed of this process until it was over.

I hated my not being 'at the table' myself. I had to rely on my own trustees' honesty – which I did – but there was always a nagging concern that I was not being kept fully informed. In our community, deal-making behind the scenes is commonplace, and the trustees knew that successfully merging the two hospitals would be seen as a great coup among their colleagues. Finally, I had been told that the group believed the new organization would require new leadership – it would be politically unacceptable to either Board to allow the other's incumbent CEO to head the new organization. I had no personal relationship with any of the Catholic hospital's trustees, so I felt that I would be considered completely expendable by that body. While I understood that the business community desired a merger, and that the two organizations might gain many benefits from consolidation, it was difficult to approach this transaction from an objective standpoint while I constantly worried about my own fate. I had been assured that I would be provided for financially, and I knew that I was hardly without career options, but I found my inability to control events and my exclusion from the process to be especially galling and frustrating. Worse, because the process was conducted in secrecy, I did not have the opportunity to discuss the matter with others who might have helped me to relieve my own anxiety. I worked with my trustees and expressed support for a merger because it was unwise to be seen as an obstructionist, but I was greatly relieved when the bishop rejected the trustees' proposal and put an end to the episode.

Pressure to consolidate the two institutions arose again in 2001, this time from the state regulatory authority responsible for hospitals. This time I was determined, as was my colleague from the Catholic institution, not to allow a repetition of the secret meetings. We resolved that the management teams would take the lead and we developed a time line to bring our trustees into the process only after we had framed the transaction conceptually. In the years following the first episode, collaboration between the two hospitals had become substantial, including the building of a large, free-standing cancer treatment center. Trustees and senior executives from both institutions had had the opportunity to work together on this significant project for an extended period and the two management teams had developed a relationship of respect and trust for each other. I was no longer an unknown quantity to the Catholic hospital's trustees and knew that I was well regarded by those who participated in the cancer center project. I no longer worried about becoming a casualty of a merger. Besides, I was a bit older, I was pursuing the Doctor of Management degree at the University of Hertfordshire, and the idea of a career change, however late in my working life, seemed much less ominous. The advantages of a merger were now clear and compelling, and I was able to pursue that goal with honest enthusiasm. However, this process also came to an abrupt end when the bishop intervened a second time, but the idea of consolidating the hospitals, despite the challenges and barriers, remains very much alive today.

There were several lessons to be learned from this episode. One of the most stark and frequently exercised expressions of power differences in any organization is the power to include or exclude, yet executives rarely think much about inclusion/exclusion dynamics and their destructive potential. Inclusion or exclusion from a group immediately distinguishes an 'in' group from an 'out', and the ability to define who is or is not 'in' is the prerogative of, and essential to the self-identity of, the more powerful. Most hospital CEOs, including me, are members of their boards of trustees, but my exclusion from the process immediately established my subordinate status. Further, my inability to influence, if not control, a process in which I had so much at stake, both personally and professionally, was a source of great anxiety for several weeks.

For all of these reasons, I could not have been more 'involved' in the proceedings; yet, because of my position, I was obliged to deal with it as detachedly and objectively as I could. Because of the secrecy of the process, I was unable to discuss the matter with colleagues – a process which may have helped me to manage my own anxiety. My experience of being excluded from the first merger talks will never be forgotten. I have tried since then to make the management processes of our organization more open and participative – but I have become increasingly sensitive also to the difficulties in changing such a fundamental feature of organizational life, mostly to do with how people feel.

In this chapter I will explore the everyday experience of leading in an organization, focusing on the role which emotion, involvement, plays in that activity and the relationship with detachment. At their most basic, emotions are the sensations we experience as our bodies respond to stimuli from our environment, the 'feeling states' rooted in neural impulses and changes in body chemistry as we encounter and respond to people, places, objects and situations – and also react to the memory images these encounters stimulate. Intense or unusual experiences will stimulate feeling states that we notice, but, for the most part, we experience a continuous flow of feeling states at or below our level of attention.

Emotions once had no place in rational, 'by the numbers' scientific management, so emotions were not studied extensively. However, because some management thinkers now recognize the importance of emotions in management practice, there is a small but significant body of literature on 'emotional intelligence'. In the mainstream literature, leading is inevitably presented as an activity of individuals, and leadership is a cluster of skills and traits possessed by individual leaders. In this paradigm, emotional intelligence is described as a characteristic or a learned skill – enabling leaders to attune their behaviors to specific situations or co-workers.

I believe leading is an activity that emerges in groups of interacting individuals engaged in collaborative action – a totally social perspective. From this perspective, emotions become a far more significant phenomenon and a worthy subject of study and understanding. Emotions, feeling states, are not skills or traits. Feeling states are essential to the life processes of the complex human organism. Studies have shown that emotions, feelings, are essential to our ability to think rationally. Rational, 'by the numbers' scientific management is impossible without emotions. Emotions perform an evaluative function – helping us to choose optimally from among the many action options we face continually throughout the working day. As such, they play an important role in helping us make ethical choices as well as 'operational' ones. Finally, emotional 'resonance' in a group of collaborators plays an important role in coordinating human action, the very essence of organizing and managing. The question before us, when we consider emotions from this perspective, is whether or not a leader can learn to focus more attention on feeling states and, through that enhanced attention, gain a better understanding of what is going on in a social interaction, thereby participating in the process in a way that improves outcomes.

Elias and complex processes

Sociologist Norbert Elias, whose work is an important source for the theory of complex processes of relating, was also indispensable to my own exploration of the role of emotions in executive practice from a complexity perspective. In 1939, Elias wrote:

> what we lack – let us freely admit it – are conceptual models and an overall vision by which we can make comprehensible in thought what we experience daily in reality, by which we could understand how a large number of individuals form with each other something that is more and other than a collection of separate individuals – how they form a 'society', and how it comes about that this society can change in specific ways, that it has a history which takes a course which has not been intended or planned by any of the individuals making it up.
>
> (Elias 1991, p. 7)

While Elias wrote these words long before chaos and complexity began to receive attention in the 1960s, first in mathematics and the natural sciences, and, later, in the social sciences, in all of his major works Elias describes and studies what are certainly complex, nonlinear dynamical processes among humans. Perhaps more importantly, Elias describes how we experience living in such processes, and how our selves, our personalities as individuals, arise from the process of human relating.

I believe that insights from the complexity sciences may strengthen the explanatory power of the conceptual models Elias was attempting to develop for sociology in particular, and for the human sciences in general, and thus may become the conceptual model Elias found lacking in contemporary social sciences. If so, interpreting Elias' concepts with insights from the complexity sciences may open new ways to understanding how organizational processes work, and the implications such new understanding may have for those who lead organizations.

Organizations and the societies in which they are embedded are complex, nonlinear, relational processes. The increasing complexity of organizations is a manifestation of the increasing complexity of Western society. The 'opacity' of the process is a source of anxiety in organizations as it is in society as a whole. Elias describes the experience in vivid language:

> It is as if first thousands, then millions, then more and more millions walked through this world with their hands and feet chained together

by invisible ties. No one is in charge. No one stands outside. Some want to go this way, others that. They fall upon each other and, vanquished or defeated, still remain chained to each other. No one can regulate the movements of the whole unless a greater part of them are able to understand, to see, as it were from the outside, the whole patterns they form together. And they are not able to visualize themselves as part of those large patterns because, being hemmed in and moved uncomprehendingly hither and thither in ways in which none of them intended, they cannot help being preoccupied with the urgent, narrow and parochial problems which each of them has to face. They can only look at whatever happens to them from their narrow location within the system. They are too deeply involved to look at themselves from without. Thus what is formed of nothing but human beings acts upon each of them, and is experienced by many as an alien external force not unlike the forces of nature.

(Elias 1987, p. 10)

Elias and the dynamic of involvement and detachment

According to Elias, societies, their structures and their institutions evolve. Simpler societies have simpler social structures. Historically, primitive societies consisted of small groupings where largely self-sufficient individuals lived very close to nature. In this situation, the threat of physical harm from other human beings, wild animals or other natural phenomena such as storms were a constant threat to human survival. According to Elias, both historically and today, the more we fear or lack control over the phenomena we encounter in our natural environment, the greater our tendency to think about them through fantasy and emotion. For Elias, humankind's inability to comprehend and control the forces of nature required a more 'involved mode of thinking.' 'Magico-mythical' thinking provides emotional relief to the constant threat. In this sense, a capacity for involved thinking confers survival advantage, and has become an innate capacity of human thought processes.

The evolution of Western society into the complex web of interdependencies we experience today was also accompanied by a growth in the fund of human knowledge (especially scientific knowledge) – a growing ability to achieve substantial control over our natural environment – and the gradual pacification of Western society. This process results in a growing sense of security. We experience diminishing fear of threats from nature and diminishing fear of direct physical violence at the hands of others in our immediate, everyday environment. At the same time, navigating this complex web of interdependencies requires a far greater degree of control over our natural impulses and also a much greater degree of foresight and of understanding the motives and likely reactions of others, so that we can adjust ourselves to our place within the social structure. Elias referred to the requisite mode of controlled, observant, non-impulsive behavior as 'ambivalence' or 'detachment'.

In summary, knowledge development is a process relationship. As our power over our non-human environment, through scientific advances, has grown, we are able to consider natural phenomena in an increasingly detached way. At the same time, the danger human beings represent to each other has grown. Although the civilizing process has been characterized by increasing pacification within human groupings, the level of violence between groupings (or at least the potential for violence) has grown. Further, in a complex society such as ours, threats to our status, identity and economic well-being are just as unsettling to us as threats of physical violence. The incredibly complex webs of interdependency of modern society have become so incomprehensible to us that these threats can be just as mysterious in origin as earthquakes and typhoons were to our forebears. 'Tensions, power differences, wins and losses associated with interdependence create insecurity and thus make it difficult to deal with social change in a detached way' (Elias 1987, p. 11).

Concept of the 'double bind'

The concept of the double bind is closely related to involvement and detachment. Elias defines the circular process of double bind succinctly:

> High exposure to the danger of the process tends to heighten the emotivity of human responses. High emotivity of responses lessens the chance of a realistic assessment of the critical processes, hence of a realistic practice in relation to it. Relatively unrealistic practice, under the pressure of strong affects, lessens the chance of bringing the critical process under control.

> (Elias 1987, p. 98)

The basic idea of the double bind is that the more we lack control over phenomena, the greater our fear and anxiety concerning these phenomena and the greater our tendency to think about them through fantasy and emotion-laden ideation. Our need for relief from the stresses and anxieties caused by fear keeps us 'locked' in this type of thinking, making it very difficult to approach these kinds of phenomena in a detached way. Throughout history, this has retarded the general advancement of knowledge, and continues to operate to a greater extent today than we might assume to be true in our technologically advanced society.

Elias argued that it is difficult for human beings to break out of the double-bind problem in our social relationships for several reasons. Because we have gained a significant level of control over the non-human aspects of our environment through advances in the natural sciences – and thus the ability to view natural phenomena in a more detached way – we tend to assume that this mode of thinking is universal. In fact, we do not have the same level of control over social processes, and thus are 'blind' to our own tendency to approach social intercourse in a more involved way. We also have a millennia-long philosophical and religious tradition that causes us to think of ourselves as endowed by God or Nature with special human attributes, including the power of rational thinking and behavior that is totally within our control through the exercise of free will. Finally, we have no good theoretical models for unplanned social processes driven by their own internal dynamics and with immanent structures of their own – complex relational processes. 'All planned social practices take place within a stream of unplanned and aimless, though structured, processes at a variety of interdependent levels' (Elias 1987, p. 49).

Since learning and adaptation to change in organizations goes hand in hand, Elias' concept of involvement and detachment has relevance to an exploration of leading in complex processes of relating. Because we lack (perhaps up until now) a useful conceptual framework for dealing with complex processes, Elias says we tend to comprehend them at either of two extremes: as completely unplanned, random processes over which we have no control, or, because we know social processes involve human action and human intention, as processes driven by the intention and planning of individuals or groups (leaders). Insights from the complexity sciences suggest a perspective falling between these extremes: in a complex process of relating, human intent and human action certainly matter, but it is the nonlinear interaction of the actions of many human beings that drives the process into an unknowable future.

The implication for leadership, then, must also lie somewhere between the extremes of control, and 'going with the flow'. Elias argues that it is possible, through a 'detour via detachment', to better understand the structure and the dynamics of the processes in which we are embedded and thereby be able to 'position' ourselves (for lack of a better term) within those processes in ways that will improve our chances of reaching a desired future. Elias cautions, however, that these are, after all, group processes. The ability of any individual to think in a more detached way and to act accordingly will be constrained by the process itself, the nonlinear interaction of individual actions with those of others.

Many popular interpretations of the implications of insights from the complexity sciences suggest that modern organizations are oppressive places. Structure, control and 'linear thinking' are sources of anxiety and stifle creativity in organizations. Elias presents a compelling argument for an opposite interpretation: structure and control mechanisms may be essential for the successful evolution of human processes. Elias argued that anxiety inhibits learning, which is essential for adaptation and change. This implies that a crucial role of leaders is helping organizations adapt to a changing environment by enabling what Elias called 'detached' thinking, not only on the part of formal leaders, but of all members of the organization. Formal roles, clear lines of authority and responsibility, boundaries, hierarchy, control systems and other characteristics of organizations may serve a useful purpose in anxiety control/reduction. Some argue that 'complexity-inspired' management means less hierarchy. They often cite the spontaneous emergence of organized collaboration at, for example, a disaster scene. On the other hand, we have thousands of years of historical record which suggests that hierarchies with structural power differences are the normal patterns of human organizing.

One could argue that a stable, structured, corporate environment can provide a safe, relatively secure environment in a sea of uncertainty. Thus corporate structure becomes, in fact, an essential enabler for the expression of creativity and individuality of organizational members.

The problem with 'involvement' and 'detachment'

Elias took pains to make clear that involvement and detachment are not either/or options, but rather some blend of thought, action and impulse that tend towards either involvement or detachment but that never reach either pole.

One cannot say of a person's outlook in any absolute sense that it is detached or involved (or, if one prefers, 'irrational', 'objective' or 'subjective'). Only small babies, and among adults perhaps only insane people, become involved in whatever they experience with complete abandon to their feelings here and now, and again only the insane can remain totally unmoved by what goes on around them.

(Elias 1987, p. 3)

Nevertheless, perhaps due to the limitations of language in adequately expressing the continually shifting, subtle interplay of emotions and rationality that Elias had in mind, the concept easily lends itself to either/or expression. In writing about this, I find myself describing individual behavior as 'detached' or 'more involved' as if the complementary element of the process were absent. I have found no easy way to resolve the terminology problem.

Elias treats the concepts of involvement and detachment differently in his earlier and later works. Only in *Problems of Involvement and Detachment* does he emphasize the emotional content of the 'involved' state of mind. In his other works he stresses detachment and self-distancing as means to gain a perspective, very much in the way I apply this concept to 'sense-making' throughout this chapter. For example, in *The Society of Individuals*, Elias does not use the term 'involved'. He speaks of two perspectives one might have in experiencing a social process – a detached perspective, and a perspective realized from being 'in the flow' of the process itself. Certainly 'participation' is a synonym for one sense of involvement as we use that term today.

In *The Society of Individuals*, Elias uses detachment, the setting aside of 'personal wishes and impulses', in a sense that is consistent with my own use of the term as a skill of leaders. Elias stresses the importance of observation and action from within the flow of events, and the concomitant need for a 'longer-sighted perspective' in comprehending the paradox of social processes – how little control individuals have over events, and yet the importance of choosing 'that which is perceived to be better and more easily in the moment of action itself' (Elias 1991, pp. 47ff.). Nevertheless, there is no doubt, both in personal experience and in the literature, that emotions play an important role in thought processes, and therefore in our actions.

Damasio's (1994, 1999) work on emotions and cognition are helpful in thinking about involvement and detachment in this way more fully. Drawing on an extensive body of research, Damasio argues persuasively that emotions are an essential component of the human body's self-regulatory mechanisms, aimed at maintaining homeostasis and, therefore, life itself. Emotions also play a fundamental role in consciousness, our sense of self and cognition.

Cognitive processes require attention and working memory, scarce resources in our central nervous systems. When we engage with objects and situations in our environment, emotions, 'gut feelings', give us automated signals of 'good' or 'bad', 'relevant' or 'irrelevant' – focusing our attention, and helping us to rapidly sort through possible responses. 'Emotion is critical for the appropriate direction of attention since it provides an automated signal about the organism's past experience with given objects and thus provides a basis for assigning or withholding attention relative to a given object' (Damasio 1999, p. 273). In addition to focusing our attention, the physiological processes associated with emotion affect the rapidity of mental image formation within the central nervous system, the diversity of these images and the efficiency of our thought processes, and thus are basic to human creativity and adaptability (ibid., pp. 145–7). (Interestingly, body states associated with positive, 'happy' emotions enhance our cognitive processes, while body states associated with negative emotions – depression, anxiety – are characterized by diminished cognition.)

At the most basic level, we experience emotions as a feeling of physiological change juxtaposed with images of the object that induced the change. Damasio distinguishes among three levels of feeling: background feelings (such as fatigue, excitement, wellness, tension) which are mostly privately experienced indications of body state; basic, or universal, emotions (such as happiness, fear, anger, disgust); and, secondary, or social, emotions (such as embarrassment, jealousy, guilt or pride). All are complicated collections of chemical or neural responses forming a pattern, and all have a role of some sort in creating conditions favorable to the organism, to help it maintain life.

While all have a common biological origin, background feelings and primary emotions are most directly connected to physiological states. Learning, experience and other social processes further shape secondary emotions. In a further elaboration of the role of secondary emotions, Damasio offers what he calls the 'somatic marker' hypothesis. Somatic markers are feeling states which we learn to associate with certain scenarios, through social processes beginning in childhood. Somatic markers place a good/bad value on the outcome of possible responses to those situations, and thus bias our actions towards the 'good' option(s). Somatic markers have a physiological origin and purpose, but are shaped by social conventions and ethical rules.

Mead on the role of emotions in social conduct

Mead is another theorist whose work is crucial to the theory of complex responsive processes of relating. In a 1910 paper, 'Social Consciousness and Consciousness of Meaning', Mead wrote about the importance of emotions in co-ordinating human action. Mead described human interaction as a seamless process of gesture and response between at least two people (and this includes a silent, internal conversation with the self) and 'the first function of the gesture is the mutual adjustment of changing response to changing social stimulation, when stimulation and response are to be found in the first overt phases of the act' (Mead 1910, p. 398).

In Mead's theory, each gesture is made with the intention of evoking a specific response in the other actor. As the first actor gestures, he is watching the other for clues (words, body language, facial expressions and so on – all outward manifestations of emotions) as to actual response, and immediately adjusts his own action – as he is making it – according to the actual response evoked. Both (or multiple) actors are all doing the same thing, forcing us into this process of continual adjustment.

In this 'conversation of gestures', we have the ability to call out in ourselves the responses we evoke (or intend to evoke) in others. Thus our adjustments to their changing reactions take place, by a process of analysis of our own responses to their stimulations. In these social situations appear not only conflicting acts with the increased definition of elements in the stimulation, but also a consciousness of one's own attitude as an interpretation of the meaning of the social stimulus. We are conscious of our attitudes because they are responsible for the changes in the conduct of other individuals. Mead wrote that when we are in harmony with our environment, our response to environmental stimuli becomes more or less subconscious. Our ability to deal with many situations in a habitual way, below the level of consciousness, is an important element of the 'economy of our conduct'. Since our environment includes other human beings, this same tendency towards habitual, subconscious response to others' gestures obtains. The more perfect the adjustment between the stimulation and response within the act, the less conscious are we of the response itself.

Damasio's views on emotion are quite consistent with those of Mead, who would not have had the advantage of nearly a century's-worth of neurobiological and cognitive science research. For Mead, emotion is the feeling of changes in body state induced by engagement with an object in the environment, or by the thought of such an object. In his concept of emotions, emotions arise only when there is tension between a habitual response to the encounter and cognitive recognition that the response must be modified by new circumstances, or where tension arises because there are choices between possible responses. In either case the result is a felt change in body state. In Mead's own words, 'It is under the influence of stimuli . . . that the emotional states and their physiological parallels arise. The teleology of these states is that of giving the organism an evaluation of the act before the coordination that leads to the particular reaction has been completed' (Mead 1895, p. 164). This concept finds its full expression in Mead's gesture–response dialectic. The essence of intelligent behavior is in delayed response to an encounter with an object in experience while choices among possible responses are being weighed. This process is 'made possible physiologically through the mechanism of the central nervous system, and socially through the mechanism of language' (Mead 1934, note, p. 254).

Mead wrote relatively little about emotion in any comprehensive way, and his writings on the subject are scattered among several articles and books. In 1904, in an article on whether linguistics was an appropriate field of study for psychologists, Mead wrote that the language of gestures was in the first case an expression of affect.

> The gesture is first of all and originally an affective expression. However necessary it is for a language of gesture that should raise itself above this stage, it remains true that it would never have arisen without the original emotional impulse. Only secondarily, in so far as every affective state contains ideas charged with emotion, does the gesture become an expression of an idea. . . . It is, above all, as a conveyor of ideas that the expressive movement of one calls out the like affective states in others because only through the passage of constant ideas from one to the other can the actual agreement of their emotions take place. Expressions of feeling are able to give and recreate only the like fundamental direction of emotional change.
>
> (Mead 1904, p. 381)

Mead maintained that emotions rise when a human being encounters a problem which cannot be resolved through instinctive action. The physiological stress that results from our checking of impulsive or habitual behavior is felt as emotion. In such a situation, the feeling of a change in body state focuses our attention on the problem encountered, and the gesture/response process rises to the level of consciousness: the feel of one's own attitude arising spontaneously to meet the gesture of the other. Again, our own emotional response to another's gesture is crucial in our analysis and interpretation of the other actor's intention, and thereby in our selection of an appropriate response. As Mead puts it,

> Within social conduct the feel of one's own responses become the natural objects of attention, since they interpret first of all attitudes of others which have called them out, in the second place, because they give the material in which one can state his own value as a stimulus to the conduct of others. Thus we find here the opportunity and the means for analyzing and bringing consciousness to our responses, our habits of conduct, as distinguished from the stimulations that call them out. The opportunity is found in the import of the response in determining the conduct of others. The means are our gestures as they appear in the feel of our own attitudes and moves, which are the beginnings of social reaction.
>
> (Ibid.)

Emotions provide an evaluative function. This 'feeling' establishes the relationship between gesture and the mental 'imagery' of an appropriate response in this continuous process of mutual adjustment and thus establishes the meaning of mutual interaction – the

> consciousness of meaning. In this fashion finally the individual emotional state, under the influence of the backward and forward interchange of gestures, has passed into a common affective experience. As, through this pronounced emphasis on the contents of ideas, the affective elements and thus the emotions themselves are moderated, the common emotional experience with the backward and forward interchange of gestures passes into a common thought process, taking place with the exchange of gesture expression.
>
> (Mead 1904, p. 383)

In summary, then, in a collaborative situation, such as an organization or a team with specific goals to accomplish, human emotional response is essential to the necessary mutual social adjustments that make collaboration possible.

Detached involvement

Bringing this overview of emotions back to the issue of involvement and detachment, it appears that it would be possible for a human being to exhibit totally impulsive, totally emotion driven behavior (and this is certainly consistent with everyday experience) while the opposite could not be true. Rational thought processes cannot occur without substantial emotional content. Thus, in the involvement and detachment concept, involvement must have some priority and the idea must be captured that involvement and detachment are totally intertwined and interdependent, rather than poles in a continuum or even a 'blend'. Perhaps Elias' concept would be better named 'the paradox of detached involvement', and conceived of as an entirely different dynamic in which the meanings of 'involvement' and 'detachment' are transformed.

The essential notion is that through 'self-distancing', and by bringing our feelings and emotional responses within the scope of our rational thought processes, we are able to experience our emotions in a different way – as an object of our experience. We are better able to control impulsive, habitual behaviors and responses. We can enable better comprehension of the processes in which we are embedded, and thus cope better with the sense of being impelled and constrained by forces we cannot control or even experience directly. We can plan and act in a way that is more likely to produce a desirable outcome. Self-distancing through detached involvement gives us the capacity to become engaged without being overwhelmed.

Emotional intelligence versus detached involvement

The mainstream management literature does not pay much attention to the role of emotions in management practice. However, Daniel Goleman's work on emotional intelligence is a noteworthy exception. According to Goleman, emotional intelligence consists of five (competencies): self-awareness (the ability to recognize one's own moods and emotions as well as their effect on others); self-regulation (the ability to control or redirect 'disruptive impulses and moods' and the ability to 'suspend judgment, that is to think before acting'); motivation; empathy (the ability to understand and respond to the emotions of others); and social skill (proficiency in managing relationships) (Goleman 1998, p. 97) .

To some extent, Goleman's ideas are consistent with Mead's and Elias' conceptions of emotions in social discourse. Self-regulation is reminiscent of Elias' 'affect control' and 'self-distancing'. We human beings navigate a complex social environment by gaining sufficient control over emotional responses and by concealing our feelings from others while we weigh our options more thoughtfully and plan our next moves. For Goleman, self-awareness also means understanding that our own emotional states expressed through our bodily actions and speech will have a profound effect on others and this is also an idea that is entirely consistent with the theme of this chapter. Similarly empathy, 'considering others' feelings . . .' (ibid., p. 98) in the process of making intelligent decisions, is related to Elias' concept of detachment.

Despite the superficial resemblance of some of Goleman's ideas to those argued in this chapter, there are important differences. In a perpetuation of 'Descartes' error', Goleman refers to brain research that locates emotions in the limbic system, while the neocortex governs rational thinking. According to Damasio and others, the limbic system (the brain stem and immediately adjacent structures of the brain – from an evolutionary standpoint, the most primitive part of the human brain) is indeed associated with our core emotions, such as anger or fear. However, Damasio makes a compelling case that human emotional response is far more complex, involving widely distributed areas of the brain as well as biochemical and neurological connections with the whole organism. Damasio argues for an expanded level of 'socialized' emotions (envy, for example) which involve, again, a more generalized bodily response, including the brain structures associated with both emotional and cognitive processes. Finally, and most importantly, Damasio argues that human emotional response and cognition are completely integrated – the theme of his book, *Descartes' Error* – such that central nervous system disease or injury that impairs emotional response will also impair rationality.

Again, drawing on brain science, Goleman says that while our emotional skills have a genetic component, our emotional skills (which he defines here as the attitude and abilities with which someone approaches life and work) are not genetically 'hard wired' (Goleman *et al.* 2001, p. 47), and thus may be changed through learning. This learning involves coaching, mentoring and feedback around specific skills. As an example of this mixing and combining, Goleman asserts, in arguing that emotional intelligence can be learned, that 'organizations must refocus their training to include the limbic system. They must help people break old habits and establish new ones' (Goleman 1998, p. 97). In the example given of such training, the author equates 'low empathy' with poor listening skills, and suggests that improving listening skills will also improve empathy.

Goleman's splitting of emotional and cognitive structures of the brain is completely consistent with the mainstream management perspective and leads inevitably to the notion that emotions are something to be managed. Our emotional response is completely subordinate to our rational capacities and our emotions cannot only be controlled, but can be deliberately manipulated in order to influence others. Emotions become a management tool of sorts. Again, consistent with mainstream discourse, Goleman's frame of reference is clearly the autonomous individual, rather than the social organism. This is especially evident in later articles, such as 'Leadership That Gets Results' (2000), which deals with leadership styles, and 'Primal Leadership' (Goleman et al. 2001), which deals with emotional intelligence and the chief executive.

For Goleman, emotional intelligence is clearly a top-down phenomenon because 'everyone watches the boss'. Consider: 'a leader's emotional intelligence creates a certain cultural work environment'; 'emotional intelligence drives performance – in particular, at how it travels from the leader throughout the organization to bottom-line results'; and 'the leader's mood is quite literally contagious, spreading quickly and inexorably throughout the business' (Goleman et al. 2001, p. 44).

In the perspective of this chapter, human emotional response, including the CEO's, is shaped through interaction with our environment, including other people, and is not subject to complete control by an individual. Goleman ignores the social aspect of emotions. Emotions are to be used as a tool, never truly shared, and he barely touches on the notion that an executive's emotions and moods can be influenced by factors outside of social interaction, as well (even the boss can have a bad day). Goleman urges executives to 'get happy, carefully', to 'display moods and behaviors that match the situation at hand' (Goleman et al. 2001, p. 49).

Goleman also tells us that emotional intelligence may be quantified, analyzed and modeled, and that emotional intelligence is a driver of management style. In the end, Goleman summarizes his point of view succinctly:

> That's why emotional intelligence matters so much for a leader. An emotionally intelligent leader can monitor his or her moods through self-awareness, change them for the better through self-management,

understand their impact through empathy, and act in ways to boost
others' moods through relationship management.

(Ibid., p. 48).

Goleman offers some useful ideas to help the executive improve his or
her emotional intelligence – for example, the use of mentors or a trusted
group of advisers to assist in improving these skills. However, such skill
building is always a special effort outside of everyday social interaction,
since subordinates cannot be trusted to speak with candor about the boss's
shortcomings. Self-awareness and empathy never seem to imply a
different level of awareness towards emotional expression as it emerges
and changes in a process of social intercourse.

Druskat and Wollf apply Goleman's concept of emotional intelligence
to groups. According to them, team success is based on trust among the
members of the group, a sense of group identity and a sense of group
efficacy (that is, an understanding that the members of the group can
accomplish more by working collaboratively than they could by working
independently). These factors are enhanced by the group members'
developing 'emotionally intelligent norms – attitudes and behaviors
that eventually become habit' (Druskat and Wolff 2001, p. 82). In the
development of these norms, any sense of social construction or group
process is ignored. Such norms do not emerge in social interaction, but
are 'introduced from any of five basic directions: by formal team leaders,
by informal team leaders, by courageous followers, through training,
or from the large organizational culture' (ibid., p. 89).

In addition to the foregoing, this work falls into the mainstream,
system-thinking paradigm in two other important ways. 'Group' is clearly
a collection of individuals, so individual group intelligence matters.
However, the group members as 'the group' also:

> must attend to yet another level of awareness and regulation. It must
> be mindful of the emotions of its own members, its own group
> emotions or moods, and the emotions of other groups and individuals
> outside of its boundaries.

(Ibid., p. 82)

The group becomes an 'it' capable of expressing and regulating emotions
as if it were a living being. By contrast, from the perspective of groups as
a process of communicative interaction, rather than a 'group mind', one
would interpret this phenomenon as a pattern of emotional resonance
emerging in the interaction of the participants.

Second, the theme of the article is the control and use of emotions as a means to achieve group members' (or 'the group's') goals. Like Goleman, these authors apparently make a split between emotional and rational aspects of thinking, with emotional response subordinate to rational, cognitive processes, rather than seeing emotion as an integral aspect of human thought, including cognition. In this article, the word 'regulation', in the sense of controlling rather than adjusting, is used repeatedly. For example, the authors posit certain competencies: '"personal competence" comes from being aware of and regulating one's own emotions' while '"social competence" is awareness and regulation of others' emotions' (Druskat and Wolff 2001, p. 82). The authors also make it clear that the purpose of developing group emotional intelligence is to achieve harmony among group members. They write of 'emotional capacity (the ability to respond constructively in emotionally uncomfortable situations) and to influence emotions in constructive ways' (ibid., p. 82). If emotional intelligence is to be a path to harmony and achievement, it must be a quest to have the right group norms – in this case optimism, and positive images and interpretations rather than negative ones. Here, of course, 'right' is the key word. The authors also see no benefit to diversity, individual expression or conflict as potential sources of creativity, although their position is expressed somewhat covertly. They maintain that the regulation of emotions is not about imposing 'groupthink'. The goal 'must be to balance the team's cohesion with members' individuality' (ibid., p. 84). However, the authors go on to suggest a number of techniques for confronting and correcting 'errant' behavior.

The paradox of detached involvement in everyday practice

My organization has a small executive team, namely myself and four vice-presidents. Our meetings follow a fairly consistent format. We usually have an agenda, but we follow it loosely or, perhaps, not at all. In reality, the 'agenda' is simply a list of issues one or another member of the team wishes or needs to discuss, and we manage to get around to every issue, although not always at a given meeting. We always review our list at the beginning of each meeting. We add or delete items and change the order of topics based on priority. As the meeting progresses, if we find that some conversations last longer than anticipated, we may have topics 'jump' the list if a member of the team is particularly anxious that we address an important issue during that meeting. Sometimes, I use my role as chair to make sure that we get to a topic that I know one of the members is worried about but who may not wish to introduce the topic.

Reality testing in an organizational conversation is an aspect of involvement and detachment. A leader, or other members of a group, can serve as the 'reality tester' for individuals or the group as a whole, keeping the group focused on the task at hand and forcing the group to confront difficult issues. One of the most difficult challenges any group faces is dealing effectively with performance concerns among its own members.

Within our executive team recently, complaints about our Human Resources Department had become frequent and intense. Mary, our Chief Operating Officer, was particularly troubled and insisted we do something. The HR Department was seen as rigid, rule-bound and unresponsive. In a time of severe shortages of nurses and other critically skilled health care workers, the HR Department was painfully slow to respond to changing job market conditions and unimaginative in its recruiting campaigns. Perhaps most importantly, the HR department is responsible for the hospital's in-service training programs, headed by a training director who reports directly to Paul, Vice-president of Human Resources. Mary and her staff felt educational support to the front-line staff, especially recently hired nurses, was woefully inadequate. Mary in particular, and Steve to some extent, had been complaining privately to me with an increasing sense of urgency and frustration. They had discussed the problem among themselves and both had been receiving complaints from their operating managers but both were reluctant to confront Paul directly, since we are all personally fond of him and value the relationships we have among ourselves as an executive team. My response was always to insist that we had to discuss this as a team. If we are, in fact, a team, it is crucial for us to be able to deal constructively with a problem concerning one of our own members and we have to be able to hold each other accountable for performance. The matter was added to our 'to do' list.

The issue was brought to a head when we engaged in a project to develop a human resources strategic plan, working with some other hospitals and a consultant expert in this field. The project was to begin with an employee survey and Mary was very concerned that the survey would create expectations within our workforce that we were in no position to respond to. We decided to put the question of participation to our department directors, since they were the ones who would have to do the work and deal with any workforce concerns. When the directors enthusiastically endorsed the project, the executive team could no longer avoid confronting our own concerns about HR's ability to 'deliver'.

We decided to devote one of our regularly scheduled meetings to this issue, without warning Paul in advance. Mary opened the discussion by laying out her concerns in considerable detail, especially the training director's shortcomings. Paul responded by saying that it was really a problem of resources. As part of a mid-1990s re-engineering project, the HR Department had been reduced in size. He felt it was easy to blame his director, who would gladly do what was expected if only she had adequate staff herself. Mary then asked Paul what staff resources he needed. Paul responded and Mary began to make a list of the types and numbers of new staff that the HR Department required. I let the discussion continue in this vein for a few minutes and then cut in. We had started a conversation about leadership and we had almost instantly shifted to a much less intense discussion of resources. Talking critically about leadership and performance is hard, especially when the issues are pointedly directed at a member of the executive team. Paul is directly responsible and we were implying that he had failed to deal with issues vital to the success of the organization.

Following that intervention, the conversation immediately shifted back to the education director and the perception of the HR Department that is widespread in the organization. Both Mary and Steve now gave specific examples – delays in recruitment, lost opportunities, issues with educational support. Paul defended the director and continued to hang on to the resources argument. Colleen, the Chief Financial Officer, remarked that we all thought HR was inadequately staffed and that Paul had had, but not taken advantage of, opportunities to budget for additional staff. Paul responded that he had been trying to set a good example during lean times. The conversation again shifted into a discussion of staffing requirements and I intervened again. This time I reminded the group that we had recovered from a huge financial loss in the prior fiscal year by being disciplined with regard to expenditures. I would not consider additional staffing for HR as long as I felt the other issues in HR were not being attended to – as an executive team it would be irresponsible of us to try to solve a difficult problem by throwing money at it.

The conversation then immediately went back to the performance issues. This pattern persisted for nearly two hours. Each time the conversation wandered from the real issues I would intervene. My contributions were either that I would not allow Mary, Paul and Steve to sidestep the director's performance matter – we were not leaving this meeting until all had agreed on the next steps – or I reminded the group of our fiscal responsibility – resource decisions had to be made wisely and for legitimate purpose. Adding staff to see if the education director's performance would then improve was not acceptable. (It is difficult to convey here the stress levels of all participants. We finally took a quick break that relieved the tension, but returned to the discussion during a working lunch.)

Paul gradually, but reluctantly, agreed that the education director's style was a problem and that perhaps she did not have the skills needed to perform the job we expected of her in the way we expected her to do it. We all agreed that, as a long-time veteran employee of Waterbury Hospital, we had to find another role for her (rather than firing her). Mary insisted that Paul agree to some next steps – both with the director and with the resource issue – which he did. Members of the group also contributed several helpful suggestions.

With the matter resolved – at least as far as we could for the present – the group then engaged in some healing conversation. Everyone said something about how difficult this must have been for Paul to hear and how much we all valued him as a colleague. Steve reminded everyone of an incident in which a mishandled recruitment had resulted in a serious problem between Colleen and some of our Trustees. Steve reminded the group of how completely dependent each of us is on the other members of the team and how crucial it was for all of us to be sure that the whole team was pulling together. I commented on how pleased I was. I had known how strongly Mary and Steve felt about the issues and knew it would be very difficult for Paul to be the focus, but everyone kept their emotions under control, and the discussion was factual and thoughtful. I felt it was a hallmark of a high performance team to be able to deal with internal conflict in a forthright but constructive way. I was especially pleased that the meeting had ended on a caring note.

In reflecting on this meeting, and the notion of a group member's forming and being formed by the group process, I was highly aware of the role I played in that meeting and made the interventions I made in a very deliberate way and with the expectation that they would have the effect they did. How difficult it is to persist with a difficult conversation and my interventions had kept us 'on task' until we had reached a conclusion. Action and awareness go hand in hand.

The important learning in all of this is that the authority figure in a conversation is not the only person making contributions to the achievement of a more self-distanced perspective for the group as a whole. In this episode, individuals making more 'objective' observations changed in the course of this conversation. It is also clear that authority figures benefit from free-flowing conversations in which others feel free to make more detached observations, thus contributing to the authority figure's own learning.

Leading is an emergent role

Human beings form collectives – groups, families, tribes, organizations and so forth – for collaborative action. Collaboration enables us to achieve goals and to solve problems that no individual could solve alone, or, at least to accomplish these goals in a more efficient, effective and labor-saving way. Collectives are characterized by a division of labor and mutual interdependence. Leading is a role that emerges in collaborative interaction when that interaction is sufficiently complex to require such a role (that is, of some form of centralized co-ordination of activity). The role of the leader has to do with achievement of the purposes of the collective, whatever those may be. That role may encompass many tasks (sense-making, anxiety reduction, resource allocation, conflict adjudication and so on), but all of these are achieved through ordinary conversation 'in the moment' as the work collective unfolds.

Human social interaction is a complex process involving the nonlinear interaction of many 'agents' and countless variables. As such, human social interaction exhibits complex dynamics, including self-patterning of themes and emergent properties. Leading – and being led – is one of those emergent patterns. It does seem clear that, especially in conditions of change and uncertainty, a primary function of leaders is helping organizational members to perceive the realities of the situations they are in, and the problems they are attempting to solve, through the enabling of what Elias refers to as 'detached' thinking. Detachment, in other disciplines and writings, is also referred to as sense-making, reality testing, therapeutic insight, or personal mastery in some forms of system thinking.

It is important to think of leading not as one person making sense for others, but rather of emerging from the communicative interaction of all members of a collectivity. From the perspective of participative relational processes, it may be more useful to think of leading as an emergent phenomenon in which some individuals possessing certain attributes – a capacity for mental self-distancing, a greater capacity for self control, physical strength, formal authority, special skills or knowledge, the 'value' of any of these being contextual – will pattern the iterative communicative interactions through their participation and expression of those skills and traits. Such participation will thus have greater impact on the course of events. Other actors in the group will recognize this greater contribution to the outcome as leading. Leading is a social process in which the one(s) recognized as leading are also actively engaged in the sense-making process themselves and in which their own sense-making is developed in their interaction with others. In modern society, the concept of leadership has become formalized and institutionalized – but its 'raw' form, its emergent nature, may be seen in many situations, even within the context of formal hierarchies.

The central role of emotion in the process of leading

Emotion and bodily feeling states are crucial to our successfully engaging our environment because they play an essential role in our cognitive and reasoning processes. 'Well-targeted and well-deployed emotion seems to be a support system without which the edifice of reason cannot operate properly' (Damasio 1999, pp. 41–2). Emotions give us enhanced attention, enhanced working memory, and increase the rapidity and variety of mental image formation. The feeling states associated specifically with negative emotions can disturb and diminish our cognitive powers. On the interconnectedness of reason and feelings, Damasio writes:

> taking stock of the pervasive role of feelings may give us a chance of enhancing their positive effects and reducing their potential harm. Specifically, without diminishing the orienting value of normal feelings, one would want to protect reason from the weakness that abnormal feelings or the manipulation of normal feelings can introduce into the process of planning and deciding.
>
> (Damasio 1994, p. 246).

Hence the need for self-control and 'self-distancing' in leaders not only to enhance the leaders' own cognitive powers but also to help others achieve the adequate self-distancing needed to enhance their thought processes and powers of reason. By planning and deciding, I mean not only the planning and deciding as we think of those actions in business and organizations, but also as they occur continually in the gesture/ response process described by Mead: gesture made in anticipation of a specific response, observation of the beginning phase of the response (act) of the other for clues as to actual response, delay while response options are weighed, action (response), and so on *ad infinitum*. Emotions are automatic bodily signals that bias our actions towards choices which are in our own best interests and, because human beings' social nature is a survival advantage, our own best interest is usually the best interest of others in our group. Thus emotions also play a role in ethical behavior and the maintenance of social conventions.

Emotional resonance and collaborative action

Damasio's ideas about secondary emotions and 'somatic markers' are consistent with Elias' and Mead's concept of the internalization of social controls. Damasio argues that somatic markers – or some comparable process – play an important role in the co-ordination of human action in social processes. Somatic markers 'are consistent with the notion that effective personal and social behavior requires individuals to form adequate "theories" of their own minds and of the minds of others. On the basis of those theories, we can predict what theories others are forming about our own mind. The detail and accuracy of such prediction is, of course, critical as we approach a critical decision in a social situation' (Damasio 1994, p. 174). Paying attention to our own feelings (our emotional responses, our background feelings) gives us essential clues to the mental state of others with whom we are relating.

Our emotions are essential to effective human collaboration. We only have unfettered access to our own feeling states, the 'private' aspect of emotional expression. The outward expression of emotional states that is observable by others through body language, facial expressions and so on can be effectively masked. This 'affect control' is amply documented in the literature, and is a key theme of Elias' in many of his important works. The executive's paying close attention to his or her own feelings is the best clue to the emotional state of others with whom the executive is interacting. This is because we are able to evoke in ourselves the same responses that we are engendering in others.

Paying attention to, achieving heightened awareness of, our own feelings (our body states, our emotional responses to given situations) provides the clues we need to assess the mental state and likely actions/responses of others. Awareness of our own feelings is essential to effective social interaction, collaboration and co-ordination. In Mead's gesture–response dialectic, our gesture calls out in ourselves a similar response that we intend to call out in the other(s) to which our gesture is directed. We are able to experience, simultaneously and in a bodily, visceral way, the feelings, emotions and body states of others – we have the same experience, with all that this implies.

Mead has written very little about leadership, but when he does so he mentions both detachment ('Occasionally a person arises who is able to take in more than others of an act in process') and emotional resonance ('the statesman who is able to enter into the attitudes of the group and to mediate between them by making his own experience universal, so that others can enter into this form of communication through him') (Mead 1934, pp. 256–7).

The role of the group

My experience with my own executive team suggests that it is possible for a group, with no special training in group process or self-distancing, to fulfill its own leading function. It seems likely that, in any group of humans engaged in collaborative work, each individual will have a different level of emotional involvement with respect to any specific problem the group is dealing with. In free-flowing dialogue, the less involved (in Elias' sense) can help the more involved to achieve a more rational, less emotion-laden perspective. The capacity for detached involvement exists continually within the process and is available to all as the conversation proceeds from problem to problem. This self-organizing process may also explain why some teams are effective while others fail to gel.

In the story of Paul and the HR Department, the members of the executive team were not just aware of Paul's feelings; we were also able to experience those same feelings directly ourselves. However, because we were not threatened by the challenge posed to Paul's thinking and management of the HR Department, we were able to experience those feelings in a more objective way and our participation in the discussion thus patterned the interactions in a different way.

Paying attention to the dynamics of involvement and detachment 'in the moment' during social interaction will heighten our awareness and appreciation of what is going on at a much deeper level. Our experience with the participants and the issues under discussion, our own feelings as the conversation progresses, and the sometimes subtle indications of the emotional states of other participants, such as tone of voice, facial expression, body posture and so on, are all important clues we can use to enhance our participation.

Conclusion

The idea that our rational minds are separate and distinct from our feeling bodies has deep roots in Western philosophical and religious tradition and the notion of the 'objective observer' essential to the scientific process. The scientific method is intended, among other things, to minimize the observer's biases tainting results. This separation of the rational from the emotional has also found its way into scientific, by-the-numbers management thinking. Although advances in the sciences during the twentieth century have given the observer – with all of the subjectivity that implies – a central role, this is a relatively recent development which is not well understood by non-scientists, and has been slow to be recognized in the social sciences or in the popular media. The dualistic tradition was certainly the one in which executives of my generation were trained.

In this chapter, I cite principally the work of Damasio, Mead and Elias to argue that rationality and emotionality are deeply intertwined in the thinking processes of healthy humans – there cannot be one without the other – and that emotion and feeling states are essential to rational thinking.

In conditions of uncertainty and stress, the emotional content of our thinking has a tendency to overwhelm the cognitive and rational. Thus I argue that a skill of leaders in complex relational processes is one of 'detached involvement'. By detached involvement I mean that a leader exercises enough self-control to provide some degree of mental 'distancing' from one's current situation in order to achieve a somewhat broader perspective than others. Through detached involvement the leader may apprehend more possibilities offered by a given situation than others are able to, and thus the leader has more possibilities for action, more options, because of this broader perspective. Through detached involvement, the leader is also able to attune him or herself emotionally with the other members of the group, without becoming overly caught up in impulsive responses, and thus facilitate group collaboration more effectively.

Finally, although I have not developed it here, there is a significant body of research (e.g. Schore (2001), Gabbard (1997), Damasio (1994, 1999), and even Goleman (1998)) suggesting that 'neuroplasticity' – physiological changes in our central nervous systems in response to social experience – persists throughout our lives. This phenomenon suggests that we can continue to develop our ability to co-ordinate our emotional responses with those of others in the process of human communicative interaction. This, in turn, suggests to me that our capacity for detached involvement may be learned, enhanced and developed through everyday social interaction.

References

Damasio, A. (1994) *Descartes' Error: Emotion, Reason, and the Human Brain*, New York: Avon Books, Inc.

Damasio, A. (1999) *The Feeling of What Happens: Body and Emotion in the Making of Consciousness*, San Diego, CA, New York, and London: Harcourt, Inc.

Dewey, J. (1894) 'The Theory of Emotion. (1) Emotional Attitudes', *Psychological Review* Volume 1, pp. 553–69, available from the Mead Project website: http://spartan.ac.brocku.ca/~lward/mead.pubs/Mead.

Dewey, J. (1895) 'The Theory of Emotion. (2) The Significance of Emotion', *Psychological Review* Volume 2, pp. 13–25, available from The Mead Project website: http://spartan.ac.brocku.ca/~lward/mead.pubs/Mead.

Dewey, J. (1896) 'The Reflex Arc Concept in Psychology', *Psychological Review* Volume 3, pp. 357–70, available from the Mead Project website: http://spartan.ac.brocku.ca/~lward/mead.pubs/Mead.

Druskat, V. and Wolff, S. (2001) 'Building the Emotional Intelligence of Groups', *Harvard Business Review*, March, pp. 44–53.

Elias, N. (1987) *Involvement and Detachment*, New York: Blackwell.

Elias, N. (1991) *The Society of Individuals*, New York: Continuum.

Elias, N. (1998) *Norbert Elias On Civilization, Power and Knowledge: Selected Writings*, ed. S. Mennel and J. Goudsblom. Chicago and London: The University of Chicago Press.

Elias, N. (2000) *The Civilizing Process*, Oxford: Blackwell.

Elias, N. and Scotson, J. (1994) *The Established and the Outsiders*, London: Sage.

Gabbard, G. (1997) 'Dynamic Therapy in the Decade of the Brain', *Connecticut Medicine*, Vol. 61, No. 9, September, pp. 37–49.

Goleman, G. (1998) 'What Makes a Leader?', *Harvard Business Review*, November–December, pp. 93–102.

Goleman, G. (2000) 'Leadership that Gets Results', *Harvard Business Review*, March–April, pp. 79–90.

Goleman, G., Boyatzis, R. and McKee, A. (2001) 'Primal Leadership: The Hidden Driver of Great Performance', *Harvard Business Review*, December (special issue on Breakthrough Leadership), pp. 43–51.

Goudsblom, J. and Mennell, S. (1998) *The Norbert Elias Reader*, Oxford: Blackwell.

Griffin, D. (2002) *The Emergence of Leadership: Linking self-organization and ethics*, London: Routledge.

Hallowell, E. (1999) 'The Human Moment at Work', *Harvard Business Review*, January–February, pp. 55–63.

Mead, G. H. (1895) 'A Theory of Emotions from the Physiological Standpoint' (abstract of a paper read to the third annual meeting of the American Psychological Association, 1894), *Psychological Review* Volume 2, pp. 162–5, available from The Mead Project website, http://spartan.ac.brocku.ca/~lward/mead.pubs/Mead.

Mead, G. H. (1904) 'The Relations of Psychology to Philology', *Psychological Bulletin 1*, pp. 375–91, available from the Mead Project website, http://spartan.ac.brocku.ca/~lward/mead.pubs/Mead.

Mead, G. H. (1910) 'Social Consciousness and the Consciousness of Meaning', *Psychological Bulletin*, Vol. 7, pp. 397–405.

Mead, G. H. (1934) *Mind, Self and Society*, Chicago: Chicago University Press.

Schore, A. (2001) 'Minds in the Making: Attachment, The Self-organizing Brain, and Developmentally-oriented Psychoanalytic Psychotherapy', *British Journal of Psychotherapy*, Vol. 17, No. 3, pp. 103–17.

Short, D. and Yorks, L. (2002) 'Analyzing Training From an Emotions Perspective', *Advances in Developing Human Resources*, Vol. 4, No. 1, February, pp. 80–97.

Stacey, R. D. (2000) *Organisational Dynamics: The Challenge of Complexity* (3rd edn), London: Pearson Education.

Stacey, R., Griffin, D. and Shaw, P. (2000) *Complexity and Management: Fad or radical challenge to systems thinking?*, London: Routledge.

Senge, P. (1990) *The Fifth Discipline: The Art and Practice of the Learning Organization*, New York: Doubleday/Currency.

Zimmerman, B., Lindberg, C. and Plsek, P. (1998) *Edgeware: Insights from Complexity Science for Health Care Leaders*, Irving, TX: VHA Inc.

5 Values, spirituality and organizations: a complex responsive processes perspective

Ralph Stacey

- Complex responsive processes
- Desires, values and norms
- Complex responsive processes and spirituality
- Values and spirituality in the literature on organizations
- Values and organizational practice

For some years now, theorists and practitioners have taken up questions to do with values, and also spirituality, in relation to leadership in organizations. This chapter explores how one might understand these matters from the perspective of the theory of complex responsive processes (Stacey *et al.*, 2000; Stacey, 2001; Griffin, 2002). I start with a brief outline of this theory and then draw on the work of Joas to understand the role of values, and the link with spirituality, in organizational life. I conclude with a brief review of other approaches and how the complex responsive processes perspective differs from them.

Complex responsive processes

Complex responsive processes of relating are continually iterated nonlinear interactions, in both verbal and non-verbal forms, between human bodies. Such interactions always involve feelings because a body is never without feelings. These interactions constitute the social, which is public and vocal, and at the same time mind, which is the private and silent interaction of each body with itself. The social and individual mind are thus the same processes of bodily interaction. As social structures, organizations may be understood as the patterning of complex responsive processes of relating. These processes, as with all social interactions, have three fundamental and inextricably interlinked aspects, the first being communicative interaction, the second power relating, and the third the evaluative choices people make. The main focus of this chapter is on the third aspect.

Communicative interaction

In the theory of complex responsive processes, communicative interaction is understood primarily in terms of Mead's (1934) theory of the conversation of gestures. According to Mead, human communication takes place in the medium of significant symbols; that is, gestures in which one body has the physiological capacity to call forth in itself similar responses to those being called forth in others. Together, gesture and response constitute the social act of which they are inseparable aspects. In other words, communicative interaction constitutes consciousness, the ability to know what we are doing. It is this consciousness that enables us to cooperate and compete with each other in sophisticated ways and at the same time constrains us from doing whatever we want – we must take the attitude of the other if we are to communicate.

Central to Mead's theory is the process of generalization in which each body evokes in itself similar responses not only to the specific others present in current interaction but, at the same time, to the group or society. Mead uses a number of terms to refer to these generalizing processes, namely the 'generalized other', the 'social object', 'cult values', and the 'me'. A brief description of each of these terms follows.

Social objects/the generalized other

Mead distinguishes between physical objects which are to be found in nature and social objects which are to be found only in the human experience of interaction (Mead, 1938a). Social objects are generalized tendencies by large numbers of people to act in similar ways in similar situations. These generalized tendencies to act are iterated in each present as rather repetitive, habitual and thus largely unconscious patterns of action. However, in their continual iteration, these general tendencies to act are normally particularized in the specific situation and the specific present the actors find themselves in, with its specific understanding of the past and its specific expectations for the future. Such particularization is inevitably a conflictual process of interpretation as the meaning of the generalization is established in a specific situation. The possibility of transformation – that is, further evolution of the social object – arises in this conflictual particularizing of the generalization because of the potential for human spontaneity to generate variety in human action and the capacity of nonlinear interaction to amplify consequent small differences. Social objects do not have any existence outside of particularizing social acts. It is important to notice how Mead used the term 'object' in a social sense as a 'tendency to act' rather than as a concept or a thing, which are meanings appropriate to physical objects. In a social setting, then, Mead used the term 'object' in tension with the usual understanding of object as a thing in nature. The pattern, or tendency, what Mead calls an object, is only an object in the sense that it is what we perceive in taking it up in our acting but this is a perception of our own acting, not a thing.

Mead refers to market exchange as an example of a social object. When one person offers to buy food, this act obviously involves a complex range of responses from other people to provide the food. However, it involves more than this because the one making the offer can only know how to make the offer and what to expect in making it if he or she is able to take the attitude of the other parties to the bargain. All essential phases of the complex social act of exchange must appear in the actions of all involved and appear as essential features of each individual's actions. Social objects with these characteristics evolve in the history of a society and each individual is born into such a world of social objects, learning to take them up in his or her conduct in ways that are largely unconscious. However, social objects are not simply forming action because they are at the same time formed by human action. In other words, individuals are forming social objects while being formed by them in evolutionary processes.

Cult values

In addition to pointing to the importance of the generalizing and particularizing characteristics of human interaction, Mead also saw the importance of its idealizing tendencies. He expressed this in the closely interlinked concepts of cult values, which may be thought of as a particular type of social object, and functionalized values (Mead, 1923).

Mead pointed to how people have a tendency to individualize and idealize a collective and treat it 'as if' *it* had overriding motives or values, amounting to a process in which the collective constitutes a 'cult'. Members of 'cults' forget the 'as if' nature of their construct and act in a manner driven by the cult's values. Cults are maintained when leaders present to people's imagination a future free from obstacles that could prevent them from being what they all want to be. The visions which leaders are currently meant to have are examples of this. A cult provides a feeling of enlarged personality in which individuals participate and from which they derive their value as persons. It is important to stress that cult values can be good or bad or both. Cult values would include 'ethnic purity' and 'loving your neighbor'. Mead points out that the process of idealization is far from unproblematic and could easily lead to actions that others outside the cult will come to regard as bad, even evil. Mead was pointing to the dangers of focusing on the cult values themselves, on the values of the personalized institution or system, and directly applying them as overriding universal norms, conformity to which constitutes the requirement of continuing membership of the institution.

Normally, however, idealization is accompanied by functionalization. Idealizations, or cult values, emerge in the historical evolution of any group or institution to which they are ascribed, and they can become functional values in the everyday interactions between members of the institution rather than being simply applied in a way that enforces the conformity of a cult. For example, the cult value of a hospital might be to 'provide each patient with the best possible care'. However, such a cult value has to be repeatedly functionalized in many unique specific situations throughout the day. As soon as cult values become functional values in real daily interaction, conflict arises, and it is this conflict that must be negotiated by people in their practical interaction with each other.

Self-consciousness and the 'I–me' dialectic

So, Mead explains how consciousness arises in the capacity of each human being to take the attitude of both specific others and the generalized/idealized other at the same time. Consciousness and mind are processes of private role play and silent conversation of a body with itself. As such, conscious individual minds are fundamentally social processes. There is no consciousness without society. Individual mind is social through and through because it is patterns of interaction of the body with itself that always involve the generalized/idealized tendencies to act to be found in the experience of the group or society. Furthermore, self-consciousness is also fundamentally social. Self-consciousness means that a subject can take itself as object to itself. Thus to be self-conscious, to be a self, the subjective 'I' must take itself as the objective 'me'. The 'I' can only understand itself as 'me'. Mead explained that the 'me' is the gesture of society to the 'I' and the 'I' is the individual's response to that gesture. To put this another way, the 'me' is one's *perception of the generalized tendency* of numbers of people to act towards one as an 'I' in similar ways in similar situations, a generalized tendency that one takes up in interactions with oneself. The self can only be formed through interaction with others. However, this is not social determinism because the 'I' has the capacity for spontaneous responses, a matter I will return to below. Furthermore, the 'I' and the 'me' have to be understood as inseparable phases of one act. Mead presents a dialectical account of self-formation in which the opposition (negation) of subject and object is transformed (*Aufhebung* or negation of the negation) as self-consciousness. It is not that the 'I' in some sense converses with the 'me' as separate 'voices'. Together they are the processes, or 'voices', of self.

Mead's concept of the 'I' is sometimes interpreted as the spontaneous impulse of the body (Joas, 2000). However, in complex responsive processes terms, the 'I' is no less social than the 'me' simply because they cannot be separated from each other. The dialectical 'I–me' process evolves – it has a history. This means that in any present, the 'I' response reflects a history of social engagement. It is the capacity for imagination and reflection that brings small differences in the 'I' response to the 'me' gesture from one present to another and it is the amplifying propensity of nonlinear interaction that escalates these small differences into transformations of the self.

The ongoing dialectical iteration of self-formation implies a particular view of the nature of time (Mead, 1938b). Interaction occurs in the living present (Stacey *et al.*, 2000), which means that each person in the interaction is acting in the present on the basis of expectations for the future that arise in accounts of the past. These accounts of the past influence expectations for the future but the expectations are also, at the same time, affecting the accounts of the past. The living present, therefore, has a circular time structure in which the past changes the future and the future simultaneously changes the past, all in the action of the present. This view of time will provide an important differentiation when it comes to comparing mainstream views on values in organizations.

From a complex responsive processes perspective, ordinary everyday conversation, with its always intertwined non-verbal 'body language' and feelings, is extremely important for the sophisticated ways in which humans cooperate and conflict with each other in order to accomplish their tasks, their living together, and the formation of their very identities or selves.

Power relations

The second fundamental aspect of complex responsive processes is power relating, and this is understood from the work of Elias (Elias, 1939; Elias and Scotson, 1994). He argues that power relations are an inescapable aspect of all human relations because when one enters into a relationship with another one is constrained by, and at the same time constrains, that other. However, in our relating we also enable each other, at the same time. Power, therefore, is the paradoxical enabling-constraining property of human action which is an irremovable aspect of all human relating. Elias pointed to how patterns of power relations, which he called figurations, emerge in human interaction such that power ratios are tilted in favor of some and against others. Power relations arise in communicative interaction because its turn-taking and turn-making structure immediately establishes patterns of inclusion and exclusion. Power figurations, therefore, inevitably create patterns of inclusion and exclusion. In this way, groupings are created to which people feel they belong and this belonging provides an essential aspect of personal identity. Elias refers to the inextricably interwoven aspects of 'I' and 'we' identities. Identity and self, therefore, emerge in social processes of power relating.

As people cohere in groups and collectively identify with them, they develop gratifying feelings of belonging to a group of higher status inevitably accompanied by contempt for other groups. In other words, they establish an idealized 'we' identity. Less cohesive groups with little history of being together are vulnerable to denigration by more cohesive groups, so establishing the dynamics of 'us' and 'them'. In this way, an ideology emerges which serves the unconscious purpose of sustaining a particular pattern of power relations (Dalal, 1998). A key aspect of ideology, then, is the binary oppositions that characterize it, and the most basic of these is the distinction between 'them' and 'us' (Dalal, 1998). Ideology is thus a form of communication that preserves the current pattern of power relations by making it seem natural.

Together, communicative interaction and power relating constitute the iterative, self-organizing processes in which the social, collective and individual identities, individual minds and selves, all emerge, change and are sustained. As people interact, they develop habitual, repetitive patterns of interaction which they continually iterate, but never in exactly the same way. In other words, there are always small differences in the interaction and it is a property of nonlinear interaction that small differences can be escalated into qualitative changes that are unknowable in advance. This is a central insight derived by analogy from the natural complexity sciences. The iterative processes are understood in terms of transformative causality which is paradoxical, in that individuals are forming the social while being formed by it at the same time, and what is thus formed as mind, self/identity and society is always iterated as both repetition and potential transformation at the same time. Interaction is communicative and power relating at the same time. Transformative causality has another important feature in that the cause of the patterning of interaction is the patterning of interaction itself. Patterns of human interaction lead to further patterns of interaction, not the creation of some 'whole' outside of that interaction. Any notion of a 'whole', from this perspective, would be understood as an imaginative construct, a point to be discussed below.

The patterning of interaction

The patterns of communicative interaction and power relating take the form of narrative and propositional themes that organize the experience of being together. In a history of social evolution, some themes become repetitive and habitual, taken up anew by each generation in processes of socialization – this is what we mean by social structure. But such social structure does not exist anywhere other than in ordinary everyday experience of relating. The themes that organize experience are what provide meaning. Individual identities, individual selves, are clusters of these themes. Organizations are particular patterns of narrative and propositional themes that organize the experience of being together.

The themes I have been referring to are essentially self-organizing. However, here, self-organizing has a particular meaning. The term is easily misunderstood as a kind of free-for-all in which individuals organize themselves, doing whatever they like. In using the term to understand complex responsive processes of relating, however, self-organization does not mean a free-for-all and emergence does not mean that it 'just happens'. On the contrary, self-organizing processes are characterized by constraints which often conflict with each other, so that those interacting cannot do whatever they like. Patterns of interaction do not 'just happen' but rather emerge precisely because of what those interacting do and do not do. In fact, it is not individuals organizing themselves at all but, rather, it is only the thematic patterning of interaction, the patterns of meaning that emerge, which may be said to organize themselves. Self-organization means that individuals are interacting with each other on a local basis and it is widespread thematic patterns of meaning that emerge without a blueprint or plan for those widespread patterns. However, in their local interaction, individuals are expressing impulses, obsessions, compulsions, desires, preferences, intentions, expectations and plans in the living present. What emerges, what organizes itself, is the interplay of all of these individual intentions, desires and so on.

What the theory of complex responsive processes presents, therefore, is a paradoxically cooperative and conflictual perspective on human action. If humans are not simply enabling but also constraining each other at the same time, they will inevitably be trying to constrain each other in ways that conflict. If the patterning of interaction, of identity/self and the social, evolves through the amplification of small differences, then that too implies conflict. In other words, as they interact with each other, individual selves will be continually faced with the problem of choosing between conflicting desires, preferences, impulses, intentions and plans. This means that human action is fundamentally evaluative and that human interaction must itself produce the evaluative criteria upon which choices of action are made. The narrative and propositional themes that are the patterns of human interaction must, therefore, involve themes of values and norms. It becomes important, then, in understanding societies, organizations and groups as complex responsive processes of relating to explore the nature of human desires, the normative constraints (morals) on those desires and the values (ethics) according to which they are judged and evaluated as the basis of acting. The work of Joas is particularly helpful in this regard.

Desires, values and norms

Joas (2000) draws on the work of the America pragmatists (James, 1902; Dewey, 1934; Mead, 1934) to make a distinction between desires/preferences, values/ideals and norms.

A distinction may be made between first and second order desires (Frankfurt, 1971). First order desires or preferences are:

- fluid and particular bodily impulses expressed as unreflective action;
- experienced as compulsive motivations for actions;
- lacking in evaluative criteria and so not intrinsically linked to ethics or morals.

However, human beings also have desires directed to their desires, second order desires. In other words, humans can desire to have desires, or not, and they can desire that their desire be strong enough to influence their will. We can desire to be different to what we are. Desires directed to our desires arise in reflective self-evaluation so that human desiring is essentially reflective and self-evaluative and so essentially social, in the way described in the previous section. For human action it is not possible to take desire (bodily impulse, or first order desire) on its own due to the human capacity, essentially social, to formulate the desirable and the judgment or evaluation that this always involves. Only in the rarest of circumstances, I would argue, do humans simply act on bodily impulse – there is almost always some kind of discrimination arising in a history of social interaction, although that discrimination could quite easily have become unconscious. This discrimination inevitably implicates norms and values. So what are they and how do they arise?

Norms are:

- evaluative in that they provide criteria for judging desires and actions;
- obligatory and constraining. They therefore restrict opportunities for action. We experience them as compelling in a restrictive sense;
- intimately connected with morals in that they provide criteria for what *ought* to be done, what is *right*.

Norms, then, provide a basis for evaluating and choosing between desires and actions. Elias (1939) was particularly concerned with how norms emerge and evolve as people in a society become more and more interdependent and as the use of violence is monopolized by the state. He explained how desires are taken more and more behind the scenes of daily life as more detailed norms emerge about what can and cannot be done in public. These norms become part of individual personality structures, and adherence to such norms is sustained by the social process of shame. Norms, therefore, are constraints arising in social evolution that act to restrain the actions and even desires of interdependent individuals, so much so that the constraints become thematic patterns of individual identities. In complex responsive process terms, norms are themes organizing experience in a constraining way. However, norms are inseparable although different from values. First, consider how values differ from norms and then how inseparable they are, despite the differences.

Joas uses the words 'values' and 'ideals' interchangeably and identifies their characteristics as:

- evaluative in that they provide general and durable criteria for judging desires, norms and actions;
- attractive and compelling in a voluntary, committed sense. They motivate action and open up opportunities for action. Values attract us, giving life meaning and purpose, and so are not experienced as restrictive. They are the highest expression of our free will, presenting a paradox of compulsion and voluntary commitment at the same time;
- intimately connected with ethics in that they provide criteria for judging what *is* the *good* in action, differentiating between good and bad desires, good and bad norms.

Values are essentially concerned with what it is good to desire. When we reject a perfectly realizable desire because we believe it is unacceptable, we are distinguishing between higher and lower virtues or vices, profound and superficial feelings, noble and base desires. Such evaluations refer to feelings such as outrage, guilt and admiration, and they indicate a life we hold to be of higher value, a view of the kind of person we want to be.

Joas draws on Dewey (1934), who was heavily influenced by Mead, to argue that values, as inspiring, attractively compelling motivations to act towards the good, are continually arising in social interaction as inescapable aspects of self-formation. Values are continually arising in our ongoing negotiation with each other, and ourselves, in our going on together. It follows that values are contingent upon the particular action situations in which we find ourselves. Although values have general and durable qualities, their motivational impact on action must be negotiated afresh, must be particularized, in each action situation. Dewey combines such an intersubjective understanding of self and value formation with experiences of self-transcendence. The communicative interaction, in which self is formed, is more than a means to coordinating action; it opens up human beings to each other, making possible the experience in which values and commitments to them arise. Shared experiences overcome self-centeredness producing altruism, which is a radical readiness to be shaken by the other in order to realize oneself in and through others. This opening, or transcending, of the self is the decentering of the self towards others and it is in this process that values arise.

Dewey also brings in the role of imagination and creativity in the genesis of values and value commitments. Imagination idealizes contingent possibilities and creates an imaginary relation to a holistic self. While imaginary, this relation is not an illusion or a fantasy. Idealization allows us to imagine a wholeness which does not exist and never will, but it seems real because we have experienced it so intensely. This is not a solitary but a social process. The will does not bring about the imagined wholeness; rather, the will is possessed by it.

The description of values and value commitments so far may easily be taken as meaning that values are unequivocally good. However, as indicated in the above discussion, this is not so. The notions of cult values, the power dynamics of inclusion and exclusion, and the way in which groups of people may get caught up in destructive unconscious processes of self-loss, focus our attention on the darker aspects of values/ideals and value commitments. These processes point to the particular problems that arise from the tendencies to idealize imagined wholes and submerge in imagined participation in them.

Notice the paradoxical nature of the theory of values outlined so far. Values arise in processes of self-formation and self-transcendence at the same time. Values arise in critical reflection and in experience beyond conscious deliberation at the same time. Values arise in intense actual experience of interaction and in idealizing acts of imagination at the same time. Values may be good or bad or both, depending upon who is doing the judging. Values arise in processes in which the self is simultaneously formed and transcended.

Values arise in interaction between people but are experienced by them as beyond their own positing. Values do not arise either from conscious intentions or through justification and discussion, although such intention, justification and discussion may be applied later. Values cannot be produced rationally and they cannot be disseminated through indoctrination. A purpose in life cannot be prescribed. Instead, the subjective experience of values arises in specific action contexts and types of intense experience. Values and value commitments arise in the process of self-formation through processes of idealizing key intense experiences and through the imaginative construction of a whole self to yield general and durable motivations for action directed towards what is judged as the good. These generalized idealizations must always be particularized in specific action situations as people negotiate their going on together.

Values cannot be prescribed or deliberately chosen by anyone because they emerge, and continue to be iterated, in intense interactive experiences involving self-formation and self-transcendence. To claim that someone could choose values for others would be to claim that this someone could form the identity, or self, of others and form the self-transcendence of others.

Norms, values and ideology

In complex responsive processes terms, values are themes organizing the experience of being together in a voluntary compelling, ethical manner, while norms are themes of being together in an obligatory, restrictive way. Furthermore, in complex responsive process terms, norms and values constitute a paradox. As I have already pointed out, when humans interact, they enable and constrain each other at the same time. It is the actions of human bodies that enable and constrain. However, in their ongoing negotiation of the enabling-constraining actions they choose, all are taking the attitude of others both specifically and in a generalized/idealized way. In other words, they are continually negotiating the evaluations of their actions. The criteria for evaluation are at the same time both obligatory restrictions taking the form of what they ought and ought not to do (norms) and voluntary compulsions, taking the form of what they are judging it good to do (values). The evaluative themes forming and being formed by human interaction are norms and values at the same time, together constituting ideology. How is this so?

The generalization/idealization (the whole) has the qualities of obligatory restriction (norm) and, at the same time, the qualities of voluntary compulsion (values) and so is evaluative. In dialectical terms, the opposition (negation) of norm and value, of restricting and opening up, is transformed (*Aufhebung* or negation of negation) as ideology. Ideology, a whole that is simultaneously the obligatory restriction of the norm and the voluntary compulsion of value, constitutes the evaluative criteria for the choice of communicative interactions and the sustaining of power relations. As such it is largely habitual and so unconscious processes of self and social at the same time. If people in a group rigidly apply the ideological whole to their interactions in all specific, contingent situations they co-create fascist power relations and cults which can easily be taken over by collective ecstasies. The result is to alienate people from their ordinary everyday experience and so create a false consciousness. Alternatively, if the ideological whole is so fragmented that there is little generalized tendency to act, then people will be interacting in ways that are almost entirely contingent on the situation, resulting in anarchy. Usually, however, people particularize/functionalize some ideological wholes in contingent situations and this is essentially a conflictual process of negating the whole, which always involves critical reflection.

The discussion of norms and values can, I think, further illuminate the nature of the 'I–me' dialectic. The 'I' may be thought of as the voluntary compulsion that arises in intense iterative experience, grasped by the imagination and idealized in a manner that opens up possibilities for action. Spontaneity, imagination and idealization, voluntary compulsion impervious to argument, are all characteristics of the 'I'. On the other hand, one can think of the 'me' in terms of the obligatory restriction of the ought/right (norm). However, 'I' as value and 'me' as norm can never be separated in the process of self-formation. In dialectical terms, the opposition (negation) of voluntary compulsion ('I') and obligatory restriction ('me') is transformed (*Aufhebung* or negation of negation) as self. Self-formation is thus a fundamentally social process and this is a fundamentally evaluative process of norm and value. But there is further negation because in altruistic social interaction, the self is opened up to others and it is in this experience of self-transcendence that values arise. I would argue that, for human beings, the spontaneity of the 'I' has little to do with bodily impulses as such because bodily impulses are already socially formed. Furthermore, I would argue that human spontaneity is not the opposite of reflection. Dewey, James and Joas all link the experience of value with the critical examination of action, with reflection. One might think of the 'I' as the impulsion to enact values and this inevitably involves reflection. For me, the spontaneity of the 'I' refers to the feeling that I must respond, even in ways that surprise and frighten me, if I am to be able to live with myself.

From a complex responsive processes perspective there are no universals outside of human interaction, but this does not mean that norms and values are purely relative in an 'anything goes' kind of way because generalizations and idealizations may only be found in their particularization in specific interactive situations. This always involves negotiation of conflict, power relating, in which 'anything goes' is impossible.

From a complex responsive processes perspective, desires, values and norms are all understood to be particular narrative and propositional themes emerging in interaction and at the same time patterning that interaction. Norms are constraining aspects of themes, providing criteria for judging desires and actions. Emotions, such as shame and fear of punishment or exclusion, provide the main constraining force. Values, on the other hand, are highly motivating aspects of themes that arise in particularly intense collective and individual experience, involving imagination and idealization, and serve as the basis for evaluating and justifying desires and actions, as well as the norms constraining them. Emotions such as gratitude, humility, altruism, guilt and feelings of self-worth provide the attractive, compelling force of value experiences. For each person, these intense value experiences are particularly linked to interactions over a life history with important others, such as parents, who are perceived to enact values ascribed to them. These important others cannot unilaterally prescribe such values because they emerge in the relationship. However, while the separation of values and norms is an aid to understanding, it is an abstraction from lived, practical experience in which norms and values are inseparable aspects of the evaluative themes, the ideologies, which are choices of actions.

What part does a leader play in all of this? Leadership arises in social processes of recognition (Griffin, 2002) in which, in imagination, the leader may be recognized as embodying the idealized whole. Here the leader is not designing the value and persuading others to commit to them. The leader is participating in the intense experience in which the values are arising and in which he or she comes to be imagined as embodying them. He or she and the others may be so caught up in the process that they all lose sight of the imaginative nature of their construct. The leader is then idealized as a person and denigration is never far away. Leadership is a social object and cult value.

I want to turn now to the connections between the above theory of value/norm genesis and the spiritual.

Complex responsive processes and spirituality

In talking about the spiritual, or as he calls it, religious experience, Joas relies heavily on Dewey and James, who both argue that such experience is an aspect of 'values in general'. Exploration of the nature of religious experience, therefore, brings deeper insight into the genesis of values and value commitments. Consider first the views of Dewey.

In 1934, Dewey published *A Common Faith* setting out his theory of religion. Having broken away from his own religious background and belief in any supernatural being, he was not concerned with institutionalized religion but, rather, the experience of religious feeling, which many refer to as the spiritual. Furthermore, he did not believe in specifically religious or aesthetic experience but saw them as dimensions of all experience. For him, religious experience was real but was culturally mediated without supernatural origin. Both religious and aesthetic experiences are imaginary orientations to a whole self, which is an ideal or imaginative projection that permeates and transforms life, bringing a sense of security and peace.

Dewey held that participation in communication/conversation could lead to the experience of wholeness and he regarded this as an ideal inspiring reverence, thereby sacralizing community and democracy. For Dewey, then, religious experience is a social experience of value involving self-formation and self-transcendence.

In his *Varieties of Religious Experience* (1902), James seeks to understand the religious by taking the religious experience of the solitary individual seriously. Unlike Dewey, therefore, James does not take a social perspective on self-formation but focuses on the given individual. However, like Dewey, he sees self-transcendence, self-opening, as the process in which 'values in general' arise and faith, like love, is a special case of this. He too broke away from his own religious background and was not concerned with theology or religious institutions but with personal religious experience, which he defined as the feelings and acts of people in their solitude as they understand themselves in relation to the divine. To study such experience is to study human experience in one of its most intense and universal manifestations. To understand religious experience, he studied accounts of conversion experiences, prayer, mystical experiences and personal rebirth. He concluded from his studies that the religious is always experienced anew by living individuals as religious emotions, which are natural emotions directed towards religious objects. James said that the divine is a primal reality which one feels impelled to respond to gravely and solemnly. James distinguished religious experience from moral experience. The moral person concentrates the will in order to lead a moral life and this morality restricts possibilities for action. The religious person lives life with passion, excitement and fervor, and this experience is liberating, empowering and morality transcending, so increasing possibilities for action. This experience of religiosity arises in the impulse to yield the self to the Self.

James then explains what he means by religiosity. Religiosity is a state of assurance and certainty in which there is a loss of worry, and a feeling of peace, harmony and willingness to be. It is a passion of acquiescence and admiration involving the perception of truths impossible to articulate in language. The appearance of the world is altered and a feeling of bliss or ecstasy flows through one, involving the conviction of the presence of a stronger power than oneself. Conversion is a unification of the self and prayer opens one up to supra-individual forms of power. Such experience cannot be instilled by proof and is impervious to argument.

Religious and closely related aesthetic experiences are, therefore, particularly intense examples of the experience of values in general. Religious experience, as an experience of value, has particular qualities and emotions to do with awe, reverence and love, accompanied by feelings of peace and assurance that give meaning to life. For Dewey this has nothing to do with anything supernatural but arises as idealization of an imagined whole, while for James the divine is a primal reality.

From a complex responsive processes perspective, religious or spiritual experiences, as described by Dewey and James, are easily understood as particularly intense and powerfully attractive experiences of value in just the way Joas argues for. I include James' work in this claim despite the fact that he saw religious experience in terms of the solitary individual. Joas makes the point that although Mead's theory is one of the social formation of the self, he is not thereby dismissing the notion of unique individuality. Similarly, I would argue that this theory of self-formation does not exclude the notion of solitariness or the capacity to be alone (Winnicott, 1965). One can only become a unique self in social interaction but that self certainly also experiences being alone or solitary. I would argue that this is an essential aspect of the religious experience, alongside its social aspect. The key aspect, perhaps, of religious and spiritual experience is a particularly powerful experience of that self-transcendence, the emptying, losing and opening the self to otherness and so finding the self, which Joas holds to be common to all experiences of value. Without this we get the cult and collective ecstasy with its loss of self. For some, the experience of self-transcendence is not accompanied by the need to postulate some transcendent divine and is presumably, therefore, not accompanied by any experience of the transcendent divine. For others, however, the spiritual experience of self-transcendence and the experience of the transcendent divine are inseparable. The theory of complex responsive processes has, of course, absolutely nothing whatsoever to say about the question of whether there is, or is not, a transcendent divine or what the nature of that transcendent divine might be. The theory is concerned with how either or both of these beliefs are taken up in action.

However, the theory of complex responsive processes rests upon a theory of causality in which there is no causal power outside human interaction accounting for the patterning of that interaction because interaction patterns itself. The theory is, then, saying that any transcendent divine is not the cause of human interactions. It is we who cause our interactions through individual evaluations and choices of action but not simply as individuals for, although each of us may evaluate and choose our next action, the pattern that emerges is the result of the interplay of all those evaluations and choices and none of us can choose that interplay. To say that God is the cause of an individual's actions or the cause of the interplay of individual actions would be to escape our own ethical responsibility for what we do in particular situations and run into the unsolved problem of how a loving God could choose the terrible things we do to each other. Furthermore, just as with any value, the spiritual value experience has its dark side. Those who have powerful spiritual experiences may well come to believe that this entitles them to occupy the moral high ground, leading to the dynamics of inclusion and exclusion, with its often terrible consequences. The result is a loss of negotiated value orientations in highly normative institutional structures with the direct application of cult values.

It might be objected that denying a causal role for the divine in the patterning of human interactions amounts to claiming either that God is irrelevant or that religious experience is being split off from all other experience. I argue that this objection is unfounded. Those who believe in God and experience the religious are experiencing what is, for them, the most powerful and motivating of all values. This experience, therefore, infuses all their actions and evaluations. The religious experience is thus taken up in the actions of those who are religious, and this must play its part in what emerges in the interaction between them and others who will have different or no religious experience, but will all, nevertheless, experience value in some way. It is from negotiations of these differences, and the conflict they bring, that human futures emerge. The religious experience is not split off from the other actions of the religious person and the belief in God is not irrelevant to them. They play their part through the actions of religious persons in ways that cannot be understood in terms of simple causality.

When I talk to groups of managers about understanding organizations as complex responsive processes, I am frequently asked about the connection with the spiritual. When I ask people what they mean by the spiritual, they reply that it has to do with personal peak or ecstatic experiences often related to nature; the connectedness of everything to everything forming a whole; the infinite; and a higher purpose, the ultimate meaning of life. What is it about the theory of complex responsive processes that triggers this question of spirituality for managers in organizations that ostensibly have nothing to do with spirituality? I think it is because this theory emphasizes the unpredictability of human futures. When I talk about the unknowable, the perpetual construction of the future in the never-ending iterative processes of the present, this is easily linked in the hearer's perception to some notion of the infinite. I also talk about the emergence of individual and collective identity in social interaction, thereby challenging ways of thinking and talking about identity as an essence or a pre-given self existing inside an individual person. This challenge touches on questions about the meaning of life and its purpose. Furthermore, a key aspect of the theory of complex responsive processes is its notion of transformative causality where human interaction patterns itself, as repetition and potential transformation at the same time, from within that interaction. In other words, interaction is its own cause without any 'whole' having causal power above or below that interaction. It is then taken that I am denying anything mysterious, mystical or spiritual in human experience. It is taken that the notion of a transcendent divine, or any higher purpose in life, is incompatible with the perspective of complex responsive processes. It is understandable, therefore, that the theory of complex responsive processes should trigger questions to do with spirituality.

However, it is striking how often this question is raised when we are talking about organizations that have nothing to do with religion. Why does this happen? Perhaps it has something to do with the fact that most people in the West now have no religious practice and, for more than a century, sociologists, philosophers and politicians have raised concerns about the basis of ethics and values in such a secular society. There was a time when religion gave most people a sense of the ultimate meaning of life but now, in a secular society, where is one to look for such meaning? Perhaps people have come to look for some kind of ultimate purpose in life in the organizations for which they work, and this is why the question of spirituality quickly comes to mind when taken-for-granted notions of the nature of organizations are questioned.

For me, there are a number of reasons for not appealing to the mythological and the mystical in our explanatory frameworks relating to organizations. First, when we move to the mystical, to an ineffable and unknowable God, for example, we move away from the possibility of rationally articulated explanation because, by definition, we cannot articulate explanations of the ineffable and unknowable. In relation to the mystical, we have to move away from explanation to intuitive experience which we might try to talk about in terms of mythology or theology and experience in ritual. However, when talking about human organizations, I feel it is incumbent upon us to explain what we think we are doing together, rather than pointing to mythology or engaging in ritual. Second, some of those importing notions of the spiritual into their discussions about organizations seem to me to use the spiritual in a prescriptive, instrumental or utopian way, thereby positing a cause of human interaction which lies outside that interaction. For me, this is a debasing of the most precious aspect of human experience and an easy way out of taking ethical responsibility for what we are doing in the ordinary daily conduct of our lives. Third, it seems to me that most organizations exist in order to provide goods and services of many different kinds. Most organizations do not exist to meet people's spiritual needs – for these we have religious organizations.

I now turn to how norms, values and the spiritual are dealt with in the organizational literature, and in the section after that to how people take up these matters in organizational practice.

Values and spirituality in the literature on organizations

Among the most influential thinkers about values and organizations in recent times are Schein (1985), who understands values in terms of organizational culture and links this closely to the role of leaders, and Senge (1990), who sees values as part of the learning organization.

Schein on values and culture

Schein distinguishes three elements of culture, which he locates at different levels:

1 At the most superficial level culture is displayed in the form of visible artifacts, such as art and technology, and visible behavior patterns. However, although visible, it is difficult to understand what these mean, and to achieve a deeper understanding one has to move to the next level, namely the core *values* that produce the day-to-day operating principles according to which members of a particular culture govern their behavior.

2 At the next level culture reflects someone's original *values*, and by values Schein means what *ought* to be rather than what *is good*. Schein proposes a theory of the genesis of such values, which occurs as follows. When people face a new task, the first solution they adopt is a value because there is as yet no shared basis for determining what is factual and real. Someone, usually the founder of an organization, has a conviction about what to do and proposes a solution. When the group believes this conviction, it is acted upon and cognitively transferred to, and reflected in, the observable behavior of the first level described above. The observed behavior then becomes habitual and its value basis falls below the level of awareness, so constituting a deeper, third level.

3 At the deepest level culture consists of shared values below the level of awareness, which Schein refers to as basic assumptions. These basic assumptions are so deeply shared, as a non-confrontable theory-in-use, that there is little variation in the behavior of the members of a cultural unit. When these basic assumptions, or deep values, cease to be reality congruent, they must be brought to the surface and made conscious. This usually requires the assistance of some objective third party to act as facilitator. The basic assumptions are about the relationships to the environment; the nature of reality, time and space; the nature of being human; the nature of human activity; and the nature of human relationships.

What Schein calls values, which he contrasts with the factual and the real, first arise as the response of some individual to a problem. If successful they are then reflected in the observable behavior of other members of the group and then, as they become habits, they fall below the level of awareness to become the cause of ongoing patterns of group behavior. If these deep underlying values become inappropriate then they need to be deliberately changed by leaders. Deep values are unconsciously shared, and it is possible to make them conscious and engineer changes in them.

In some places, Schein says that culture evolves and cannot be changed to suit our purposes (p. 5). He refers to the psychoanalyst Bion (1961) to draw attention to the complex interplay between individuals struggling for leadership in a group. However, despite this he locates the origin of culture/norm/value in the founder of a group and the possibility of changing culture in leaders. He says that the importance of shared basic assumptions in the emotional life of a group will depend upon the stage it has reached in its development, and this will determine whether the leader can change the culture. When a group reaches a mature stage, its culture predisposes it to certain kinds of leadership – the group creates its own leaders. However, if a mature organization is to avoid blindly perpetuating itself and the leadership it has created, then the leader must break the tyranny of the old culture. Such a leader must acquire objectivity and insight into the elements of culture (p. 321), and it is his essential function to manipulate the culture (p. 317).

This is completely different to the theory of values set out in the previous section. First, Schein uses the term 'value' to mean what *ought* to be, rather than what *is*. In this chapter, a norm is what ought to be and a value is about what is judged to be good. Schein, therefore, makes no distinction between values and norms and loses the attractive, motivating nature of values in the obligatory and restrictive nature of norms. Second, Schein locates the genesis of values–norms quite clearly in the individual arising as a rational solution to a problem. From a complex responsive processes perspective, values arise in social processes of self/identity formation and self-transcendence. Third, complex responsive processes are continuous temporal processes rather than the notion of system underlying Schein's view. Fourth, Schein holds that deep-seated norms can be changed by deliberate choice, which is explicitly rejected as a possibility in this chapter because values and norms both arise in social interaction which no one can control. They have to do with self and identity, both individual and collective, and these cannot be deliberately chosen or engineered. Schein has no notion of functionalization and so ends up talking about cult values. For Schein, it is the rational individual choice that generates values rather than the conflictual interaction between people with its potential for amplification as in the theory of complex responsive processes.

Senge on values and spirituality

Senge (1990), with his theory of the learning organization, is another organization theorist concerned with the matter of values, and he has been just as influential as Schein. Senge specifies what he calls the five disciplines of the learning organization: systems thinking, mental models, shared vision, personal mastery and team learning. The matter of values is relevant to the discipline of personal mastery and also to that of shared vision. He talks about a subtle aspect of personal mastery being the experience of increased connectedness between people, and between people and their environment. This experience of connectedness leads to the values of compassion and a genuine commitment to something larger than us, namely the whole. This is a commitment of the heart and a sincere desire to serve the world, naturally leading beyond self- interest to a broader vision. He quotes CEOs who talk about important discoveries being those that arise in the experience of spiritual power with the will of a person committed to a higher purpose being a cry from the soul that has been awakened and shaken. The CEOs he quotes see spiritual welfare, the self-actualization of their people, as part of their task. The discipline of personal mastery requires spiritual growth but goes beyond it to approach life from a creative viewpoint. Those who display personal mastery have a special sense of purpose and for them vision is a calling. They are called to work creatively with the tension between vision, what we want for the future, and current reality. Senge stresses that this discipline of personal mastery is not a soft option but one that leads to better organizational performance and higher profit.

Senge distinguishes between:

- vision, which is the picture of the future we wish to create, answering to the question of *what* to do;
- purpose, being a larger sense of purpose to contribute to the world, answering to the question of *why* we exist;
- values, which are about how a company wants life to be on a day-to-day basis while pursuing the vision, answering the question of *how* it wants people to act consistent with the mission. The kinds of values Senge specifies are fairness, harmony, humility and gratitude.

He talks about building a vision as one element of the 'governing ideas' of the organization, the others being purpose and values, with the three elements together answering to the question of what we believe in. He provides examples of companies which have deliberately constructed values and taught their people in training sessions to act according to those values. However, he also says that no one can give another a vision so that organizations need to take steps to encourage personal vision. The leader's vision is one such personal vision and he or she then asks others to follow him or her so that they come to share commitment to that vision, which should flow naturally from genuine enthusiasm for the vision. Although vision can start anywhere, managers must be skilled in building shared visions. Such sharing takes time to emerge as products of interaction taking the form of ongoing dialogue. Such dialogue is a facilitated conversation in which people suspend their assumptions and listen to each other, thus getting in touch with a common pool of meaning which is said to flow through them. Senge then goes on to describe leaders as integrators of the five disciplines, who design the governing ideas and the learning process, act as stewards of the vision through their purpose story and also take on the role of teachers.

Senge, then, presents a view of organizational life and the role of values in it, which is clearly in the same tradition of thought as Schein. For both, the leader is the one who designs the values and must manage their widespread sharing on the part of organizational members. Both talk somewhat ambivalently about values emerging, but at the same time they claim that in successful organizations leaders design them and persuade or train others to follow them. They see nothing contradictory about this – all it means is that it is difficult to achieve. Both, therefore, locate the genesis of values in individuals with any social process coming into the sharing phase. Where they differ is as follows. For Schein the process of value genesis and commitment is largely a rational one, and although he does talk about the impact of emotions, he does not refer to spirituality. For Senge, however, there is a strong spiritual aspect to the learning organization. He talks about serving a higher purpose, about interconnectedness and wholes, and sees dialogue as a form of communication that causes a common pool of meaning to flow through people. He refers to meditation, which a later writer in this tradition advocates for managers as a way of discovering what they should do (Scharmer, 2000). Senge links his views on personal mastery to the great religions of Buddhism, Hinduism and Christianity. Furthermore, he argues that these spiritual aspects are not to be dismissed as soft because they lead to superior performance and so greater profit.

Unlike Schein, therefore, Senge does introduce the strongly attractive, motivating nature of values in the form of spirituality. However, he sees the kind of climactic experience leading to the experience of value as an individual act of self-mastery. From a complex responsive processes perspective, such moments are not simply individual choices but, rather, they have to do with values arising in social processes of self-formation and self-transcendence. Values cannot be deliberately designed or rationally chosen because they arise in interaction, and spiritual experience has the quality of a gift rather than a choice. Senge does not distinguish between values and norms – he talks about values as motivators in relation to personal mastery and then also uses the word 'values' to cover how a company wants people to act, which is a norm. Senge does not ignore interaction but that interaction which produces values and visions takes the special form of dialogue with its rather mystical undertones. For Senge, values and visions can be designed and built, and this becomes a prescription for successful organizations. Implicitly, the suggestion is that organizations should use what Senge describes as spiritual to improve their performance. The spiritual is then being dealt with in a prescriptive and instrumental manner to secure improved organizational performance. In the approach taken in this paper, there is no prescription or instrumentalization because I argue that all values, including the spiritual, cannot be designed and built in the first place. Senge ascribes a pivotal role to the leader, which is very different to the role of leader from a complex responsive processes perspective.

Senge and Schein present a view of value and organizations in terms of what might be thought of as a gap analysis. This involves analyzing what the current values are, how they affect behavior, and what is disadvantageous about this. The next step is to identify what would be advantageous, what kind of future people would like to have, and this is usually seen as the task of the leader. The gap between what they have and what they would like is thus identified as the basis for taking action to close the gap. However, the envisioned future is usually an idealization, some kind of hypothetical utopia. The hypothetical nature of this utopia is then easily forgotten and it is taken as a reality that can be discovered or realized. This is a linear view of time in which there is a presumed movement from a past that has yielded the present to a future identified in advance. This is a completely different view to the circular view of time taken in the concept of the living present in complex responsive processes theory. What results from this linear view of time and its hypothetical utopian future is a kind of false consciousness in which people are alienated from their ordinary lived experience of the present.

The complex responsive processes perspective focuses on how values, both positive and negative, emerge as motivators in ordinary everyday interaction between human bodies. In contrast to this emphasis on the ordinary in all its good and bad, Senge focuses on the good, and presents a thoroughly utopian view of the possibilities for organizational life. Neither Schein nor Senge link values to self-formation. Senge never explains how voluntary commitment to a leader's vision and values arises so that they become compelling, attractive motivations. The theory of complex responsive processes points to how this happens in interactive experiences of self-formation and transcendence rather than self-loss. Both Senge and Schein confuse norms and values and end up suggesting cult values.

Some other examples of values and spirituality in the literature

Some other writers take the emphasis on spiritual matters in relation to organizations even further than Senge. In his book *The Reinvention of Work*, Fox (1995) points to the enormous increase in unemployment that took place over the 1980s and early 1990s, to the clash between work and family life, to the despair of young people and to the impact of economic growth on the planet, talking about the wounded Earth and the ignored needs of other species. He claims that current economic and organizational systems are not working and calls for a metanoia, a change of mindsets, hearts and ways of acting. At the centre of this metanoia he sees the need for a new definition of work and the way we create and compensate for it, as well as a need to let go of work and infuse it with play and ritual. He argues that life and livelihood should not be separated but that we should see them as flowing from one source namely, Spirit, so enabling us to live with meaning and purpose, contributing to the greater community and the sustainability of Earth. He calls for a spirituality of work. In presenting his arguments he refers to mysticism and mythology, calling for re-sacralization of work after the machine age to reclaim the sacredness of work that permeates the universe and contributes to growth, justice and compassion. He calls for the greater work of the inner, the development of our souls and selves, and also for a more relational world. He wants to bring together inner and outer work because in doing this we are creating cosmology, a making whole.

What we see here is the bringing together of a number of themes that constitute what many are now talking about when they link spirituality with organizations. There is the call for organizations to meet the spiritual needs of individuals, the development of the individual's soul. This is linked to a relational world, the community and the sacralization of community and work. Relationships are taken to be entirely good. Soul and community are then closely linked to deep ecology and sustainability, often understood in mythological, even mystical, terms, and this in turn calls for a return to ancient wisdom. Nature too is to be re-sacralized. These are all elements of a whole that is unquestionably good, so establishing a particular ethics of a universalist kind in that those who participate in this whole are good and those who do not are bad (Griffin, 2002). All of this points to the need for a sense of higher purpose and creates a utopian prescription for organizational success, thereby instrumentalizing the spiritual. What is so created is what Mead called 'cult values', and those putting them forward pay no attention to just how these cult values are functionalized as good and bad in ordinary daily life. This is in sharp contrast to the perspective of complex responsive processes theory, which seeks to understand just how such cult values are functionalized in ordinary, everyday conflictual social life as both good and bad.

While complex responsive processes theory draws on the natural complexity sciences for analogies with human interaction understood in the terms of Mead and Elias, others see in the complexity sciences a direct justification of the view of values and spirituality summarized in previous paragraphs. They understand the insights from the complexity sciences in systemic terms and apply them directly to human action. In doing this, they take up the emphasis that the natural complexity sciences place on systems, wholes, interconnectedness, relational, emergence, self-organization, unpredictability, and the possibility of highly complex patterns emerging from the interaction of simple rules. All of this resonates with the particular view of spirituality outlined above.

For example, Wheatley (1992) argues that the new sciences are making us more aware of our yearning for simplicity and how we share this yearning with natural systems. Such simplicity takes the form of a few guiding formulae or principles rather than complex controls – simple rules. She calls for a focus on relationships and how this means that we have to give up the predictable for the potential. She says that self-organization succeeds when the system supports the individual activities of its members by giving them a strong frame of reference. Creative individuals can have an enormous impact on such systems by attracting the attention of the organization and then watching it amplify into new developments.

When she talks about meaning, Wheatley starts with the mythology of chaos, a yawning chasm, and Gaia, the mother of Earth. In their partnership they created everything we know and they continue to inhabit our imagination. She says that this mythology has now taken on a new life in the new sciences and she finds this return to ancient wisdom comforting. She likens humans to Gaia, a generative force that gives meaning to life and dispels chaos in our creative expression.

According to Wheatley, one can tell what an organization's values are by watching anyone working in it because they will all display a consistent and predictable quality of behavior. This quality is produced by simply expressing expectations of acceptable behavior and giving the freedom for individuals to assert themselves. Successful organizations must: 'trust in the power of guiding principles or values, knowing that they are strong enough influencers of behavior to shape every employee into a desired representative of the organization' (p. 132).

Effective leadership communicates these simple rules, guiding visions, inspiring values, and then allows individuals in the system to meander in seemingly random, chaotic ways. She also says that the movement to participative management is rooted in the changing perception of the organizing principles of the universe.

Here we see the mythological elevation of nature to the status of some whole that we must all participate in, since it provides our higher purpose. The effect is to hold out the hope of a utopia, a hopelessly idealized future, if only we would all conform. This is, of course, Mead's definition of a cult value. Rather than the self-transcendence that Dewey talks about in his view of the genesis of values, we have in the perspective of Wheatley and others what may only be described as the loss of self in participation in a whole.

Another example of complexity writers directly importing notions from the complexity sciences to justify their prescriptions of the spiritual for organizations is provided by *The Soul at Work* by Lewin and Regine (2000). They point to how pervasive the feeling of not being valued at work has become, leading to reduced job satisfaction and morale, frustration and anger that is detrimental to business. To reverse this, they call for organizations to nurture people's souls at work and to allow their souls to emerge, linking this to improved business results. They say that the complexity sciences see the world as composed of complex adaptive systems, which are living, interconnected, dynamic entities. Like Wheatley, they argue that the complexity of relationships and businesses comes from deep simplicity, a principle applying to the universe. They conclude that when relationships in an organization are care-full then a community of care develops, creating space for the soul at work to emerge. The soul at work is both an individual and a collective phenomenon. When the individual soul is engaged, people naturally want to add value. The collective soul is where people become connected to a larger purpose, transforming the 'protean' spirit of the organization to infinite possibilities through a culture of care, support and fulfillment. The collective soul benefits the whole.

Here once again we see the use of the natural complexity sciences to justify particular cult values without any interpretation of what the insights of those sciences may mean in human terms or any attempt to explain how such cult values are functionalized in daily life. There are the same ethical implications as before, namely that those ascribing to the cult of care are good and those not ascribing to it are bad (Griffin, 2002). Compared to Dewey, the writers reviewed in this section lose sight of the imaginary nature of the whole and of the role of self-transcendence or altruism, the opening of the self, in the genesis of values. For Dewey, care means opening the self to others rather than participation in some actual whole in which the self is lost rather than transcended. A view of care as the opening of the self to others does not exclude conflict. The writers reviewed in this section miss the contingent, conflictual and negotiated nature of values but see them rather as universals. They confuse ethics and norms and do not see the link between idealization and denigration.

Values and organizational practice

The literature on spirituality and organizations, examples of which were discussed in the above section, may not have had a major impact on how practitioners in organizations think and act, but the views of those writing about values in general, particularly Schein and Senge, certainly have. Most large organizations now pay attention to their values, taken as synonymous with norms, and seek to specify those that should govern the behavior of their members. The questions of values/norms and leadership feature prominently in a great many of the management and leadership development programs through which organizations put their most promising managers.

For example, General Electric (GE) has specified in great detail what it calls 'The GE Values', so taking seriously the views of Schein and Senge that it is the role of leaders to design the values/norms that members of an organization are to live by. GE requires all employees to sign a form undertaking to abide by the 'GE Values' which are specified in a large volume given to each employee. Employees are also given 'Blue Forms' which they are encouraged to use to report on those who are infringing these values in some way. Such reports initiate disciplinary procedures against those infringing the values. These are, of course, not values in the terms of this chapter but norms constraining what people can do, and the use of procedures to inform on people breaking the norms is the practical illustration of the point made above on the conformist ethics that this promotes.

Many companies mount initiatives to develop new values, so carrying out the prescriptions of Schein, Senge and others that it is the role of leaders to redesign the values when the old ones are no longer appropriate. For example, the chief executive of one major company I worked with appointed a task force of 'high-flyer' managers to identify a new set of values for their organization so that people would act in more entrepreneurial ways. Despite intense effort, this task force could not come up with a new value set that they felt to be meaningful, and they floundered in trying to identify how they could get everyone to behave according to such a value set even if they could come up with one. What I found intriguing about this attempt to carry out the prescriptions of Schein, Senge and others was that the members of the task force showed no signs of reflecting on what the concept of 'values' might mean or how values might arise and be sustained or change. They simply took the prescription for granted.

Given the presumably unwanted consequences of a conformist ethics and the enormous difficulty, I would say impossibility, of carrying out the mainstream prescriptions to do with values in organizations, the question arises as to why managers still try. Furthermore, why is there a considerable interest expressed by many in organizations in that form of value called the spiritual, most commonly meaning higher purpose and the 'whole', linked to nature? The reason probably has to do with the experience of many of a loss of value in their lives. The response to this loss may well be reflected as a call for the organizations in which they work to fill this loss. However, the resulting mythological and utopian thinking amounts, for me, to an escape from explanation, and in practice leads to an ethics of conformity.

From the perspective of complex responsive processes, the value statements produced by organizations amount to gestures, and although such gestures can be designed, the response to them cannot. What kind of response might one expect? One response would be cynical disregard. However, if the publication of a value statement, a list of desired behaviors, is accompanied by strong pressures to conform, then the value statement amounts to an articulation of norms, and fear and shame may lead people to be seen to conform even though they do not really agree. The inspirational qualities of values simply do not arise. Finally, if accompanied by sufficient rhetorical skill on the part of leaders, the response may be some kind of collective ecstasy, some kind of cult. What one would not get from designed values is the compelling and attractive force of authentic values which arise in intense interactions between people in processes of self-formation and self-transcendence.

References

Bion, W. (1961) *Experiences in Groups and Other Papers*, London: Tavistock.

Dalal, F. (1998) *Taking the Group Seriously*, London: Jessica Kingsley.

Dewey, J. (1934) *A Common Faith*, New Haven, CT: Yale University Press.

Elias, N. (1939) *The Civilizing Process*, Oxford: Blackwell.

Elias, N. and Scotson, J. (1994) *The Established and the Outsiders*, London: Sage.

Fox, M. (1995) *The Reinvention of Work*, San Francisco, CA: HarperCollins.

Frankfurt, H. (1971) 'Freedom of the will and the concept of a person', *Journal of Philosophy*, 67:1, pp. 5–20.

Griffin, D. (2002) *The Emergence of Leadership: Linking self-organization and ethics*, London: Routledge.

James, W. (1902) *The Varieties of Religious Life*, Cambridge, MA: Harvard University Press.

Joas, H. (2000) *The Genesis of Values*, Cambridge: Polity Press.

Le Bon, G. (1920) *The Crowd: A Study of the Popular Mind*, New York: Ballantine.

Lewin, R. and Regine, B. (2000) *The Soul at Work*, London: Orion Business Books.

Mead, G. H. (1923) 'Scientific method and the moral sciences', *International Journal of Ethics*, 33, pp. 229–47.

Mead, G. H. (1934) *Mind, Self and Society*, Chicago, IL: Chicago University Press.

Mead, G. H. (1938a) *The Philosophy of the Act*, Chicago, IL: Chicago University Press.

Mead, G. H. (1938b) *The Philosophy of the Present*, Chicago, IL: Chicago University Press.

Scharmer, C. O. (2000) 'Presencing: using the self as gate for the coming-into-presence of the future'. Paper presented at conference on Knowledge and Innovation, May 25–6, 2000, Helsinki, Finland.

Schein, E. H. (1885) *Organizational Culture and Leadership*, San Francisco, CA: Jossey-Bass.

Senge, P. M. (1990) *The Fifth Discipline: The Art and Practice of the Learning Organization*, New York: Doubleday.

Stacey, R. (2001) *Complex Responsive Processes in Organizations: Learning and knowledge creation*, London: Routledge.

Stacey, R. (2003) *Complexity and Group Processes: A radically social understanding of individuals*, London: Brunner-Routledge.

Stacey, R., Griffin, D. and Shaw, P. (2000) *Complexity and Management: Fad or radical challenge to systems thinking?*, London: Routledge.

Wheatley, M. J. (1992) *Leadership and the New Science: Learning about Organization from an Orderly Universe*, San Francisco, CA: Berrett-Koehler.

Winnicott, D. W. (1965) *The Maturational Processes and the Facilitating Environment*, London: Hogarth Press.

Editors' introduction to Chapter 6

James Taylor is CEO of a hospital in the USA. In this chapter he recounts three short stories of the everyday experience of being a leader. The first concerns a crisis arising from relations with the heath regulatory system, vividly bringing out the fear and anxiety which threatening encounters with quality assurance systems arouse, rather similar to Williams' account of such encounters in the UK. The second is concerned with negotiations around the use of financial resources and the third is about an encounter with a consultant. Like Williams, in Chapter 3, and Tobin, in Chapter 4, Taylor makes us aware of the strong emotions involved in acting as a leader.

What Taylor is emphasizing in this chapter is the ordinary relational nature of leading where the skill of leading resides in the capacity to pay ongoing, careful attention to the present. This is a rather different view to the mainstream one in which the leader is often presented as an extraordinary, even heroic, person who pays attention to the future. In his stories, Taylor shows how the role of leader does not simply reside in him but moves around a group as different people are recognized as having a contribution to make. Taylor sees his role as being present but not intruding until some crisis requires him to, and then he offers assistance rather than intrusion. Taylor is also very aware of the movement of power relations in the role of leading.

An important part of this chapter relates to the notions of cult and functionalized values, described in Chapter 6 of this volume. He argues that mainstream views of leadership present leadership as if it were a commodity that could be owned by an individual. He holds that this view arises in the manner in which leadership is reified, generalized and idealized. In doing this, mainstream writers on leadership are articulating leadership as a cult value, that is, an idealized value that can never be directly realized in ordinary life but must always be functionalized in specific situations if we are to avoid forming a cult. Taylor recognizes the inevitability of people idealizing leadership but is interested in understanding how this idealization, or cult value, is functionalized in the ordinary everyday activities of leaders. He argues that this provides us with a more meaningful way of talking about what it means, in experience, to lead because it focuses our attention on the inevitably conflictual nature of functionalized leadership.

The particular influence of a leader arises in his or her displaying an enhanced capacity to pay attention in the moment, taking the attitude of others, as well as the attitude of the group and society. The leader is able to generalize his or her experience in a specific situation and so enable others to communicate through him or her. The leader is an influential contributor to the social process of making sense of collective experience. He or she does this by taking in more of the act in process than do others and by being able to put him or herself more into relation with the whole group/community. In his narrative about the crisis he faced he displays, as leader, the kind of detached involvement that Tobin writes about in Chapter 4.

For him, leadership is a role which emerges in conversation in which he plays an influential part:

I understand that our conversation, however punctuated by my exercise of my formal organizational power, will inform other conversations in ways that I will never know and cannot use my organizational power to control. Again, my leadership experience is paradoxical; at the same time I have the power to seemingly control the conversation, I know that I am no more in control of the meaning being made than any other participant. The meaning I make of the conversation and the meaning others make is informed by our participation together while at the same time our participation together is informed by the meaning we make (see p. 148 below).

6 Leadership and cult values: moving from the idealized to the experienced

James Taylor

While waiting for the coffee machine to fill my cup one last time on the Thursday afternoon before the New Year's weekend, I noticed a letter addressed to me, CEO of a university teaching hospital in the USA, coming off the fax machine from the federal government's agency that runs the Medicare program and regulates hospitals at the federal level. I took the fax and my coffee back to my office and sat down to read what I assumed would be an announcement of some new regulation. What I read, however, was quite different and very disturbing. I was being notified that the federal government had made a determination that University Hospital presented 'an immediate and serious threat to patient health and safety' and that publication in the local paper of this determination was imminent. The letter explained that as a result of a state agency inspection of a patient complaint earlier in the month, which by regulation had been forwarded to the federal government, the determination had been made of the patient safety threat and such a decision required the cessation of the federal government's Medicare funding. Notice of this action would be published in the local newspaper on the last day of the calendar year. The federal government's letter indicated that if 'a credible allegation of compliance' was received, a follow-up inspection visit would be conducted before January 15. A retraction of the action would then be possible and again a notice would be published to indicate compliance.

I immediately puzzled at the ominous-sounding governmental phrases like 'credible allegation of compliance' and 'immediate and serious threat to patient health and safety.' I was trying to make meaning of them, understanding that they symbolized someone else's previous meaning. I knew I was responding to the fax bodily, my stomach was churning, and a feeling of fear of impending disaster was very real.

As I carried the fax around the corner to a colleague's office, I was thinking of the bad timing of this problem. It was a down time at the hospital, the week in between Christmas and New Year, and many people were taking time off. Certainly the same would be true of the state and federal agencies involved. Getting anything done to avert the public relations disaster that public knowledge of this action would bring would be difficult at best and likely not possible.

I found my colleague, Barbara, in her office and handed her a copy of the fax. Barbara's responsibilities include oversight of the quality management functions. As she read the letter for the first time, I remembered she had briefed me about the state inspection weeks ago, but I had heard no more about the incident. What I remembered of the incident did not merit such a severe action on the part of the regulators. We quickly identified people to notify of the situation. The senior nursing officer, the hospital's attorney and the public relations director were at the top of the list. Discussion with this group would allow us to create a strategy to deal with what was before us. I left Barbara's office, leaving her to study the details of the inspector's findings. She would take the lead in gathering together the people to develop a strategy; I would consider the public relations implications. Several hours later I spoke with the group of clinicians and administrative people who had gathered in a large conference room next to my office. They had already made significant progress in assessing the details of the inspector's report and gathering information about our policies and practices that could be used to make a 'credible allegation of compliance' to the federal government.

I wondered at the ability of a group of people to come together and so quickly organize themselves so as to be able to take up work they had never done together before. While everyone in the room knew everyone else, not all had worked directly with each other before, but everyone had worked previously with someone who was present. The current relating now drew on those previous patterns of relating to create new and stable patterns at the same time, enough stability to go on, and enough novelty to adjust to a new situation. I observed the natural flow of communicative interaction in the gestures and responses, the questions and answers, and the announcements and acknowledgments of the turn-taking/turn-making of the conversations (Boden, 1994; Stacey, 2001a). While there was a convener in Barbara, there was a movement in who was leading the work that emerged from the conversation. Leading was a natural part of the conversational process, taking its form in what response one person's gesture called forth from the others.

By this time Barbara and I had also talked with the hospital's attorney who had spoken with a federal government attorney with whom he had worked before. We learned from this conversation that it might be possible to head off the public notification of this situation if we could provide persuasive and credible information by 1 p.m. on Friday to the federal government official responsible for this matter. For the first time since my initial reading of the fax, I had some hope that we could come through this situation without significant damage to University Hospital's reputation and standing in the community. The question was: Could we get the work done in the time we had and would it prove to be compelling to the federal government agency?

Barbara had explained to the people assembled in the conference room what the attorney had told us. Everyone seemed to understand the opportunity we had to 'dodge the bullet' headed towards us. The group decided they had a good start on what would be required to make our case and agreed to gather again in the morning, knowing that they needed to complete their work by noon to allow it to be assembled and faxed by 1 p.m. Barbara was uneasy with not continuing on into the evening but yielded to the confidence of the others that there was sufficient time on Friday to complete the task before them. Many people would be coming to work on a day they had planned off for the New Year's holiday. I had spent my afternoon encouraging the group and working with the public relations director on a communications strategy which would be needed should notification finally occur in spite of our best efforts to avoid it. As we ended our day, written communications to our employees, the medical staff, the governing body and the media were close to final form. I was feeling upbeat about our chances of getting through this mess without any damage.

I was at work early the next morning, excited by what the day might bring and the challenge that was before us. I was surprised to find that by 8 a.m. only Barbara and I and one other person from her work group were present and ready to work. By 8.45 a.m. everyone was at work, but Barbara was beginning to show, in her body language and tone of voice, signs of concern. I tried to be present but not intrusive in the work of the group, but I was paying close attention to the progress the group were making towards the noon deadline. The work was technical and there was not much I could do to contribute to getting it done, except for offering encouragement and being available to remove any organizational barriers that might crop up.

By 11.30 a.m. three administrative assistants were fully engaged in word processing work and a fourth was standing by to do the faxing. The work came from the work group in pieces which needed to be typed and formatted to fit the governmentally mandated report style. There was much moving about, taking work from person to person, interpreting handwritten notes, and trying to get a lengthy form completed with the substance that would convince the federal government that we were compliant enough with their rules and regulations so that the drastic action which was about to be initiated was unnecessary.

Again, I tried to be present without being intrusive or giving the work group the impression that I was looking over their shoulders. As the noon hour came and went, I sensed a rising tension in the group. Their work was not quite done and the three people word processing were having difficulties dealing with the government forms. Standing beside Barbara as she worked with one of the women word processing, I saw in her facial expressions anxiety that was bordering on panic. Getting the substance of the work in the proper form was the problem. It was now 12.40 p.m., and it was apparent to me we were going to miss the 1 p.m. deadline for faxing information to the federal government.

Barbara and I had related in a non-verbal, but very important way. I sensed that she was not going to admit failure and would have pushed the administrative assistants as best she could. Her body was gesturing in what Stacey has called 'protosymbols', non-verbal representations of bodily rhythmic changes whose meaning was made in the gesture/ response process with me (Stacey, 2001a: 103). For me, the meaning made was that she needed help. I suggested to Barbara that we call the federal government official waiting for our information and tell her we were faxing our work in a format that did not conform to the government report format but did provide the substance of our case for compliance and that we would send the properly formatted report by overnight mail. Barbara, looking relieved, went to her office to make the phone call. She returned a few minutes later with a smile on her face. We would make the deadline after all. By 1.15 p.m. we had confirmation from the federal government that they had received all of our information and would call us before 3 p.m. with their decision. With no more work to do, the group of people who had worked so closely together over the last day went their own ways, some to start their holiday weekend a half day behind what they had planned and others to return to their offices to finish up the week's and the year's work. The women doing the word processing, however, still had to contend with getting the overnight package assembled, which meant fitting the work to the government forms.

As 3 p.m. approached, I was in the office next door to Barbara's, sneaking a look at the televised football game that our university was playing. Barbara came to the door and asked to talk with me. We went to her office and she reported that she had just talked to the federal government official deciding our case. There was a question about the intent of our response. Were we contesting the federal government findings or were we making a case that we were now in compliance? We got the hospital's attorney on the phone and agreed that we needed to talk again with the federal government official.

Our three-way phone conversation took just a few minutes. We agreed that we were not contesting the federal government's findings and were attempting to make a 'credible allegation of compliance.' The federal government official explained that she had the authority to rule on the compliance issue and was prepared to do so, but she did not have authority to deal with an appeal that would result if we contested this issue. Furthermore, if we were going to contest, the notice would be published and it would take weeks to schedule the appeal and hold the hearing. Our attorney noted that we could appeal later if we chose but that was not our concern as the work week neared its end. The conversation ended with the federal government official telling us she would have her decision to us before 4 p.m., assuming we e-mailed her our position on our submission within the next fifteen minutes. My e-mail was sent ten minutes later, and again we waited for a decision that would either end our year on a disappointing and negative note or allow the year to finish out quietly and without unwanted attention. Barbara and I helped finish assembling the overnight packet of information that we hoped would need to be sent to the federal government. Even though our phone call had given us some optimism that the decision would be favorable, the uncertainty of the moment restricted our conversation; there was no end-of-the-day joviality.

A few minutes after 4 p.m., Barbara received the decision. We had satisfied the federal government that no 'immediate or serious threat to patient health or safety' existed at University Hospital. Our year would end quietly. Within minutes, the hospital's attorney arrived with two bottles of champagne. We toasted our good work and our good fortune. The mood was one of relief more than victory. We talked briefly about how to thank and recognize the people who had worked so hard to get us past this threat. We congratulated each other one more time and departed for our holiday weekends.

The leader as an emerging role in everyday experience

In coming to understand the nature of leadership in the above incident, I believe that it is important to pay attention to the theories we are using to make sense of our experience with others. These theories are how we make sense of our experiences together and result from the experiences of being together. Complexity theory leads me to a different sense of what leadership means. Rather than trying to emphasize what from the past may be applied to the future, attention to the present becomes the focus. Dominant views of leadership, in essence, urge the identification of skills and knowledge understood from past experience and their application to a future envisioned as either different from or the same as the present. The present is important only as a time and place for studying the past and planning the future; it is not where action is occurring. Action has occurred in the past and will occur in the future, so the past and future are the subject of attention.

My perspective is that attention to the present must be the focus of leadership, where the present is understood to be where the past is understood and the future created in the interaction of human persons. This different sense of the present leads me to participate in a different way in the everyday interactions with others that constitutes my organizational experience. The two everyday organizational experiences that follow explore how I find myself participating in everyday organizational activity. First, I want to be more explicit about what I am trying to draw attention to.

Mead wrote the following about the present and its relation to the past and future:

> A present then, as contrasted with the abstraction of mere passage,
> is not a piece cut out anywhere from the temporal dimensions of

uniformly passing reality. Its chief reference is to the emergent event, that is, to the occurrence of something which is more than the processes that have led up to it and which by its change, continuance, or disappearance, adds to later passages a content they would not otherwise have possessed.

(Mead, 2002: 52)

It is in the present that one constructs the past and future. The focus on the present does not mean a lack of attention to the past or future, only an understanding that it is only in the present that the past and future are knowable. Writing about the past and future, Mead said:

We extend them out in memory and history, in anticipation and forecast. They are preeminently the field of ideation, and find their locus in what is called mind. While they are in the present, they refer to that which is not in that present, as is indicated by their relation to past and future.

(Ibid.: 53)

I am not saying that I am not informed by my past experiences, nor that I am acting without intent for the future. What I am saying is that my influence, my contribution to meaning-making about what the past was or towards what the future will be, is only made in the present. If the role of leader is an emergent phenomenon, then participating in the movement of the present, from which the role arises, is where a contribution may be made. Only with attention to what is happening in the moment can I influence the movement, which is one definition of leading. It is the everyday interactions with others that have become my focus of attention even as those interactions are about what has happened in the past or may happen in the future.

What follows is an account of conversations in which I participated over a period of several weeks. These conversations concerned identifying cash balances determined to be in excess of what had been anticipated in the annual budgeting process and deciding how to allocate the cash to competing organizational needs. This kind of conversation in my organization occurs annually. I have included this experience because it is typical for me of my organizational experience in that so much of that experience is doing what has been done before, but doing it again and knowing from doing it many times before that what will result will not be the same as before and what will result cannot be known apart from the doing of it. That is not to say, however, that there will not be similarities which will be experienced in the present of doing what has been done before. This perspective, informed by complex responsive processes theory, leads then to a very different approach to participating than would a systems thinking informed approach.

The difference that is most important for me, as I participate in this kind of organizational experience, is the sense that something novel can emerge from a process that is repetitive. Without such a possibility, organizational life could easily become rote and uninteresting. Systems thinking and its formative and rational teleology means playing out a pattern of activity to allow the embedded conclusion to occur (Stacey *et al.*, 2000: 52–55). While that end may or may not be knowable, depending on the branch of systems theory one holds, it offers no theoretical place for the participants in the process to influence the result through their participation.

Managing the cash balance

The first conversation about distribution of excess cash occurred, as in previous years, during the final Board of Directors' finance committee meeting of the fiscal year. I participate in this conversation as the organization's CEO and as the individual charged by the committee to cause an analysis of the cash balances to be made and to bring back a recommendation to the committee at their next monthly meeting. I recognize that the role I have here is as the formal leader of the management team which will provide an analysis and recommendation, and as the individual who will be held accountable by the governing body's finance oversight group.

At this particular meeting, the issue of excess cash distribution is not on the agenda. It is a meeting that is quite upbeat, since the chief financial officer reports on what everyone has watched building during the year, namely very strong financial results. Bill, the CFO, is just finishing his first full year on the job and I can sense, from his very relaxed presentation, pride in what has been achieved. While outside of formal meetings he is chatty and animated in his interactions with others, in finance committee meetings he is usually very careful as to what he says and how he says it. Today, however, he speaks in a seemingly more spontaneous way. Perhaps picking up on the CFO's less constrained speech, the other members of the committee diverge from the published agenda and John, the chair, does not attempt to hold them to the agenda topics.

George, a member of the Board, advocates strongly for the building of a reserve account, necessary, he argues, for a 'rainy day'. This is a position he takes often with this committee, and I find myself looking around at the others to see their responses. I agree with what he is saying and yet I am annoyed by the soliloquy he delivers. Susan, the Medical School Dean and a committee member, responds with a supportive statement about establishing a responsible reserve but then advocates for the maximum distribution possible to the university. Susan cites the difficulties the Medical School faces with state government-imposed cutbacks in funding due to state budget problems. This, too, is a familiar position and I know I will be spending many hours with the Dean and her staff trying to understand what these cutbacks in funding will mean for the Medical School and the hospital before I bring a recommendation before this committee.

I participate in the discussion, trying to be at once the assertive and confidence-inspiring CEO while also being responsive and deferential to those ultimately legally responsible for the well-being of the organization. I feel a growing anxiety that this conversation may result in some official action on the use of cash balances. I know such an action will be premature. I ask the members to charge management with preparation of a recommendation for the January committee meeting. Without further discussion, John, the chair, responds by saying that my suggestion is consistent with the previous year's approach to this question and he asks that a recommendation be prepared for the next meeting. The meeting ends with several Board members expressing to me as they leave the room the need now in this, the best of financial years, to put something away for more difficult times. The Dean waits until the others are gone and asks that we talk about this issue as soon as I have the financial analysis needed to understand how much cash will be available for distribution. She then leaves the room reminding me that she needs an additional $2 to 3 million from what had been budgeted for distribution.

Following the finance committee discussion, the two senior finance staff members, Bill and Joanne, and I begin to discuss the cash balances issue, sometimes all of us together, sometimes one-on-one between any two of us. I try, however, not to talk about anything of more substance than a brief question or observation unless both Joanne and Bill are together. Bill, being relatively new, is sensitive to my interactions with Joanne, who was the acting CFO for almost a year while we searched to fill the position. While Joanne was not a candidate for his position, Bill knows she is highly respected in the organization and I do not want to act in a way that might cause him to question my confidence in him. At the same time, Bill's style is to delegate much of the detailed analytic work, and I know that Joanne is most often the person who will have the answers to my questions or be the one to translate my perspectives into financial analysis.

Over the next few days, we establish a deadline for the initial analysis and begin to talk about the relative priorities of the competing needs. Those needs typically fall into three categories: additional spending on hospital plant, equipment and programs; increased distribution of monies to support the Medical School; and funding a 'rainy day' reserve for unanticipated needs. After working many hours together, Bill and Joanne bring to me for discussion their initial analysis of cash balances. We sit down in my office around a small table and Joanne passes around the analysis. Bill offers a few comments on the process of analysis and says that they will refine what they have done as soon as they know where I want them to go with the recommendation to the finance committee. I respond by saying I hope we can have a discussion about where we think we should go. Bill asks Joanne to review their work and she does so in a straightforward, assumption-by-assumption, line-by-line way.

I ask questions of Joanne as she goes through her presentation and she responds, often looking to Bill before she speaks for a sign that she and not he should answer. Bill seems relaxed and participates easily in the conversation. I challenge the two of them, knowing from past experiences with Joanne and with other financial executives with whom I have worked that the first pass on this kind of analysis will be very conservative, seeking to retain as much flexibility for unanticipated future needs as possible. Our conversation is a good give-and-take, each of us participating without any sign I can detect of reluctance to take our turn in saying what we think should be said. We end with a revision of the initial work written on easel paper, taped to the wall beside us.

I participate in these conversations as the one whom we all recognize must make the final judgment about what is taken back to the finance committee. I know, and so do the others, that while I have that power, I am, at the same time, very dependent upon the expertise of the finance staff to provide solid analysis and to be candid about what they think is good for the organization. I know they will be conservative and protective of the hospital's financial assets and they know I will seek to find a balance between the Board members' individual perspectives, the

Medical School Dean's wishes, and our understanding of the hospital's immediate and anticipated needs. I also recognize that this is the first time our current chief financial officer has participated in this kind of conversation in our organization. He and his colleague participate as experts. He, being new to the organization, seeks to build my confidence in his capabilities while also trying to give his colleague her due, understanding her importance to this process, an importance grounded in over twenty years in the organization. Building our relationship is as much of what is going on as is the task of crafting a recommendation for the finance committee.

Having developed an initial understanding of the cash balances and worked through with Bill and Joanne an initial scheme for the allocation to the competing needs, I arrange to talk with the Dean and her senior staff. Teaching hospitals exist as part of a clinical and academic enterprise, and a major role the hospital has is to support the Medical School. In our case, the Medical School is entitled by contract to all excess cash, what is excess being a determination of the board finance committee on which the Dean is a voting member.

I go to the Medical School conversation as both the advocate for the hospital and as a member of the academic medical center leadership group, the Dean and the hospital's chief of staff (Dave, a physician who is a faculty member and the vice-dean of the Medical School) being the others. At this conversation, I am the expert on hospital finances and the presenter of the scheme I have worked on with the hospital finance staff. I enter this discussion recognizing that what is going to happen is a negotiation between the Dean and myself in the presence, and with the participation, of the others. We assemble in the Dean's conference room on the third floor of the Medical School's administrative building. The walls are covered with pictures of the old, long-torn-down hospital, whose restored administrative building is where we are today. Susan, Dave and I are joined by Kevin and Linda, the Medical School's senior administrative and financial officers, respectively. It is a group where people participate freely and, while not without deference to Susan and myself, each person's point of view is sought. Susan takes her customary seat at the head of the table and I take a seat at the end facing her and next to the white board where I have written out the analysis. Dave, Kevin and Linda fill in around the table and I begin to explain the cash position and my sense of how it should be distributed.

A familiar pattern of conversation is talked out as I try to walk the fine line between advocating for hospital needs and being a constructive member of the academic medical center leadership group. I have the power of being the recognized authority on what the numbers say and the constraint of trying to be a team player, which means balancing hospital and Medical School needs. The Dean, the most powerful person present, pushes back and tests assumptions as she seeks to also find a balance between hospital and Medical School needs. The others speak freely and our hour-long conversation produces a modified scheme that I support as a responsible approach to the allocation of the $16 million of cash balances, and one I can take as the hospital management's recommendation to the Board finance committee.

While the conversation had a pattern of sameness to it, it also produced several new and useful approaches to talking about the cash balances and about how to present the recommendation to the finance committee. There was a back-and-forth, give-and-take rhythm to the conversation which did not feel like a negotiation at all. As I have thought about the conversation, I recognize that for each person present there was not a clear-cut my-side and your-side reality that we assume to characterize negotiations. Susan pushes for as much as she can extract from the hospital's cash balances, but she also knows that without a financially healthy hospital there will be no cash in the future for the Medical School. Dave as vice-dean is responsible to Susan, but as hospital chief of staff is also responsible to the faculty who practice at the hospital and to the hospital Board of Directors for advocating for safe and up-to-date services and facilities. I have already talked about the fine line which I try to walk between hospital and Medical School needs.

I returned to my office, and waiting for me were Bill and Joanne. We had not scheduled a meeting but they were anxious to know what had happened in my just concluded discussion at the Medical School. Standing in the doorway of my office, I verbally outlined the modified scheme, pointing out the differences from what we had produced together. The numbers looked acceptable to them; what they were really interested in was the conversation that produced the numbers. Bill particularly wanted to understand what the Dean and her staff members were saying. Our conversation turned to getting ready for the finance committee meeting which is now just half of a working day away.

We quickly agreed on how to present our proposal and spent the next twenty minutes speculating about how it would be received by the committee members. I was to be the presenter since I was the only one of the three of us present when the latest version of the recommendation was constructed. Our conversation ended, Joanne returned to her office to give the numbers one last going over. I asked Bill if he was OK with me doing the presentation, given that I usually do not present to the finance committee and that he is recognized as the primary staff to the committee. His response was, yes, he was OK with me taking this before the committee. He said he sees this as more of a political issue than a finance one and that he considers political issues to be my purview.

The finance committee members assembled mid-morning on Monday in our conference room whose walls are also covered with pictures of the old hospital. The committee chair, John, was not present at this meeting, having undergone surgery the week before. Mary, chair of the Board, sat down in the chair's seat and, without ceremony, announced the start of the meeting. I sat at the other end of the table, placing myself close to the easel which contained my presentation to the committee.

I stood up to make my recommendation to the group. I summarized the process by which the recommendation was built and recognized that we were engaging in what had become an annual decision about distribution of cash balances. I was holding back revealing the first of two pages of presentation contained on the flip chart until I had a chance to sense how each Board member was participating. I sensed nothing out of the ordinary. I made my presentation without interruption and asked if there were any questions. George responded as he has many times before by stating his support for a reserve fund. My recommendation had proposed $1 million of the $16 million cash be placed in reserve. Questions were asked about how such a reserve would be treated from an accounting perspective and who would have the authority to spend the reserve. Susan was asked about why the Medical School needed the $10 million I had proposed in my recommendation and she responded by saying that the hospital's monies were vital to supporting the growing research agenda, and that the research agenda had a direct and supportive impact on the hospital. I answered several questions about the other components of my recommendation and then George made the motion to accept the recommendation as presented. It passed with unanimous support. Susan looked relieved.

Leadership and power relations

Let me reflect here on what my participating in this everyday kind of experience might inform me about leading and leadership. I want to say something about what was happening as I, a recognized organizational leader, participated in the experiences I have related above.

I notice first the differences in how I describe my role in each of the conversations. I have recognized how previous years' conversations have similarity to the current year's. My experience is that there are patterns of conversation that repeat themselves even as novel actions emerge from those patterned discussions. It is this recognition which brings me to understand leading as an emergent phenomenon with roles of those participating being constantly constructed and reconstructed in the conversation. It is from the interaction of the conversation that action emerges, and for me to assert that action is attributable to a single person called the leader is to ignore my experience. To hold that the person recognized as a leader has no influence in the emergent action is also to discount my experience. Is leading not being more influential than others in the joint constructing of action? Such influence occurs in the movement of the interaction but can only be recognized in reflection in a future present.

I notice several times in this story that I have found myself in situations where how I am participating seems to be paradoxical. Trying to be assertive and deferential or trying to provide others with direction without being directive are examples, as is trying to be at once an advocate both for the hospital and the Medical School, competing entities for the cash resources to be distributed. Collins wrote about a 'duality' he observed in Level 5 leaders (Collins, 2001:22). Dualities need not be paradoxical, and I do not think being 'shy and fearless' is necessarily paradoxical, but I did experience being both assertive and deferential as paradox.

I have pointed out who was most powerful in several of the conversations. I seem to see my identity greatly influenced by my sense of the power relations existing between myself and the others in the group. Elias explained power as about dependency (Elias, 1978: 93); those upon whom we have more dependency than they on us have power over us. Elias recognized that power is a 'structural characteristic of a relationship, all-pervading and, as a structural characteristic, neither good nor bad. It may be both' (ibid.). Power here is not some thing someone has, but rather a phenomenon of people's interactions with one another. By contrast, power is usually thought of as some thing an individual can possess and can use for his own purposes. Paying attention to power relations in the present of participating seems to me to be useful in making sense of what is going on. Mead spoke of a person emerging as a leader who is 'able to take in more than others of an act in process, who can put himself into relation with whole groups in the community whose attitudes have not entered into the lives of the others in the community' (Mead, 1934: 256). Leading here becomes participating in sense-making, the role of leader emerging for the individual who is able to contribute in a significant way to individual and group sense-making.

A distinction is often made between leadership and management. Management is about hierarchies and systems, like budgets. This story was ostensibly about getting the numbers right, about deciding who received what share of available cash, about management. Leadership is about people and culture. What is clear to me as I review this experience is how artificial such a distinction really is. This experience points out rather nicely what happens when we think that what is going on is about numbers, systems, hierarchies and cultures. We take our eyes off people in interaction with each other and themselves. We stand outside and away from what is happening between people, thinking we can observe and understand without being present. We come to believe that systems and cultures are real and have features that we can discover and control, and we become frustrated as we fail to achieve the control that such a perspective promises.

For me, this story is about people constantly negotiating their identities, while seeking to find ways to act together. In their interactions together, numbers and words are a medium of their transactions with one another and themselves. Leadership and management become useless distinctions; both are about people working together and the roles that emerge as they do so. Rather than focusing on these reified concepts constructed to achieve a desired future, but in my experience consistently failing to do so, what is called for is attention to what is happening, rather than what should be happening. It is by attention to and participation in the everyday human interactions which constitute organizational life that I have come to make better sense of what the role of leader is.

Leadership – movement from idealized to lived experience

Reflecting upon the mainstream leadership literature and thinking about how I am talking with others has helped me to see a pattern in how leadership is treated. It is generalized, idealized and reified. This process then makes it possible to view leadership as if it were a commodity or object that might be held by a person. It was this kind of process that

Mead wrote about when he introduced the idea of cult and functionalized values. Griffin's discussion of Mead's ideas of cult and functionalized values has suggested for me a way to think about what is going on when I am talking with others about leadership (Griffin, 2002: 194).

Writing about how nations had come to seemingly espouse national values to justify their actions, Mead introduced the notion of cult and functionalized values (Mead, 1915, 1923). Cult values are possible if nations are thought of as if they were objects. Reification makes possible the assignment of characteristics of behavior or belief as if a nation were a real and mindful being. A cult value then is a broadly generalized idea, such as a nation acting in its self-defense or a national commitment to democracy. A value addresses a motivation for action or a justification of a belief that a mindful person might have and that, by reification, a nation too can exhibit.

Cult values, being highly idealized, are subject to interpretation in the social interaction of people with one another and themselves. It is here that these generalized and idealized ideas become functional as they are acted on in the moment of human interaction. The emergent meanings that people make of these idealized cult values create conflict because the idealized meaning gives way to local meanings which emerge with sameness and difference in the localized settings of interaction. These cult values, then, play an important role. As people negotiate the meaning of the cult values in the local setting, identity arises and the future is constructed.

Talking about leadership as if it were something someone can possess requires it to be objectified. Leadership is not, however, an object whose tangible characteristics can be dissected and reproduced. In complex responsive processes theory it is a role that arises from human interaction which has been given 'as if' qualities by accepted convention of our linguistic practices. Just as nations are generalized and idealized in the cult and functional value concepts of Mead, leadership and the organizations that leaders lead are generalized and idealized in the dominant systems theories. The importance of this generalization was explained by Mead as being able to see in ourselves what we see in others, here others being the reified concept of nation or leadership. He wrote: 'Nations, like individuals, can become objects to themselves only as they see themselves through the eyes of others. Every appeal to public sentiment is an effort to justify oneself to oneself' (Mead, 1915: 604).

What if we take leadership to be, in essence, a cult value and examine the functionalization of the cult value of leadership in everyday organizational life? Can the idealization of leadership be serving a useful purpose in the everyday conversation of people as they negotiate their differences, seeking identity and creating the future? I do not believe that Mead was suggesting that cult values arise only because of the existence of one theory of social or natural action or another, but rather that cult values arise as humans in interaction with one another struggle to be together and maintain identity of the group and self at the same time.

What I am interested in here is the process of movement from the idealized to the functional. Is this process common to what we, as human beings, do as we seek to interact with others and make meaning of our experiences together? Do we idealize as a way of seeking to talk about an important aspect of our experience together, and is the localized meaning we make of the ideal the next phase of the interaction? Is this the same phenomenon Mead was talking about as the 'generalized other' in his discussion of the gesture/response process? Mead defines the generalized other as 'the attitude of the whole community' (Mead, 1934: 154), but a community does not actually exist as a mindful embodied person, capable of an articulated attitude. Thus if a gesture is made based on a generalized or idealized sense of an attitude of others, the response it seeks will be realized by the person responding who locally interprets the ideal or generalized. This completes the gesture/response cycle with the generalized having been functionalized in the process of the gesture/response (ibid.: 173–178).

The importance of this for me lies in understanding the communicative process as one of constant clarifying of meaning, one that necessarily goes from what we can say to one another with the word and bodily symbols we have to the meaning we make of our interactions with each other through our private conversations with ourselves. This perspective allows me to participate in organizational life with all its dominant theories and language without withdrawing because I can make sense of what is happening as the movement from the generalized, idealized to the functional. I further understand that staying in the present is necessary to participating in that movement. The importance of this understanding to my leadership inquiry is apparent to me as I now re-examine what Mead said about leaders. 'Occasionally a person arises who is able to take in more than others of an act in progress, who can put himself into relation with whole groups in the community whose attitudes have not entered into the lives of the others in the community, he becomes a leader' (ibid.: 256). Here Mead sees the leader as emergent in the present. A few sentences later he clarifies the role of the leader (there as a statesman) as 'able to enter into the attitude of the group and to mediate between them by making his own experience universal, so that others can enter into this form of communication through him' (ibid.: 257). We see a process of generalizing that allows others to participate where they would not have done so otherwise. The leader, having emerged in and from interaction, has contributed to the robustness of the interaction through his abilities to generalize and, in doing so, engages others as they seek their own meaning in the functionalizing of the generalization.

How I was participating in a conversation in which I was engaged recently suggests to me that I am finding a way to better talk about leading as I am increasingly informed by this theme of the functionalization of cult values. I find myself more able to work within the paradoxes I have identified above and to better say what I mean by my attention being focused in the present. For me, this is a theme about people constantly negotiating identity for themselves and their group as they seek to address the conflict that arises when the generalized or idealized must be acted upon in everyday, local situations. What follows is an example of how this theory helps me go on with my everyday organizational life.

Presentation by a consultant

I was invited to hear a presentation by a consultant who had been working with several senior managers to review the progress of a consolidation and refocusing of several hospital departments. The consultant had interviewed over fifty people involved in the change. She had said to me that I should hear what was really occurring in my organization, making me stop and consider if she thought I was not paying attention or did not think such information worthy of my time. I accepted the invitation. As I did so, I wondered if I was going to hear a typical consultant's report, which for me means a diagnostic opinion with action steps designed to cure the cause of the organizational disease.

Barbara, Jean, Tom, Bill and I are joined by Harry, the departmental manager responsible for the newly configured departments. Barbara, Jean, Tom and Bill are the senior managers in University Hospital who together constitute what amounts to an operations committee. Harry works directly for both Jean and Barbara and has been in our organization for a little more than one year, being hired to consolidate the departments about to be reviewed and to reorient their functions. Mona, the consultant, has often worked in our organization over the past several years and she knows each of us well.

We assemble in the conference room in our administrative suite, a modular building officially known as the m.o.b., but called 'the trailer' by most. Reformulating the care management functions under Harry's direction has been a prolonged and difficult process. Many people involved in the reorganized departments have left the organization, and turnover of newly retained replacements has also been high. Mona was asked to help us understand what issues remain now that the planned changes are completed. As we gather, I sense no tension or anticipation from the others; they are relaxed and talkative. Knowing Mona's style, I guess that I am the only one present who has not seen what is about to be presented.

Mona has posted on the meeting room walls selected comments of those interviewed. Her presentation is a PowerPoint of what she had heard and her suggestions about what action is needed. She tells us that while most people with whom she had talked are committed to the hospital and its work, they are not clear about management's intent in directing the reorganization of their departments and feel that communication has broken down and has led to the conflict that is now being experienced as they attempt to adjust to the change in organization.

As the consultant works her way through her presentation, I find myself headed for familiar territory, a place detached from the present of what is occurring in the room, a place of my own focus on something other than that which is happening before me. I know that my tendency is to tune out when I begin to experience a systems oriented approach to organizational issues. I catch myself and try to stay with the presentation. Mona finishes her remarks in about twenty-five minutes and, turning off her computer, asks me directly what I think about what she has said. I respond by saying I am not surprised that people are feeling uneasy with the changes nor that they attribute the problem to a breakdown in communications. We begin to talk about what is happening with and between the people involved directly in the change. Harry says that he has explained to the staff involved the need for change based on the organization's values of teamwork and continuous improvement. He observes that some staff have had difficulty in understanding how these values apply to their daily activities and the changes the reorganization has tried to bring about. Tom, the HR executive, reports that many of the involved staff have talked with him about their anxiety with the changes, not knowing what is going to ultimately result for them from the changes.

A theme emerges in our conversation about the importance of Harry and his supervisors talking with the staff about what is really going on. We talk about how to involve the staff in shaping the new organizational situation. Someone says that the anxiety is to be expected from the conflicts present as staff try to understand what the changes will mean to them, but that anxiety can also be a topic of conversation for Harry and a way to engage people to work out the new way of doing business. Our conversation ends with Harry saying he thinks that more attention to day-to-day interactions with the people involved in the changed structure is where he needs to focus his efforts.

As the meeting breaks up and I head back to my office at the other end of 'the trailer,' I find myself wondering why I was invited to this meeting. If I was correct about being the only one present who had not seen the information presented, what had been going on over the past hour? I was not directly asked to approve any course of action; there were no significant requests for expenditure of resources nor the initiation of any new organizational strategy. What meaning am I to make of Mona's rather direct question to me at the end of her presentation? Would this meeting have been held had I not been available to attend it?

Was the meeting about Mona's need to exhibit her work to me, the formal leader? Was this the consultant's and the other senior staff's need to bring me to a different level of awareness of a long and difficult process, seeking to include me so as to fortify their position and insulate them from criticism for all that had happened that was not planned? Was there a split between the group as to what should be done next and an attempt to find out what I thought should be done? Was this just a time when those involved wanted to bring some closure to the consultative process and I was invited to participate because my participation was thought to be either valuable or necessary by the group?

Neither Mona nor the senior staff should have been surprised by my response to Mona's question about what I thought about what had been presented. What would have been surprising to those present (especially me) would have been a lengthy pronouncement from me of what should be done, how it should be done, who should do what, and a detailed timetable in which to complete the prescribed actions. My response was to attempt to engage others in a discussion of what was happening and how we might participate with others, understanding what intents we might bring to our participation and knowing that the outcome of our participating was knowable only as we participated and co-constructed the future in the present of our participating.

Deirdre Boden writes that 'membership of meetings is quite a calculated affair; in effect, it elaborates the actual activity of the meeting by including and excluding various potential members or subunits of the organization' (Boden, 1994: 89). Elias' themes of inclusion and exclusion and the seeking of identity through recognition that comes with being in or out are suggested by Boden's statement (Stacey, 2001a: 149). Was the importance to the others of my attendance as CEO at this meeting about recognizing the difficult work done and validating the decisions made, even though turmoil and conflict had resulted? Was it really my presence rather than my participating in the discussion that was being sought?

Reflecting later on the meeting, I was pleased that I had avoided tuning out as I had almost done. By staying with the conversation, I had contributed in a way I felt better about than I do when I have disengaged. I recognize that tuning out does not remove me from the process of relating, it only makes my participating in that process different. It is that recognition and my resolve to stay in these kinds of conversations that have come from my thinking about leading and participating. Rather than tune out of the conversation, I had a way to talk about what was being said because I had a way to think about what I could not say, which was that I did not find the consultant's report useful because of the systems theory that informed it. I saw management's idealized goals for the organizational change creating conflict for people as they tried to implement them in their local setting. I was able to respond to the question from the consultant about what I thought about what she was saying by recognizing that the conflict, while anxiety-inducing for those involved, was understandable, predictable and probably helpful. I was able to go on to say that the intensity of anxiety would likely diminish as people negotiated their own identities in the new organizational circumstance. I did not say, but was thinking, that conflict here is paradoxical in that it is both constraining in the anxiety it creates but, at the same time, it is enabling the movement of people as they seek to constantly create their own and their group's identity. We were able then to go on and talk about the importance of managers paying attention to conversations with staff so as to participate fully in that emergent identity for themselves and the involved staff.

Elias wrote about the importance of conflict to the movement of individual and group identities:

> It is easy to see that tensions and conflicts between groups which are losing functions and those acquiring new or increased functions, are a vital structural feature of all development. In other words, it is not just a question of personal, mainly accidental tensions and conflicts, though people involved usually see them as such. From the viewpoint of the intermeshing groups, they can sometimes be seen as expressions of personal animosity, sometimes as consequences of the ideology of one side or the other. On the contrary, however, this is a matter of *structured* conflicts and tensions. In many cases, they and their results form the very kernel of a process of development.
>
> (Elias, 1978: 173)

In our case, we were experiencing the conflicts from people losing one organizational design of how they would work for another way. These people were being invited to participate in evolving the new order and were asked to do so in a way that would be consistent with organizational values. Conflict has arisen as they are required to give up one way of organizing their work, trying to organize a new way consistent with idealized values. New identities of individuals and their work groups are emerging in the conflict of the functionalizing of idealized values and the altering of work responsibilities and relationships.

Thinking more about what the consultant said to me when she invited me to attend her presentation has made me consider whether there is a difference in how I approach acting as the recognized, appointed leader versus when I, figuratively speaking, do not occupy the symbolic seat at the head of the table. Clearly the consultant had invited me because I was the organization's CEO. However, I had not participated in deciding to undertake a review of the situation, nor was I involved in selecting the consultant, nor was I necessarily going to be asked by the senior managers involved to make any final decision about what actions were needed. I came to the presentation hoping to be able to contribute through my participating and I believed at the time that such a way of participating was the expectation the senior managers present had of me.

I emphasize what the others may have been thinking about my presence as well as my own thinking because I understand leading to be an emergent phenomenon of those participating. In our working together, the senior managers and I (and in this situation, also the consultant with us) are constantly creating in the moment of our interacting together our individual identities and roles, one of which is who leads and when and how. Does exercising my formal organizational prerogative to assume the seat at the head of the meeting table mean that I will lead and others will follow? Yes and no. I can begin the conversation and I can end it, at least for the moment. I understand that our conversation, however punctuated by my exercise of my formal organizational power, will inform other conversations in ways that I will never know and cannot use my organizational power to control. Again, my leadership experience is paradoxical; at the same time I have the power to seemingly control the conversation, I know that I am no more in control of the meaning being made than any other participant. The meaning I make of the conversation and the meaning others make is informed by our participation together while at the same time our participation together is informed by the meaning we make.

The role of the leader

I have come to understand the leader as an emergent phenomenon of people in interaction. While the leader role is embodied in an individual human person, it is a social phenomenon that emerges only in interaction. My experience suggests that the leader role is closely related to an individual person and group sense-making process, which I understand to be one in the same process of interaction. In saying this, I am making a distinction from the dominant way of thinking about the leader as an assigned position of authority to oversee and, perhaps, to be among people in their work together, seeking to achieve a desired and predetermined outcome.

If the leader emerges from people's interactions together, understanding of the leader must come from attention to the emerging interaction, which is the present, the here and now, of our experience. It must come in experience, not from experience, which is already past. An active and attentive participation, then, is what at once is both research and lived, everyday experience. Here I am using Mead's sense of experience: 'The assimilation of what occurs and that which reoccurs with what is elapsing and what has elapsed is called "experience"' (Mead, 1938: 53).

Our experience tells us that our communicative process is one of constant clarification of what we are trying to say to others and they to us. We speak, hear, listen and respond trying to sense the intent of the other's words even as we speak, trying to call out in ourselves the same response we seek from the other. Language allows us to take the attitude of the other (both an individual and generalized other) towards our self, and it is through language then that we can be a self. Language is the medium of interaction of the self with itself and among selves. Language is the social process in which differences occurring as symbolic, generalized representations are experienced and identities emerge as the conflictual differences are made sense of. Language as a social process is inherently conflictual and, as such, constant attention to finding meaning in the differences is what participating in the living present of everyday life is.

I have come to see conflict not as something to be resolved or negotiated, but rather to be made sense of. If conflict is a fundamental characteristic of human interaction, meaning-making rather than resolution becomes the focus of experience. It is in and with meaning-making that identities emerge as the conflictual differences are recognized. The presence of conflictual differences between human persons is analogous to the presence of diversity between agents in the complexity sciences, where diversity of agents is necessary for novel movement to arise from and in interaction of the agents.

References

Boden, D. (1994) *The Business of Talk*, Cambridge: Polity Press.

Collins, J. (2001) *Good To Great*, New York: HarperBusiness.

Elias, N. (1978) *What Is Sociology?*, New York: Columbia University Press.

Griffin, D. (2002) *The Emergence of Leadership: Linking self-organization and ethics*, London: Routledge.

Mead, G. H. (1913) 'The social self', *Journal of Philosophy, Psychology and Scientific Method* 10: 374–380.

Mead, G. H. (1915) 'The psychological bases for internationalism', *Survey* 33: 604–607.

Mead, G. H. (1923) 'Scientific method and the moral sciences', *International Journal of Ethics* 23: 229–247.

Mead, G. H. (1934) *Mind, Self and Society*, Chicago, IL: The University of Chicago Press.

Mead, G. H. (1938) *The Philosophy of the Act*, Chicago, IL: Chicago University Press.

Mead, G. H. (2002) *The Philosophy of The Present*, Amherst, NY: Prometheus Books.

Stacey, R. (2001a) *Complex Responsive Processes in Organizations: Learning and knowledge creation*, London: Routledge.

Stacey, R. (2001b) 'Systems, complex responsive processes, and the spiritual', unpublished, Centre for Management and Complexity, University of Hertfordshire.

Stacey, R., Griffin, D. and Shaw, P. (2000) *Complexity and Management: Fad or radical challenge to systems thinking?*, London: Routledge.

Editors' introduction to Chapter 7

Andrew Lee, HR Director of Unite plc, presents an understanding of both executive coaching and the activity of leading from the perspective of complex responsive processes of relating. He moves from a notion of coach/leader as detached, objective observer of those he or she is dealing with to a more relational, involved perspective. In Chapter 4 of this volume, John Tobin explores the relationship between involvement and detachment, suggesting that effective leadership requires acting in a paradoxically detached involved manner. Lee provides accounts of his experience in which he understands what one might call detached involvement as arising through paying attention to the micro detail of interaction with those he is coaching/leading in the living present. What he focuses attention on is the affect-laden patterns of power relations which emerge between him and others, patterns they are all co-constructing. He points to how these patterns shift in conversation and he draws attention to this as movements in meaning and inclusion-exclusion, which amount to shifts in identity. He argues that shifts in power relations, that is, changing patterns of inclusion and exclusion, differentiate identities. Focusing attention on present patterns and how they may be highly repetitive enables people to move on from the rigid, stuck patterns in which they find themselves.

Lee reviews the foundations of coaching in humanistic and cognitive psychology,, as well as in psychoanalysis. These are all individual centered psychologies, which encourage the coach to take a detached view of the interaction with the one being coached. Lee also reviews the more recent development of a dialogic approach to coaching and points to the emphasis it places on 'good' relationships and a somewhat mystic view of personal change. For Lee, all of these approaches ignore the direct, co-created pattern of relationship between coach and client, particularly the patterns of power between them. He sees personal change as essentially a shift in the patterning of power relations, in the pattern of inclusion and exclusion, where that shift involves taking risks and amounts to a change in identity. These shifts occur as small transformations that occur in striking moments in ordinary conversation. By changing his perspective, Lee changes the focus of his attention to the micro details of movements in conversation which give a more helpful understanding of what he and others are doing together.

In his narrative of a conversation with two people who report to him he describes how he dealt with what many would regard as a challenge to his authority. By paying attention to the risk his subordinate was taking in confronting him and understanding something of the implications of shifting power relations, he continued to engage in a way that enabled further meaning to be made in what became a small transformation of the relationship between the two of them.

> David had taken a significant risk in intervening strongly, and we were awoken from our co-created patterns of disengagement to a way of working that felt risky and unknowable. David's remark shifted the patterns of power-relating and caused us to find a different way of being together. In addition, the relationship between David and me shifted. I now see him as stronger and more passionate about his work. He recognizes my desire to explore the immediacy of our experience rather than to think about the past or describe what 'should' and 'ought' to happen in the future. I feel that we can have more robust conversations without preparation and that our identities have shifted as we now see each other in a different way.
>
> (p. 175)

As both coach and leader Lee finds that taking a different perspective on the nature of organizations leads him to be more present and mindful of the experiences that he is co-creating, rather than thinking and speaking about events in other times and other places.

> Now, I am particularly concerned with noticing the patterning of our interaction and am attuned to the responses and gestures that are called forth in us whilst we work. This means noticing and describing how I am reacting to our conversation, drawing attention to my experience of the processes of relating.
>
> (p. 168)

7 Executive coaching and leading

Andrew Lee

- Mainstream perspectives on coaching
- Humanistic psychology
- Cognitive psychology
- Psychoanalysis and psychodynamic therapy
- A dialogic approach
- How change is understood
- Coaching from the perspective of complex responsive processes
- Power as differentiating patterns of identity
- The manager as coach
- Conclusion

According to constructivist learning theory (Dryden, 1987), learning involves individually rewriting, or reframing, his or her 'biography' in order to transform his or her 'inner reality', so enabling a more successful future. This model of learning was taken up in the development of 'life-skills coaching' in the 1960s. Adkins and Rosenberg (cited in Zeus and Skiffington, 2000) recognized that traditional models of education through teaching were not effective when used with disadvantaged adults, since attention was not paid to the emotional and cognitive barriers to learning. The life-skills model of one-to-one coaching, based on constructivist theory and Maslow's humanistic theory of motivation (Whitmore, 1996), was adopted to help disadvantaged adults in Canada as part of a public sector 'New Start' initiative. Since its inception, life-skills coaching has been developed in the USA, Canada, Australia and, to a lesser extent, Europe. The development of sports psychology also occurred in the 1960s and some of the basic principles of executive coaching originate in the sporting achievements of prominent writers on executive coaching. These principles involve developing the individual's personal best, keeping focused on the future and working through any obstacles or self-limiting beliefs. From the mid-1980s, coaching was taken up by private sector organizations (Downey, 2002). The comparison with high-achieving sports stars working with a coach may have helped senior executives to see coaching as attractive when they may not have been drawn to other forms of training or executive development. The interest in executive coaching in the corporate context occurred in parallel with the growth of leadership development programs in the 1980s. As part of developing leaders, coaching was seen as a useful support to 'facilitate the integration of learning into the day-to-day work of executives' (Hicks and Peterson, 1996: 3).

The coach, who is usually external to the organization in which the client works, agrees an agenda of planned improvements with the client and a number, often six, of one-to-one sessions to work on an agreed agenda which includes the achievement of specified quantifiable or observable objectives. Growing numbers of external coaches are now being engaged, and, in addition, many organizations aim to develop the coaching ability of their own employees as part of programs of 'management development' or 'organizational change' (Downey, 2002). Indeed, coaching is often proposed as a model for effective leadership. In all of these applications of coaching, the underpinning, but unspoken, assumptions are clear: managers and leaders should develop their coaching skills in order to 'release the potential' of the people around them and, in particular, the people who report to them in a hierarchical relationship.

The term 'mentoring' is often used interchangeably with coaching but there are a number of key distinctions between them. In mentoring, skills or knowledge are supposed to be transferred from the more experienced mentor to the more junior 'mentee'(Lewis, 1996: Parsoe, 1992; Shea, 1996), while in coaching it is the individual's own potential that is to be unlocked. The mentor often has experience at a senior management level and has knowledge of the individual's relationships and working environment. Mentors often have influence over the career decisions affecting the mentee. A less overt aspect of mentoring is that mentors can reinforce the patterns of relating within the organization, 'conveying and instilling the standards, norms and values of the organization or profession. Coaching is more about exploring the individual's standards, values and vision' (Zeus and Skiffingham, 2000: 18).

In this chapter, I intend to explore the most influential literature on coaching and relate it to my own experiences of working as an executive coach and as a manager within an organization. I will suggest an alternative way of understanding coaching as complex responsive processes of relating. In particular, I will explore how 'change' or 'transformation' is perceived to occur through coaching from this perspective and consider what light this throws on organizational encounters which are not formal coaching relationships. I will reflect on how meaning moves in conversations and how such movement brings with it shifts in power and identity which are at the heart of change. This has implications for line managers and leaders who may decide to adopt an approach to their roles that is based on coaching rather than on traditional methods of 'command and control'. First, I set out how coaching is described by a number of authors and then explore the implicit assumptions they are making. After that, I explore my own experience as coach and manager and how I make sense of this experience.

Mainstream perspectives on coaching

John Whitmore describes coaching as:

> The unlocking of a person's potential to maximize their own performance. It is helping them to learn rather than teaching them.
>
> (Whitmore, 1996: 8)

He describes his model of coaching as emerging from 'a more optimistic model of human kind than the old behaviorist view in which we are seen as empty vessels into which everything is poured' (ibid.: 9). This way of thinking, according to Whitmore, 'suggests that we are more like an acorn, which contains within it the potential to be a magnificent oak tree' (ibid.: 11). Having been trained as a coach by Whitmore in the mid-1990s, it has been interesting for me to revisit his work, and that of other leading executive coaches, to consider how I now react to their thinking, having studied for almost three years on the Doctor of Management program at Hertfordshire University. I immediately notice some of the assumptions that underpin Whitmore's approach to coaching which were not obvious to me three years ago. Clearly he views the potential of an individual as being locked or stored away somewhere and thinks that if the 'correct' approach can be found then that potential can be released to enhance performance at work. This implies causality, which Stacey *et al.* (2000) call 'formative cause', where movement into the future is the unfolding of a potential that has already been enfolded, just as the acorn unfolds as an oak tree. With this formative thinking, Whitmore argues that the role of a coach is to unfold the enfolded self as a way of accessing the hidden potential. This approach assumes that the 'self' is innate or pre-existing and not socially constructed in the way I argue it is below. The process of realizing the potential relies on the positive frame, or mental model (Senge, 1990), with which the client approaches his work. Whitmore, when quoting Gallwey, the author of *The Inner Game* series of books, expresses this idea as follows: 'The opponent within one's own head is more formidable than the one on the other side of the net' (Gallwey, 1975: 6).

Mainstream authors use the term 'coaching' to describe a process that includes many of the following elements:

- An architecture of an agreed number of sessions with predetermined goals (Bolt, 2000).
- A skilled coach who facilitates the movement of the client to achieve the agreed goals (Landsberg, 1997).
- A client who will be changed by the experience and whose work performance will be enhanced (Whitmore, 1996).
- Coaching sessions made up of discrete one-to-one conversations between coach and client (Bolt, 2000).
- The format of the sessions allowing the client to develop his or her own solutions to issues rather than the coach offering advice or suggestions (Zeus and Skiffington, 2000).
- The coach has the belief that the client has more potential than he or she currently displays (Gallwey, 1975).

This list highlights the key assumptions that underpin most descriptions of coaching offered by mainstream authors. First, the potential to perform is in some way located within each individual as 'the essence of self' (Dahler, from Dryden, 1984) or 'the true self' (ibid.) but this potential is in some way prevented from being manifest due to obstacles (Bolt, 2000) or interferences (Gallwey, 2000; Landsberg, 1997). With this stance, we are directed to a view of the process of change as occurring by the coach in some way acting to allow the unfolding of the enfolded potential that resides within the client. In addition, emphasis is placed on the architecture of the coaching arrangements and on the skills of the coach. These, along with the high regard with which the coach holds the client, allow change to occur. We are directed, by many coaches, to consider the structure of coaching sessions as being significant. The relationship between coach and client should be one based on respect and a humanistic belief in the client's latent talents.

The writers mentioned above represent what I will call the mainstream view of coaching which integrates humanistic and cognitive psychologies. These two areas, along with a psychotherapeutic and the newer dialogic approaches, make up the four main psychological roots of current approaches to coaching. I give a description of each before going on to a different way of understanding coaching.

Humanistic psychology

In the first half of the twentieth century, the main approach to academic psychology was 'behaviorism' according to which humans were thought of in terms of mechanical metaphors, where a stimulus would lead to a response. By the 1960s, a number of psychologists shared concerns that behaviorism did not adequately address important aspects of social behavior and individual experience. A 'third wave' psychological movement developed (Merry, 1999) which supplemented the behaviorist and psychoanalytic approaches to the study of psychological processes. This was later known as humanistic psychology. Carl Rogers (1961) and Abraham Maslow (1964) were amongst the first to describe its main themes:

1 Humanistic psychology takes a phenomenological approach to the person. This means that humans behave in the world in response to their personally experienced reality. The way people experience the world is made up of their individual sensing and meaning-making which is developed through their unique mixture of 'needs, history and expectations' (Merry, 1999: 15). Each of us then lives in our own subjective experience which can never be completely understood by anyone else.
2 A humanistic approach to understanding human nature places emphasis on appreciating people's personal experiences from within their own 'frame of reference', that is, from their own subjective point of view.
3 Humanistic psychology takes an essentially existential view of life and the process of living. It emphasizes the potential for individual freedom and for individual responsibility.

4 The person is always seen to be in process, always developing and never fixed, static or complete. This 'process of becoming' (Rogers, 1961) is not motivated by deficiencies but by the need for enhancement, growth and continuing development.

A key tenet of the humanistic approach, as described by Maslow and Rogers, is the concept of 'actualization'. This is a theory that describes 'the human need to move in the general direction towards the fulfillment of potential' (Merry, 1999: 16). Rogers described his view of actualization as follows:

> We are, in short, dealing with an organism which is always motivated, is always up to something, always seeing. So I would reaffirm, perhaps even more strongly after the passage of a decade, my belief that there is one central source of energy in the human organism; that this is the function of the whole organism rather than some portion of it; and that it is perhaps best conceptualized as a tendency towards fulfillment, towards actualization, towards the maintenance and enhancement of the organism.
>
> (Rogers, 1963a: 24)

The link between humanistic psychology and coaching is taken up by Rogers when he says that the 'successful coach nurtures the client' and offers what he describes as 'unconditional acceptance and warmth' (Zeus and Skiffington, 2000: 10).

The development of latent potential which is achieved by working with the coach is rooted in Maslow's model of a hierarchy of human needs, developed in the 1950s. He studied people who were seen to be mature, successful and fulfilled, and concluded that human beings only need to overcome their 'inner blocks' (Whitmore, 1996: 102) to develop and mature. Maslow's hierarchy of needs describes different categories of requirements of human beings which, once met, motivate the individual to meet his or her needs at the next level of the hierarchy. The needs are categorized as 'food and water, shelter and safety, belonging, esteem from others, self esteem and self actualization' (ibid.: 103).

Whether in the context of sport, education or business, the most common approach to coaching comes from the humanistic psychology of Rogers and Maslow (Rogers, 1980; Whitmore, 1996). The application of this work may be seen in the desire of coaches to help develop self-understanding and self-development with their clients so as to 'achieve their full potential' (Landsberg, 1997: 10).

Cognitive psychology

The humanistic approach takes the subjective experience of the client as key to the movement towards change. The cognitivist approach develops this further to change the client's interpretation of an experience. The basic tenet of this approach is that it is a person's beliefs which influence how they feel and behave, rather than events.

In coaching, the cognitive approach is seen in its related form of constructivist therapy, where how an individual constructs his or her own reality of an event determines the behaviors that will be demonstrated in response to the situation. The constructivist model underpins many related approaches and is at the core of the work of authors such as Argyris (1992), Senge (1990) and Covey (1983, 1990). The aim of the approach is to alter the client's perception of events and therefore provide alternative ways of acting. For example, Covey advises his readers to 'think win-win' in business negotiations instead of the predominant 'win-lose' approach. At it simplest, even thinking of a problem not as an obstacle but as an opportunity is an example of 'reframing' that may lead to an improved outcome. I set out below three examples of psychological practices that aim to resolve issues through changing the mental model within which the issues were originally explored.

1 Constructivist narrative therapy is seen as a way of removing problems, or self-limiting beliefs, by rewriting the individual's story or biography. In executive coaching, the technique is used to invite clients to rewrite their own story in order to 'celebrate their gifts and abilities' (Zeus and Skiffington, 2000: 11). Skiffington describes using this approach in a way that allows clients to 'transform their inner reality, to become more mindful and are better able to dictate their own stories' (ibid.: 11).

2 Transactional analysis (Berne, 1937; Harris, 1994) helps people to identify their ego states, as parent, adult or child, and focuses on evaluating how they currently function to find strategies for improvement to achieve a 'more adaptive, mature and realistic attitude to life' (Berne, 1937). This approach is particularly applied in coaching to help develop interpersonal skills and to resolve conflict.

3 Neurolinguistic programming (Kostere and Malatesta, 1989) has been used in coaching since the early 1990s and involves the linking of thinking, language and behavior. This technique is used in coaching with the intention of improving relationships and managing thoughts and emotions to lead to a desired and pre-planned outcome.

Psychoanalysis and psychodynamic therapy

Freud's emphasis on the exploration and reinterpretation of past experience provides a therapeutic approach that aims to uncover unconscious motivation and searches for deep causes and patterns of behavior that may have their roots in childhood experiences. In the USA, many coaches are trained in psychodynamic therapy. Dryden describes the therapy as helping the client 're-experience old conflicts but with a new ending' (Dryden, 1984: 32). Dryden also describes some of the intentions of the Freudian psychotherapist in relating to patients: the therapist should be neutral but not indifferent, firm but flexible, and relate to the patient in creating a working alliance. While recognizing the psychodynamic training of many coaches, Zeus and Skiffington distinguish between coaching as 'future-focused' (Zeus and Skiffington, 2000: 11) in outlook while therapy is focused on past experiences as a way of understanding the present and having a better understanding of future choices and behaviors.

A dialogic approach

The dialogic perspective is based on the idea that change is not an individual phenomenon but a process that emerges out of the encounter, or relationship, between coach and client. McKewan (2000) distances herself from the concept of coaching as two individuals working together to solve the problems of the client. She advocates an approach based on the dialogic school of writers, originating with Martin Buber's 'I–you' (1956). She makes the distinction between the individual centric approach which she calls 'I–it' relating to indicate an attitude of a coach working with a client in the person-to-person relating of 'I–you'.

> The dialogic approach proposes that the potential for change and self development arises not through you, the coach, nor even through the client alone but through what emerges in the meeting or existential encounter between the two of you. Development evolves from the inter-human or inter-subjective realm of the dialogic. The realm of the dialogic does not refer to speech in the ordinary sense but to the fact that human beings are essentially relational.
>
> (McKewan, 2000: 4)

The dialogue-based writers (Bohm, 1976; Isaacs 1999; Lewin and Regine, 1999) take the view that by focusing on the processes of relating between people and by developing a range of improved behaviors – for example, listening, respecting, suspending and voicing (Isaacs, 1999) – a more harmonious way of working and being together may be created. Isaacs also proposes that by cultivating these behaviors one learns to be open to 'the possibility that what is happening is unfolding from a common source' (Isaacs, 1999: 117).

The concept of tapping into something greater or larger than the present interaction is also a theme in the work of Lewin and Regine (1999) who extend Bortoft's (1996) analogy of a buttercup plant to represent a common source that once tapped into spreads and connects throughout an organization.

> Like the buttercup, certain behaviors and ways of thinking took root, grew and spread in these organizations. Even though the companies were very different and their behaviors were qualitatively different they all came to a similar order and gave rise to a particular quality of culture. It was the same buttercup in all these companies.
>
> (Lewin and Regine, 1999: 273–4)

For Bohm, 'the spirit of dialogue' will 'make possible the flow of meaning' (1976: 6), while McKewan (2000) suggests 'experiencing your common humanity'. Each of these authors recommends a way of behaving that will lead to a change in what happens in organizations. Each, however, assumes that new behaviors give access to some external force for good, whether the buttercup, the spirit of dialogue or common humanity.

How change is understood

In humanistic perspectives on coaching, change is perceived to occur as a result of the unfolding of the already enfolded or the release of potential that has been dormant. This way of thinking about the occurrence of change may be described as 'formative causality' (Stacey *et al.*, 2000: 52: fig. 3.3) where the movement into the future 'reveals, realizes or sustains a mature or final form of identity, of self. This is actualization of form or self that is already there in some sense.' The dialogic model, with its reliance on an external force for good and the emergence of change as a result of tapping into the external common source, may be described as both formative and rationalist causality. In rationalist causality it is the reason-based choices of people that are the cause of change. Thus in the dialogic approach, human beings decide to suspend their existing assumptions so as to gain access to 'the pool of common meaning' (Wheatley, 1999: 40), 'the spirit of dialogue' or 'the experience of common humanity', all of which are then formative causes. It is as if, by deciding to enter dialogue, change occurs due to the exercise of some spiritual or mystical phenomenon.

Mostly, the coach is seen as the objective observer, either recognizing the lack of self-awareness of the client, or deciding how the client may best be helped in the coaching session. By taking the position of objective observer, coaches distance themselves from their own part in the co-creation of the coaching conversation and the patterns of interaction that make up the experience of coaching for both coach and client. While speaking of the need for a 'participative approach' to coaching, Bolt (2000) shows his perception of his role of observer in his phrase: 'In general, the coach needs to take control of the sessions to ensure that they are useful and relevant and that time is not wasted' (Bolt, 2000: 23).

Here he sees himself as taking a stance of evaluating his perception of the success of each conversation without recognizing the part that his evaluation may play in the dynamics and power relating in the conversation with his client. Bolt does not seem aware of the continuous processes of relating that are as much part of the coaching sessions as they are in day-to-day interactions at work. It is as if he accepts that it is possible to isolate coaching in time and location from the ongoing patterns of communication and relationship that are being investigated in the coaching.

Mainstream authors do not give an impression of the dynamic, fluid nature of coaching conversations and do not attend to the movement in power between coach and client. There is little sense of risk involved where, by challenging a pattern of power relating, if one is coached by a manager, one could be expelled from the organization or find oneself in an increasingly difficult relationship.

Coaching from the perspective of complex responsive processes

Through my reflection on my work as an external coach and as a senior manager, I have developed an interest in a way of thinking and writing about coaching that is different from the approaches outlined above. I will use examples from my experience to draw attention to these differences. I first set out one of my coaching experiences from a mainstream perspective and then describe the same relationship as influenced by my experience as a participant on the Doctor of Management program.

Adrian was head of a supply chain operation for an international food production organization. He had been offered coaching by his chief executive who felt that all members of his senior team might benefit from a program of executive coaching with an external coach. Adrian had recently been promoted and had been asked to lead a major reorganization of the UK business, so he decided to take up the offer of coaching support. An objective of the coaching program was to ensure that Adrian would be able to persuade his colleagues of the need for change in the business. He, however, felt that his peers did not have the same commitment to the business as he did and was frustrated by his interactions with fellow Board members. Through the coaching conversations, Adrian developed an awareness of how his approach to his colleagues may be a part of the issue in their lack of engagement with him. Over time, Adrian developed an ability to be more open with his colleagues who responded similarly to him. The effect of this was an agreement to establish a team to work on the reorganization and Adrian was able to gain input from his colleagues in order to design a better overall solution for his business.

This description of a program of coaching is presented in the style of mainstream writers when they give examples (Bolt, 2000; Hicks and Petersen, 1995; Landsberg, 1997). By taking this stance I have located Adrian's difficulty in persuading his colleagues in himself and have suggested that by tapping into some, as yet, untapped potential he was able to find a new approach to working with his colleagues. I also imply that by 'reframing' his relationship with his colleagues he was able to attain a more successful commercial result. What is missing from the description, however, is the experience of how these changes actually occurred. We are not invited into the relationship between coach and client and are therefore unable to relate to the changes that emerged from the coaching experience. In order to provide a richer description of the dynamic experience of coaching, I set out below an extract from my session notes, focusing on the conversation that I experienced as being a moment in which transformational change occurred.

> The August session provided significant learning both for Adrian and myself. At the beginning of the session, Adrian said he wanted

techniques to 'get more out of people' when he spoke to them and, in particular, when he spoke to his colleagues on the Board about the need to improve the management of the supply chain. Initially he said that he wanted to get more out of people but still to direct the flow of conversation and its outputs. Then he reflected and said that in controlling the conversation he would only hear back six versions of his own conclusions, but he also recognized the risk of keeping the conversation open to the views of other people.

Since he had requested tools to help get people to be more open in conversations with him, I asked Adrian if he had noticed anything I had done to 'encourage' him to speak in our work together. As I asked this, Adrian looked at his watch and said that he did not know any techniques. I stayed silent and he then suggested that I used silence to encourage him to speak and that I often said: 'What else?' I then described some other ways of encouraging people to speak, such as open questions, open non-verbal communication and listening. In saying this, I felt as if the gap between my client and myself was widening. I believe I was experiencing his disinterest and my own.

A shift began to occur when I asked Adrian to do an exercise with me. I asked him to ask me only open questions. He agreed, but his first two questions were: 'Did you have a good flight?' and 'Do you enjoy your work?' The conversation flowed after his third question: 'What do you enjoy about your work?' I replied: 'I enjoy the variety of working with a range of people in different client organizations and I am fascinated by the similarities that I see in the different places that I work.' 'What similarities?' he asked. I replied, 'I seem to notice ways of behaving and of relating between people which seem to get in the way of them interacting together beyond a repetitive pattern.' Adrian asked, 'What problems does this cause organizations?' I remember feeling as if I was taking a risk, but in the moment said: 'Well, in Bravo Foods, I suspect that there is a distance between the Board members so that conversations are never really started or finished. I suspect that conversations are held around tasks and that if there is a problem, finding someone to blame becomes a major priority.'

I noticed that I was leaning forward and that Adrian sat forward and leaned on the table, listening. 'What kinds of problems do you think this causes?' he asked. I replied, 'I guess that some issues might be that the function heads work in isolation from their colleagues and that the Board doesn't represent the horizontal way of working that you are trying to generate in other parts of the business. People may feel that it is better not to take a risk and that as a result innovation and creativity are low. I imagine that the management of people is not seen to be a strength, although there are probably a number of celebrated examples of heroic recovery once things have gone wrong.'

I noticed that Adrian's breathing had deepened and I felt that I was in a place that felt significantly risky, as if to say more would be a further challenge to the status quo. However, to go back was no longer possible. I was asked: 'How would you sort some of this out?' I was now in full flow: 'I'm not sure of how I would want to "sort this" or what the outcomes might be if we tried, but there are certainly some conversations that I would want to enter into and in particular I would want to draw attention to what is happening in the moment rather than exploring what had happened historically or in planning the future. The first would be to ask the Board as a whole to enter into a conversation together around how they perceive how they are working together and collectively delivering their responsibilities as directors of the firm. I would also want to alter the agenda for November's event. I would remove the team-building "boat trip" and use the time to explore the real issues that the Board feel are blocking their progress. I also suggest that since the development of managers of the future is a significant part of the long-term supply chain strategy, you work closely with the HR Director to explore how by working together you both have a better chance of achieving your plans.'

In each of my responses to Adrian's questions, I was moving further away from the approach to coaching that I had historically used. I felt much more like a participant in a joint enquiry and less like an observer of a client. Both Adrian and I experienced a shift in our conversation and were entirely present to it. As I discussed with Adrian later, the common reference was that we were both aware of the lack of true conversation, or authentic relationship in the Board of Bravo, and that the Board were not serving the business well. In addition, that by naming this difficulty an opportunity had been created to start to engage more freely with each other.

Now I will consider how I would make sense of this different way of understanding how coaching might bring about change.

Power as differentiating patterns of identity

Mainstream authors on coaching focus on the architecture of a coaching program or the skills of coaching that may be seen to lead to change. They also focus on outputs of coaching such as increased self-awareness (Landsberg, 1997), self-understanding (Zeus and Skiffington, 2000), improved leadership (Whitmore, 1996), reduced conflict (Bolt, 2000), increased interpersonal effectiveness (Peterson and Hicks, 1994) and career planning (Whitworth *et al.*, 1998). I have taken the perspective of looking at the detail of the processes of relating that are coaching and noticing the movements that may be described as 'change'. I have not located change in Adrian but in the patterns of relating, particularly the patterns of power relations emerging from our conversation.

The most common understanding of power is as a static property contained within, or associated with, particular individuals. This is understood as the ability to influence others through some economic, expert, physical or charismatic advantage. My understanding of power is based on the theory of complex responsive processes (Stacey *et al.*, 2000) in which, drawing on the work of Elias (1939, 1978), power is understood as ongoing patterns that paradoxically both form and at the same time are formed by the processes of relating between people. The patterning of power is co-created in relationships and is experienced as the simultaneous enabling and constraining of actions. I will briefly review some elements of the thinking of Elias before returning to the sense I make of the coaching relationship.

For Elias, there is no separation between the individual and the group, the inside and outside, the mind and body. In his *Symbol Theory* (1989), he argues that language, thought and knowledge are all activities involving the use of symbols and that a distinction between speech, thought and knowledge is artificial. He says that a 'symbol' is created in relationships and that 'it exists in a place that transcends the usual internal/external dichotomy' (cited in Dalal, 1998: 88). Elias sees 'symbols' being created as social activity and power relations. The dynamic is recursive, each forming and being formed by the other at the same time and always having the potential for transformation. Communication in the medium of symbols occurs in the context of the interconnectedness of human relating, or 'figuration'.

The term 'figuration' is used by Elias to explain that all human relating involves some form of constraint and that this constraint consists of the processes of power-relating. Elias uses the phrase 'interdependent people' to focus on the idea that interconnectedness is at the core of human existence. The concept of the individual, for Elias, refers to 'interdependent people' in the singular and the concept of society to 'interdependent people' in the plural. He argues that the term 'figuration' refers to the 'pattern of bonding' (Elias, 1978: 176) or to the pattern of interconnectedness between interdependent persons and this is how he understands power.

Reliance on an individual psychology (humanistic, psychodynamic or cognitive) focuses the coach's attention on the individual client without exploring the patterning of power relating that the interdependent coach and client are co-creating in their work. It is only when a transformation in this patterning occurs that new possibilities arise. Movements in patterns of power relating are experienced as sensations of inclusion and exclusion that configure as socially created identity. Such movements, therefore, have a differentiating effect, where what is being differentiated is one identity from another. In our relating we co-create enabling constraints as self-organizing, differentiating patterns of power that form and are being formed by our identities at the same time. A movement in these patterns therefore alters our experience of being included or excluded, which may be seen as the movement of identity.

The movements that I refer to here are differentiating the structure of power relating as identity between us. The differentiating patterns of power moved during the conversation with Adrian and were experienced by me as changes in the iteration of identity. In thinking about power as a pattern rather than as being fixed and located in an individual, it becomes possible to reflect on the movements in the patterning of power as ongoing iterations of identity in the complex responsive processes of relating. By suddenly having more power in relation to another, one's identity may be seen to alter, a change in the relativity creating a movement in the shared experience of identity between the participants in conversation. In order for such shifts to occur, in my experience, some kind of risk has to be taken. This may lead to the experience of the exclusion of one or more of the interdependent people who are engaged in the ongoing conversation, frequently the person who embodies and is seen and felt to take the risk.

I suggest that the transformation which is promised by many coaches may be seen as a movement in the configurations of power, experienced as risk of exclusion from the predominant patterning of relating. A change in the patterning of power alters what is enabled and constrained, new actions emerge and identities move. Thinking in this way assumes that power and identity are not fixed or located in individuals but are inescapable patterns of the processes of relating between them. To work with this assumption, I am drawn to be more present, or mindful, of the experiences I am co-creating. I attend more clearly to my present experiences instead of thinking and speaking about events in other times and places. In my coaching, I focus on the patterns of power and the processes of relating in the immediate conversation. With my clients, I am more interested in what is occurring for us as we work together, instead of in agreeing goals and measurable outcomes to be achieved in other places. I concentrate much more on my participation in conversation, in its broadest sense, as it occurs.

Movements in the patterns of relating that occur as conversation can have unplanned and significant consequences for people in organizations. This is a very different approach to change than the usual planned program of interventions. The promise of coaching, in its rapid adoption by commercial organizations, is that it offers a form of conversation that provides change. Some coaches even promise 'transformation' (Landsberg, 1997; Whitmore, 1996). However, in my experience, the changes that have occurred have been very different from those promised by leading coaches and I believe they have come about in a different way, or originate from a different source, from those described in literature. It is not the self-contained individual who is altered by coaching but it is a movement in the patterns of power between people that is the change. The change that can happen in coaching does not result from the conscious choice to apply a particular range of skills or from the unfolding of the enfolded potential of the client. Instead, any change is a movement in the patterns of relating between coach and client, and for each with him or herself, which neither plans.

An implication of thinking in these terms is that my focus of attention changes while coaching. Previously I would have attended to the overall goals of the program and to the desired outcomes for each session. I would have exerted some control over the direction of the conversation in order to 'help' the client get closer to our agreed destination. I would not have been as focused on the intricacies of our relating in the moment. Now, I am particularly concerned with noticing the patterning of our interaction and am attuned to the responses and gestures that are called forth in us while we work. This means noticing and describing how I am reacting to our conversation, drawing attention to my experience of the processes of relating. In the example with Adrian, I risked criticism and possible exclusion due to my movement away from the pattern of being an objective coach to describing my subjective experience of the patterns of relating that I had noticed in the client organization. In this I am not appealing to any whole or common humanity outside of our interaction.

The manager as coach

Since the mid-1990s many organizations have attempted to encourage coaching in the workplace. A number of coaches describe how coaching may be applied in the workplace (Gallwey, 2000; Landsberg, 1997; Whitmore, 1996) without however considering the implications of change occurring through coaching at work. Most authors operate on the assumption that change can be brought about by the development of listening and questioning skills, combined with the application of a structure to a coaching session.

However, the line management relationship is different to the coach–client one in a number of ways. External coaches are likely to work with a client for a specified period. After this time the relationship often ends with the coach moving to work on other assignments. However, the line management relationship is ongoing, without a finite time span. The line manager is likely to spend more time with the client and be expected to play a number of roles including assessor, trainer and coach, and will work with the client in a number of settings outside of the formal coaching agreement.

The change that coaching is supposed to bring about is often described as a subordinate being able to achieve more as he or she becomes 'empowered' or 'enabled' through coaching. By taking a monadic stance it appears possible for an individual to be able to achieve more and to have more power and authority to act. However, by considering change from the perspective of the patterning of power differentiating, it is the pattern of relating between managers and subordinates that may change. For the employee to be more enabled, the manager may be more constrained in some way when power is considered as a relational phenomenon. The level of control that the manager has may diminish as the pattern of power moves. The previous patterning of power that had sustained identity as manager and subordinate may be threatened and experienced as uncertainty and discomfort for both participants. The new patterns of power emerging from coaching may not be sufficiently robust to sustain the discomfort, and the previous patterns may be reasserted to regain the sense of the known. It may therefore be helpful to draw attention to the live experience of the patterning of power as identity in working with line managers who wish to coach.

The following example of a coaching experience is between a direct report, David, and myself. David is Health and Safety Manager for Opus and began to report to myself, as HR Director, instead of to the Head of Construction, in January 2002. David had a difficult relationship with his previous line manager and was apparently pleased to report to the HR Director, since it would allow him to widen his remit to provide group-wide health and safety services instead of focusing on the construction division of the business. I was also pleased to work with David as it gave me the opportunity to be the line manager of a specialist team in an area in which I had no technical knowledge. David and I had met regularly in the first quarter of 2002. On one occasion he asked if I would like him and a colleague to present an update of health and safety requirements to me, as part of my induction into this new area. I agreed, and was keen to have some understanding of legislation and the implications for Opus. About a week before the scheduled session, I was speaking to David and asked if it would be possible for us to visit one of our construction sites as part of the update, so that I could see the health and safety requirements in a part of the business with which I was less familiar.

David looked disappointed and replied that he did not think there would be time to do this, since he and Andy had already prepared their lecture for me. Not wanting to disrupt the preparation, I suggested visiting a site in a few weeks' time. On the day of the scheduled session, members of the HR team teased me, assuming my low level of interest for a three-hour lecture on health and safety legislation. The session described below has three participants rather than the two who usually participate in coaching conversations. Another distinction is that I did not think the conversation would be of a type that may lead to change (that is, a coaching conversation) prior to my participation in it. I had imagined that the session would take the form of a presentation from David and Andy to myself.

At the scheduled time of the session, I waited for David and Andy in my office and then, after twenty minutes, was told that they were waiting for me in 'Board Room One', our most imposing venue. I went to the room, apologized for my delay and noticed a pack of bound papers entitled 'A Health and Safety Update – for Andrew Lee 26 February 2002'. I felt flattered that my colleagues had invested so much time in the preparation but I felt heavy at the thought of wading through a set of documents and slides. The six-foot plasma screen flashed into life with the first slide on it. I guessed that there must have been fifty slides in the pack and clearly David and Andy intended to speak to each of them. I scanned the table to work out how David and Andy intended to manage the afternoon.

I noticed my pack of notes and their packs, which had the addition of speakers' notes under each slide. I was to be the only audience member for a well-prepared, high-tech, set-piece presentation. My mind wandered to thinking that although I might get bored I needed to respect both the preparation and the medium that my colleagues had chosen to use in order to feel comfortable working with their new line manager.

Andy started by speaking about the first slides. Not only were there fifty of them but each was composed of lists of bullet points, or in some cases animations that would try to bring a point to life but actually killed it for me. After reviewing the key points of the Health and Safety at Work Act 1974, Andy said, 'After we have gone through the slides there are some things we want to talk to you about.' I was curious, since I sensed the possibility of a conversation instead of a presentation. The need to speak about something was referred to twice more and each time I resisted asking more in case I caused too much disruption by moving the course of the meeting away from its intended path.

On reflecting on my hesitation, I notice how I felt both enabled by my management role to intervene if I wanted to but simultaneously constrained by not wishing to interrupt and disrupt the rhythm of the prepared session. I also felt less influential due to my lack of technical knowledge of health and safety matters and concerned that I might miss something that related to my statutory obligations in this new role. From the perspective of complex responsive processes, however, power was not located in me, or in my colleagues, but in the differentials that emerged from our personal histories, our previous experiences of each other and the anticipation of our future relationship. The fluidity of such power relations is clearly illustrated later in this example.

The perspective of moving power differentials helps my understanding of my experience in the moments of deciding whether or not to intervene in David's presentation. My experience of set-piece presentations is that questions and interruptions are not desired and that any intervention would be seen as unhelpful. The effect then of a scripted, power point presentation was of constraining my contributions in a way that ensured that 'turn-taking' happened in a way that David, Andy and I co-created, based on our experiences of making and attending presentations. Simultaneously, David and Andy were both enabled to plough through their intended material while also being constrained to staying in the parameters of the pre-prepared material. The three of us were constrained by the process and prevented ourselves from moving from a predetermined path but were enabled to deliver and receive the intended material. Despite the apparent control over turn-taking in the meeting, it was not possible to control the meanings that were being made. For example, while David and Andy were able to stick to their scripts, they were not able to control how I reacted. I know that they did not intend to bore me or make me feel unengaged and excluded.

As one slide on the 157 pieces of fire legislation was displayed, I experienced a feeling that I remembered from lectures as an undergraduate, the weight of boredom as I observed a lecturer go through slides of information, watching to see the pile of slides diminish slowly as the lecture progressed. I checked myself and tried to refocus my attention on David and Andy. Within a few minutes I began to think about the factors that made this such an unengaging session for me. The subject matter was not particularly interesting, although I knew that as a provider of accommodation for 20,000 students, health and safety was of vital importance. I was curious about what was happening to make me feel so unconnected to the session. I watched Andy as he spoke towards the screen, giving examples of case law and descriptions of EU directives. I had a sense of watching a video, where the presenter is unconnected and even unaware of his audience.

I spoke after slide twenty-four: 'You've mentioned a couple of times that there is something you want to discuss. I wonder if we can make sure that we have sufficient time to do justice to that conversation.' David said, 'Um, yes, I think we'll have a few minutes left.' I asked, 'What's the topic of the conversation?' 'Well,' Andy replied, 'We want to talk about how you in HR have done so much to get the business to think about working together more effectively. At the moment everyone is doing their appraisals and we want to learn from you about how you've got everyone engaged.'

I was fascinated by this request. I had been sitting for two hours in a presentation that was most unengaging and was now hearing a request to discuss with the health and safety team how to engage their colleagues. I suggested that we have that conversation now and return to the slides later, or even allow me to read the slides overnight and come back to them with questions if I needed to. David and Andy seemed hesitant, but agreed. I asked what they had noticed about how the appraisal process had been introduced and how that might be relevant for the health and safety team. Andy said, 'Well for a start you're senior and you're behind it, so your support helps. Also everyone has been trained and there is a clear process and suggested approach. Even I, who am often cynical about these things, have been changed. I thought I'll give it a go.' I was curious, 'Andy, tell me what has happened for you so that your skepticism has changed to understanding and engagement.' Andy said, 'Well, no, it's the whole business being prepared.' I pressed on: 'Andy, help me out here. I'm really interested in hearing about what happened for you. We're talking about needing people to engage and I'd like to think about your experience.'

Andy was sitting opposite me and in my peripheral vision I became aware of David moving. I became aware of his agitation. He leaned forward and said, 'I'm not here to mess about!' I was somewhat startled by this interjection. David's threshold of intolerance had been breached and his remark made me believe that he was ready to walk out of the meeting, shifting the power differential to make him relatively more powerful, by threatening to exclude himself from Andy and myself and therefore excluding us from him. This movement in the patterns of power and the shift in the meaning that was made of our interactions resulted in us engaging with each other in a different way.

I said, 'David, I'm not here to mess about either, but I do want to explore what is happening so that you feel that people in the business are disinterested in health and safety. I feel unengaged by the process that we have followed today, when your intention today was to increase my interest in the area.'

David's challenge to me was hard. For the first time in Opus I was challenged in a way that I challenge others. The patterns of power moved so that David appeared to have more control over what happened next than I did. It was clear in his statement that he would not tolerate the questions that I had begun to ask his colleague. In this challenge, the meaning that I made of my question to Andy shifted. Andy's response to the question was: 'Well, attending the workshop and having the time to think about and discuss the important conversations that I needed to have with my line manager made the process of appraisal become more relevant to me.' The meaning of my question was 'let us see how we can compare your experience of becoming interested in something with what you are trying to achieve in your team.'

David's challenge caused the meaning of my original question to shift significantly. In the moment of hearing 'I'm not here to mess about!' I saw my experience of myself as trying to ask some artificial coaching questions to lead Andy to an insight about how he might engage others.

I recognized myself in David's assertion. I thought for a moment and said: 'Look, I don't want to mess around here, but I think that there is something important for me to say about my experiences this afternoon that may help us think about how we can engage people in the business about health and safety issues.'

I was still aware of David's tension and felt that at any moment he would walk out of the room. It felt as if the security of his carefully designed process had now evaporated and that we were in uncharted territory. Then, instead of asking Andy or David any further questions, I described my own experience of the meeting: 'Let me try to explain how I have been feeling this afternoon. I know that health and safety is really important and that we need to do much more to get to the standards that we would like to achieve. However, I don't know from this session what I now need to do or what I am doing that is OK. It feels as if you are both explaining some broad concepts but together are not looking at the impact of your information on what we are doing here.'

David used a defense that I had heard before: 'Ah, but the legislation is not prescriptive. It is goal-setting legislation and the business needs to set its own goals and agree its standards. The health and safety team can't do that for them.' I replied, 'I'm really clear that the law is about goal setting, but what I'm not clear on is how we are helping our colleagues to set those goals. How are they engaged in coming up with what they need to do to ensure compliance?' David said, 'Well we've used this presentation as a basis of a meeting with the senior managers, but I don't think that it made much impact.' I replied, 'If I think of this afternoon again, I have felt flattered by the preparation that you have done for me today and also frustrated at not being able to get to the real conversation that you wished to have. You have given me so much information but I am not clear what we need to do next. I imagine that this is a similar experience to the impact that the session would have had with the management group.'

Andy was quiet for a few minutes while David and I spoke. He then said, 'I'm just thinking that the areas where we've had most success in getting people to think about health and safety is where they have decided on the issues and actions themselves. Not when we've tried to instigate something ourselves. It's better when the managers think for themselves.' David became animated in his agreement: 'Even this afternoon, we're struggling with this issue together now instead of presenting slides.'

David's comparison of the two halves of our session was marked. He, and I, had experienced the difference between the formulaic approach to the slide-based presentation and the alert and fluid nature of our later conversation. David had taken a significant risk in intervening strongly, and we were awoken from our co-created patterns of disengagement to a way of working that felt risky and unknowable. David's remark shifted the patterns of power relating and caused us to find a different way of being together. In addition, the relationship between David and myself shifted. I now see him as stronger and more passionate about his work. He recognizes my desire to explore the immediacy of our experience rather than to think about past or describe what 'should' and 'ought' to happen in the future. I feel that we can have more robust conversations without preparation and that our identities have shifted as we now see each other in a different way.

This episode provides a strong example of my perspective on coaching, and leadership, for that matter. It is clear that change happened in the moment of David saying, 'I'm not here to mess about!' I experienced a movement in the patterns of power between us. He became stronger due to the risk he took in potentially excluding himself from our conversation. I recognized the artificiality of my earlier questioning through his interjection, and became aware of his passion to promote a healthy and safe working environment. I recognized David and myself differently in that moment. I point to the moment of David's exasperation as the time when change occurred rather than the whole session as would occur with mainstream writers. For me, it is the movement of power and identity in the micro interaction of the moment that is coaching, a shift in the patterns of relating and not the application of skills by a coach. In this example, it was my use of 'coaching skills' (asking open questions, summarizing and listening) that led to David's annoyance rather than leading to a controlled transformational outcome.

This experience of working with David and Andy points to a significant aspect not discussed in the mainstream literature. In the meeting, the dominant pattern of interaction was that of presentation. Graphics and a script were used as tools to control the conversation. In challenging the constraints of this way of communicating, I was seen to replace one formulaic approach with another. The pattern I introduced was that of 'coaching' as formulaic in the application of particular skills. I had replaced one pattern of interaction with another; one that was equally as artificial and which prevented underlying concerns from being voiced. It was only when David's tolerance threshold was breeched that we were able to speak candidly about our experiences of working together. When I reflect on the experience of working with line managers to help them develop their coaching skills, the implications of the meeting with David and Andy become clear. In attempting to replace the presentational style with a coaching conversation I had attempted to reassert the original power differential between us – regaining control of the meeting by introducing a way of speaking together with which I was more comfortable. It felt as if the presentational mode was being used to reduce the anxiety of the health and safety team and, since I felt uncomfortable with that, I had attempted to replace it with a mode of communication and control with which I felt more comfortable. Instead of coaching having the effect of reducing the power differentials, as is often intended in this 'enabling' way of working, the existing processes of power relating had been reinforced. This resulted in an increase in David's frustration.

Having had this experience, I am more aware of other situations in which the newly trained line manager may impose his coaching skills on a subordinate in a way that may be intended to 'release potential' but which has the effect of not only reinforcing existing patterns of power relating but also of creating confusion and frustration in the relationship. In my example it was David's risk-taking that caused the newly introduced coaching pattern of communicating to be replaced with a more intense and real exploration of our experience of working together.

The theme of risk-taking is present both in this example and in the earlier one with Adrian. In both situations, some sense of risk was perceived as a movement away from an existing pattern of communicative interaction. I had moved away from a passive role as the receiver of a presentation and David fought against being in the role of a reluctant client. My view is that by focusing on developing coaching skills, organizations are looking in the wrong place for the source of the desired change. They are following an approach that locates change in the client and the source of that change in the ability of the coaching line manager. I now see coaching as a relational experience in which change occurs as movement in relative power and therefore the socially created identities of the participants involved.

Conclusion

The themes in this chapter illustrate how I think about coaching in a way that is fundamentally different from that of the mainstream authors. My approach to coaching relies on a different underlying causality, transformative rather than rationalist or formative. The approach to coaching explored here is also distinct from humanistic and cognitive psychologies and dialogic practices that are at the core of much of the existing literature. Change, in the mainstream literature, is thought of as the unfolding of the enfolded potential of the client. My approach locates change in the transformative experience of movements in identities, in relation to others and to oneself, as experienced as movements in the patterning of power relating and the moment-by-moment experience of inclusion and exclusion.

References

Argyris, C. (1992) *On Organisational Learning*, Oxford: Blackwell.

Berne, E. (1937) *Games People Play*, Harmondsworth: Penguin.

Bohm, D. (1976) *On Dialogue*, London: Routledge.

Bolt, P. (2000) *Coaching for Growth*, Dublin: Oak Tree Press.

Bortoft, H. (1996) *The Wholeness of Nature*, New York: Lindesfarne Press.

Covey, S. (1983) *Seven Habits of Highly Effective People*, London: Simon & Schuster.

Covey, S. (1990) *Principle Centred Leadership*, London: Simon & Schuster.

Dalal, F. (1998) *Taking the Group Seriously*, London: Jessica Kingsley.

Downey, M. (2002) *Organisational Coaching in the United Kingdom*, London: Industrial Society.

Dryden, W. (1984) *Handbook of Individual Therapy*, London: Sage.

Dryden, W. (1987) *Cognitive Approaches to Psychotherapy*, London: Taylor & Francis.

Elias, N. (1970) *What is Sociology?*, New York: Colombia.

Elias, N. (1978) *The Civilizing Process*, Oxford: Blackwell (first published in German 1939).

Elias, N. (1987) *Involvement and Detachment*, Oxford: Blackwell.

Elias, N. (1989) *The Symbol Theory*, London: Sage.

Elias, N. (1991) *The Society of Individuals*, New York: Continuum.

Elias, N. (1998) *On Civilization, Power and Knowledge*, Chicago, IL: Chicago University Press.

Gallwey, T. (1975) *The Inner Game of Tennis*, London: Pan.

Gallwey, T. (2000) *The Inner Game of Work*, London: Random House.

Harris, T. (1994) *I'm Ok, You're Ok*, London: Arrow.

Hicks, M. and Peterson, D. (1995) *Leader as Coach*, Minneapolis: PDI.

Hicks, M. and Peterson, D. (1996) *Development First*, Minneapolis: PDI.

Isaacs, W. (1999) *Dialogue and the Art of Thinking Together*, New York: Doubleday.

Kostere, K. and Malatesta, L. (1989) *Maps, Models and Structures of Reality – NLP Techniques in Psychotherapy*, San Francisco, CA: Metamorphosis Press.

Landsberg, M. (1997) *The Tao of Coaching*, London: HarperCollins.

Lewin, R. and Regine, B. (1999) *The Soul at Work*, London: Orion.

Lewis, G. (1996) *The Mentoring Manager*, London: Pitman.

McKewan, J. (2000) 'A dialogic approach to coaching', unpublished article.

Maslow, A. (1964) *Motivation and Personality*, New York: Harper & Row.

Merry, T. (1999) *Learning and Being in Person Centred Counselling*, London: PCCS.

Parsoe, E. (1992) *Coaching Mentoring and Assessing*, London: Kogan Page.

Peterson, D. and Hicks, M. (1994) *Leader as Coach*, Minnesota: PDI.

Rogers, C. (1961) *On Becoming a Person*, London: Houghton.

Rogers, C. (1963) *The Actualizing Tendency in Relation to Motivation and Consciousness*, Nebraska: University of Nebraska Press.

Rogers, C. (1963) *Encounter Groups*, London: Pelican.

Rogers, C. (1980) *A Way of Being*, London: Houghton.

Senge, P. (1990) *The Fifth Discipline*, New York: Doubleday.

Shea, M. (1996) *Mentoring, A Practical Guide*, London: Kogan Page.

Stacey, R., Griffin, D. and Shaw, P. (2000) *Complexity and Management: Fad or radical challenge to systems thinking?*, London: Routledge.

Whitmore, J. (1996) *Coaching for Performance*, London: Nicholas Breareley.

Whitworth, L., Kimsey-House, K. and Sandahl, P. (1998) *Co-active Coaching*, London: Davis Block.

Zeus, P. and Skiffington, S. (2000) *The Complete Guide to Coaching at Work*, Sydney: McGraw Hill.

Editors' introduction
to Chapter 8

Michael Shiel, Program Director at the Irish Institute of Management, is concerned with the skill of leadership and how it might be taught or otherwise acquired. If an organization evolves into the unknown, if leaders cannot control actions or determine values, if leadership emerges in processes of mutual recognition, then what is the skill of leadership? For Shiel, the skill has to do with participation in conversations which draw attention to what is going on in the present, which influences others and so encourages the emergence of new meaning. He emphasizes the point that emergence of new meaning does not 'just' happen because emergent new meaning is co-created by what participants in a conversation are saying and doing. However, in this process of co-creation, all participants are not equal. There are not only differences of power in which the power ratio is tilted more towards some than towards others but there are also skill differences. The skill of the teacher is essentially the same as that of the leader, namely participating in ways that create wider opportunities for others. Shiel describes a workshop he led, pointing to just how this skill is exercised.

In recognizing a person as leader, people are recognizing one skilled in drawing attention to the emerging meaning in their interactions with each other. The same skill is required of one who is teaching leadership. Meaning emerges in conversations and new meaning is more likely to emerge in conversations having richer, more diverse themes and greater spontaneity. The leader's role is thus to participate in a way that deepens and widens communication. Leaders participate in a particularly influential way by drawing attention to surprises, irregularities and misunderstandings. Developing the skill of leadership means enhancing this capacity. Shiel stresses the need for leaders to be able to live with not knowing and all the anxiety this brings with it. He points to how people fill the void created by not knowing with fantasies. The leader acts with intent into this situation, helping others to learn from their own experience.

8 Leadership, learning and skill development

Michael Shiel

- A different view of knowledge
- The case of SSL
- Leadership and the move into the unknown
- Irregularity and new thought
- Novel thinking in SSL
- The capacity to direct attention
- Learning about change
- On knowledge
- On power
- Conclusion

In this chapter, I argue that management is concerned with coherent action in organizations, and that leadership concerns willing and informed participation in that action. Coherent action arises from the ways in which circumstances are understood; that is, their meaning. Mead (1934) argues that meaning arises in the social act consisting of the gesture of one and the response of the other as inseparable phases. It follows that meaning cannot be ascribed to any one individual but emerges in the processes of communicative interaction as a thematic pattern. This then makes problematic the traditional notion of a leader as one who makes meaning for others. This view of meaning is fundamental to the theory of complex responsive processes (Stacey *et al.*, 2000), a brief overview of which is given in chapters 2 and 6 of this volume. Also fundamental to this theory is individual diversity. It follows that different individuals have a different impact on the emergence of organizational futures. How does the theory of complex responsive processes in organizations account for this?

One answer to this question is that relations between individuals are such that the power ratio is tilted more towards some than towards others. However, I want to emphasize another difference between people, namely differences in skill; in particular the skills of noticing and drawing attention to what is emerging in interaction; that is, to emerging meaning. Such skilled people are particularly influential in co-creating the thematic patterning of interaction itself through the manner in which they influence other participants' responses. Leadership is concerned with this process of meaning-making. To the extent that an individual is experienced by a group as being skilled in drawing attention to what is emerging, he or she will be recognized as a leader.

My practice is concerned with the development of the skills of leadership. Using the same argument as in the above paragraph, these skills cannot be directly transferred by a teacher of leadership, but the teacher, by his or her choice of gestures, can influence the responses of the other, thereby influencing the emerging pattern of knowing; that is, the skill of the student (as well as that of the teacher!).

The central argument in this chapter is as follows:

- Leadership is concerned with participating with others in a group or organization to assist them to move into an unknown future, indeed to co-create that future. This requires the continuous emergence of meaning. New meaning cannot be commanded to appear; rather, it emerges as thematic patterning from the communicative interactions of persons, principally in conversation.
- New meaning arises from interaction and is more likely to emerge in conversation which is characterized by a richer diversity of themes and greater spontaneity than one which is characterized by static, sparse, repetitive patterns in which little new emerges.
- No one, including leaders or teachers, can take up a position outside this interaction and attempt to influence it from there. The only way to influence the emergent thematic patterning is to participate in that interaction; that is, by being there and by the particular gestures–responses one makes.
- The people participating in this process are not all the same: some are more powerful than others; some are more skilful than others in noticing and drawing attention to what is emerging between them. The more powerful or skilful people will exert more impact on the responses of other participants and hence will play a more influential role in the co-creation of the emergent thematic patterning of the

interaction in which they are engaged. Leaders are those who are experienced by the group as being skilled in this process.

- The task of a leader is to participate in particularly influential ways in the interactions (principally conversations) that constitute the life of the group, paying attention to the interactions, in particular to surprises, irregularities and misunderstandings which give rise to potential changes in the patterns of conversation. Therefore, leadership is concerned with the emergence of new patterns of thinking and knowing, that is, with joint exploratory learning.

- Developing the skill of leadership must therefore involve the enhancement of an individual's capacity to pay attention to communicative processes, to be fully present to the changing patterning of interactions as they emerge, as well as being fully present to the changing patterning of the silent conversation with oneself. In effect, since leadership concerns continuous learning, becoming a leader involves *learning to learn in a new way*.

- This change in skill is itself a change in the characteristic patterning of an individual's silent conversation. This learning is achieved through the experience of conversation in a group with skilled participants. The role of a teacher is similar to that described above for a leader. They are engaged in a similar task: participating in and contributing to conversation in skilled ways. The teacher (in this case myself), as part of the process, is also learning while helping others to learn.

A different view of knowledge

The question of knowledge creation, and the influential part that leaders play in it, is at the heart of this chapter for two reasons. First, my practice is concerned with assisting managers to learn to be effective leaders through understanding their experience and their current situations in the light of exploration with myself and with their fellow students, and with appropriate inputs of theory where this may be helpful. Learning arises in the sense we make of experience. Knowledge is created as the managers in this process gain a different understanding of their situations and how they can act effectively. My concern here is with the difference a teacher can make to a person trying to make sense of her lived experience, especially where that person herself is trying to make a difference to that experience; that is, to change something.

The second reason concerns the nature of leadership and strategy. From a complex responsive processes perspective, strategy is the evolving thematic patterning of the processes of communicative interaction, which expresses the identity of an organization (Stacey, 2003) and includes its purpose. Leaders are particularly skilful, influential participants in this process. I argue that leadership is particularly concerned with assisting a group to move purposefully into an unknown future, and that this is a creative act requiring the constant emergence of new meaning. Thus leadership itself is concerned with knowledge creation, and so, as a teacher, I am concerned that the managers with whom I work learn about this. Furthermore, I am concerned with how these managers can best learn to participate skilfully in this process of creating new knowledge and thus enhance their leadership ability.

Describing the systems view of knowledge creation, Stacey states: 'The knowledge creating system is basically one in which tacit knowledge already stored in the heads of some individuals, already enfolded as it were, is unfolded by processes of conversion. Mental models are already there, as are the learning models according to which they are supposed to be changed and so are the visions that are supposed to guide the learning and knowledge creation of the whole system' (Stacey, 2001, p. 239). One of the principal shortcomings of these theories, according to Stacey, is that they do not, on their own, account for how novel thought arises. Because of this, I cannot account for my practice solely in terms of these theories with its primary focus on how new knowledge arises. Systems thinking originates in the thinking of the philosopher Kant, who took the self, the knowing subject, as a given. The categories through which we know are given outside our experience; we come into the world with knowledge as a priori categories. Kant did not explain how new knowledge arises within the individual. It follows, therefore, that teaching and learning involve the transmission of knowledge from those who possess knowledge to those who do not. This is at the heart of the teaching/learning processes in mainstream thinking. Complex responsive processes theory is based on the work of Mead, Elias and others in the Hegelian tradition. The view of knowing presented by Hegel is fundamentally different in that it is essentially socially based. Knowing and knowledge arise through interaction with others, and this interaction inevitably involves aspects of power and conflict. Individuals do not enter social interaction with a priori identities; these arise through the interdependency and mutual recognition which are aspects of social interaction. Learning, therefore, is not a form of knowledge transmission but a social activity.

For Stacey, knowledge and its creation cannot be controlled or managed:

> Knowledge creation is an evolutionary process of reproduction and
> potential transformation at the same time. In other words knowledge
> is neither stored nor shared because it is not an 'it' at all but a process.
> It is communicative action, particularly in the form of conversation.
> Knowledge is the themes organizing the experience of being together
> and knowledge evolves as active experience. Knowledge is created as
> changes in the thematic patterning of bodies relating to each other and
> that thematic patterning organizes itself. . . . Knowledge cannot be
> grasped, owned by anyone or traded in any market and its creation is a
> process of communicating and power relating that is both stimulating
> and anxiety provoking at the same time.
>
> (Stacey, 2001, p. 220)

My argument in this chapter proceeds from this point. One of Stacey's
principal claims for the validity of the theory of complex responsive
processes in organizations is that it better accounts for the emergence of
novelty; that is, it better accounts for a critical aspect of *lived experience*.
It is central to this theory that the emergent themes in communicative
interaction cannot be controlled by anyone standing outside of the
processes of communicative interaction. However, it is a matter of lived
experience that leaders *do* influence others (in many cases), and that
(some) teachers *do* influence managers in learning to be better leaders.
That is to say, although knowing is a self-organizing pattern, this does
not mean that it just happens. The pattern of interaction which is
knowledge is being co-created by those participating in the interaction.
Leaders as powerful and skilful participants play a major role in the
patterning that emerges, although they cannot know in advance what will
emerge.

Given that my practice principally concerns helping managers to learn
from their own experiences, I must turn my attention to two related
questions. First, what is the nature of 'teaching' in processes where new
knowledge arises as the emergence of new patterns of meaning *between*
individual persons, and where knowledge itself is seen as a pattern
emerging in processes of communicative interaction? Given that a future,
including future knowledge, cannot be autonomously chosen by an
individual, what is it that I am usefully doing as a teacher participating in
a practice claiming to produce knowledge? The second question follows
from the first, and it concerns the nature of skill. I am trying to assist my

students to develop better skills as leaders and strategists, to improve their practice; what are these skills? If, as a teacher, I am employed because I have a skill in joining with others with the intention of developing their leadership skills, what skills do I employ?

The case of SSL

To explore these questions I will use the example of a company, Scully and Sons Ltd (SSL), manufacturers of materials handling equipment. The firm is now chaired by one of the sons, Steve. His father, the founder, and two brothers, have no involvement in its management. The firm had grown rapidly since Steve took over in the mid-1990s and it had developed a small range of technically advanced products. I had been contacted by the firm to give a course on strategy and leadership. I met with Ted, the CEO, at his office in a rural location and he began to speak in terms of the possible content of a course.

Leadership and the move into the unknown

We began to discuss holding a one-week workshop with the top managers in the firm. I asked Ted what he needed to achieve in the week. Above all, he emphasized, he needed the managers to gain a strong understanding of the firm's new approach to its business and a commitment to it. Up to this point, discussion had been of a one-week event which was essentially driven by a teaching agenda. Despite his professional competence and the apparently clear content requirement for the work, I began to feel something else, a kind of tension. I sensed a very deep need on Ted's part to make significant progress in this week and I tested this out with him. 'I think this is going to be a very important event for you.' He replied, 'To be honest, there's a lot riding on it. The whole future of the firm depends on this group.'

We discussed the future of the firm and the uncertainties about it. Would sales pick up after a recent lull? Would the market respond to a renewed promotional campaign? Were they investing in the right areas – market development and some product development? Did they have the right people to drive the growth of the firm?

I was struck by the sense of 'the unknown' in our conversation. Ted was trying to move SSL forward into an unknown future and was evidently trying to find a way of dealing with both the task of doing this and the feelings that accompanied it. My mind went off into a minor excursion about how this is the nature of strategic leadership: dealing with the unknown, while maintaining the purpose and identity of the organization. This is not an existing 'unknown' awaiting discovery; it is an act of creation in the moment. So many of the metaphors we use to describe strategy evoke images, such as discovering a previously unseen path through a jungle; it all seems obvious after the fact. It is said that history is written by the winners; no less so in business. Descriptions of useful strategies are not only written after the fact (Mintzberg, 1994), they completely overlook the creative moment in facing the unknown. And 'facing the unknown' is the issue – the temptations to flee it, or disguise it with a veneer of 'known' is irresistible.

Elias explores the issue of not knowing, in the context of knowing. He says that this experience is too terrifying an experience to withstand, and so the gap in knowing is filled with fantasy: 'fantasy knowledge can take deep roots in the lives of human groups. It can give to such an extent the impression of being reality-congruent that it blocks the search for more reality-congruent symbols' (Elias, 1991, p. 57). This is of particular relevance to my work because a significant aspect of managers' lives is 'not knowing', especially about the future, but also about the reality of the present and of the past.

Equally, in my own practice, it is personally and ideologically unacceptable for a teacher not to know what things mean and what is going to happen next. Yet Elias argues that it is only in the experience of staying with the 'not knowing' that fantasies can be recognized which do not serve learning or work and that new knowledge can arise. 'But without throwing oneself for a time into the sea of uncertainty one cannot escape the contradictions and inadequacies of a deceptive certainty' (Elias, 1998, p. 270). One of the temptations in dealing with uncertainty when working with SSL was to supply a reliable 'way forward', for example, a comprehensive strategy. This would have dealt with an aspect of the uncertainty of SSL's future by providing some certainty. It would also have moved the conversation away from the creative experience of staying with the unknown.

Therefore, one of the struggles in learning concerns the balance of reality-congruent knowledge and fantasy knowledge. This requires a certain measure of probing and questioning to begin to surface unquestioned assumptions and to see how this changes the picture. For example, with SSL, assumptions emerged about how success was measured, and what customers really wanted. This can be a disorienting and anxiety-provoking experience: 'Unquestioned assumptions, the basic structures of thought that we take over with the words of our language without further reflection, are among the indispensable means of orientation without which we lose our way' (ibid.). Anxiety and the responses to it are not a particular concern of Elias. In addition, it does not automatically follow that any experience, especially those intended as learning experiences, and including the experience of not knowing, will result in an increase of reality-congruent knowledge.

The principal emphasis of much of the organizational literature is one of knowledge and regularity as a way of dealing with not knowing and with 'messiness'. What I am arguing here, as a starting point, is that the reality of the situation facing a leader such as Ted is that part of the essence of leadership is in acting, with intent, into the unknown and recognizing the uniqueness of the situation, while maintaining the purpose and identity of the organization.

Irregularity and new thought

The act of creation in the strategic move into the unknown arises in interaction, principally in the form of conversation. John Shotter is a social constructionist who focuses on the 'living' quality of interaction and its capacity to create new understanding by paying attention to aspects of conversation which may ordinarily be overlooked or taken for granted. These aspects may include the use of language, connections between ideas, or simply thoughts which have a particularly noticeable or 'arresting' quality. Shotter refers to this type of thinking, in which the meaning of past and future mutually form each other continuously as they emerge from interaction, as 'relational–responsive' (Shotter, 1996).

Stacey criticizes Shotter for distinguishing this from any other kind of conversation, claiming that this creates two kinds of conversation, a 'dualism', which ignores the potential of ordinary daily conversation also to act as a source of novelty. While not denying that all interaction has the potential to pattern further interaction, what I am focusing on in this chapter is how the pattern of interaction can be skilfully influenced. I believe that what Shotter is attempting to say is that it is possible to be more (or less) present to the creative potential of a conversation, while being part of that conversation; that is, it is possible to make a difference to a conversation with skill and intent and thereby enhance its potential. This skill includes awareness and sensitivity to the living nature of the interaction. It also includes seeing the potential in going in one direction more than others, based on experience; it is not a *laissez-faire* approach. I am claiming this as my skill, both as the skill of a leader and as the skill of the teacher who seeks to assist others to learn from experience.

To express this point in complexity terms, movement into an unknowable and uncontrollable future arises continuously from multiple interactions, but this does not mean that we cannot seek to know and influence this from within the interaction. In my case I seek to influence the continuous arising of new patterns of knowing, while accepting that I cannot do this unilaterally. This is at the heart of my stance as a teacher. In the case of Ted, I sought to influence him, not towards some predetermined outcome, but in continuous response to the meanings arising in our conversation.

In discussing the organization, the conversation felt less fruitful. The conversation (and the organization) felt more than a little 'stuck'. A stable, repetitive pattern emerged and I wondered what I could do to influence it. The issue of influence is central here. As discussed earlier, it is not possible, from the perspective from which I am arguing in this chapter, to stand outside the conversation and control it; it is only possible to gesture, albeit with skill and/or power, with the intent of evoking responses in the other, and so to jointly affect the thematic patterning which arises. I was part of the conversation with Ted and I was drawing his attention to alternative perspectives, but I could not unilaterally influence how our conversation would evolve.

Novel thinking in SSL

The top twenty two managers, including the CEO, Ted, but not Steve Scully, the principal shareholder and executive chairman, gathered in a hotel on a Sunday night for the week's work. We began on Monday morning in a small meeting room with my introduction of the work. I explained that we would use the company as a 'living case' as we learned some of the principles of leadership and strategy from their actual practice of work. I gave them an outline timetable along with a caveat that we would vary this to suit needs as they arose. The mood in the room felt a little edgy with anticipation. I started by asking what had been happening in the past two to three years that they felt had been significant.

'We've been much clearer about our strategy, about what we're trying to achieve' – Brian, who manages the operation in France. 'Yeah, that's right, and the new range of machines are real winners' – Nigel, a robust north of England salesman. There are nods and murmurs of agreement on this point. 'Well, it's a different company than it was two years ago' – Dave, who manages the sales team in Ireland – 'I can see where we're trying to get to, it's much clearer to me, and the customers are really pleased with what we're producing'. There is much talk of the new range of machines and how good they are. 'A lot of that is down to you, Paschal,' says Kevin, Sales Director, nodding at the head of manufacturing, 'you're really producing the goods.' This goes on for a while and I feel irrelevant except to raise minor points of clarification. I feel some energy ebbing. The conversation feels self-congratulatory and more than a little inauthentic. Ted, the CEO, pipes up: 'We have not made our sales targets in most of our markets, it has to be said.' 'Well, that's true, but we're on the right track, and the customers are really pleased' – Nigel, again, seems to be trying to get back to the 'good place'.

I feel suddenly moved to speak about this: 'It's not your job to please customers.' I have surprised myself with this. Puzzled looks from the rest of the group. I continue: 'No, it's not – you're not Santa Claus.' I get the 'what is he on about?' looks. 'Your job is to meet certain of their needs at a profit to you. Are you doing this? I don't hear much talk of profitability or value creation.' The silence that followed reminded me of an old western movie where the stranger says something in the saloon, and the piano and all conversation stops. It felt like a crucial moment. Where will this go now?

Kevin broke the silence, saying quietly, 'He's right, that's part of our problem.' The mood had shifted. 'What do you mean, Kevin?' queries Tomás. 'Well, just that we're not guided by profitability, as if that was Ted or Neville's [the Chief Financial Officer] concern.'

The conversation continues in this readjustment to how to think about success. The pattern of conversation is now organized by a different theme. I have contributed to this shift by my interjection, which was in response to the theme organizing the conversation up to that point. I did not know when, or if, this point would arise; I was responding in the moment to something that struck me. My response was dependent on my own history, which was part of my knowing, and so part of my skill. A novel form of thought had arisen from the conversation to assist the move into the future.

Shotter (1996) asserts that it is in such 'relational–responsive' interaction that novelty can arise:

> the new ideas, or thoughts, or images, that we think of as coming
> to guide our ways of acting in the world do not just spring into our
> heads 'out of the blue'; they originate in differences (in relations)
> which have a sensed connection: whose origins are to be found in our
> spontaneous, unnoticed, responsive or dialogic reactions and relations
> to our surroundings.
>
> (Ibid.)

What is significant in Shotter's view is that the very thing which mainstream thinking, in its drive to homogenize, disparages or ignores is what gives rise to novelty, that is, *difference*. My understanding of Shotter is that it is not just the existence of differences which give rise to new thought, but the disposition of the interlocutors (or, at least, one of them), and their readiness and capacity to engage 'live' in the constantly changing landscape of meaning, a 'dialogical way of being'. Part of my unique contribution as a teacher seeking to make a difference is in my 'way of being' as a member of the group. I had a different way of looking at the situation facing SSL; something in the conversation grated with me outside my awareness and this eventually 'surfaced' as an impulse, a spontaneous act. Certainly, this act derived from my practice, but why might this have any greater validity than, say, an act which is determined from the start without any reference to what is going on in the conversation?

Part of the answer to this question is that there is so much 'going on' in daily life that we can pay attention to only part of it, but which part and why? Shotter says:

> When it comes to trying to grasp the relation between our behavior
> and its surroundings, to suggest that we behave as we do because of
> certain hypothetical mechanisms within us, is to ignore the part played
> by just those aspects of our behavior in which we relate ourselves
> to our circumstances spontaneously. Whereas: if we are to develop
> new liveable forms of life, new ways of relating ourselves to our
> surroundings, it is precisely amongst those spontaneous aspects of
> our activities, where we are already acting successfully, in practice,
> that we can find the new possibilities we require. It is only within the
> flow of our practices that we can say or do anything that can make a
> difference to them; we must work outwards from within them. Indeed,
> as Wittgenstein puts it, 'we talk, we utter words, and only *later* get a

picture of their life' (1953, p. 209); thus, you must 'let the use of words teach you their meaning' (1953, p. 220).

(Shotter, 1996, p. 225)

My spontaneous comment has come from within the flow of my practice. My history of relating and acting is now at work in the room with SSL, as are theirs, and we are producing novel thought to move into the unknown.

The capacity to direct attention

We spent a considerable amount of time exploring the practical implications of a new-found view of strategy. For some, old certainties had disappeared. SSL appeared to be facing bigger questions than many had expected to be dealing with. We spent the bulk of the second day working the issues, delving into appropriate theory to gain clarity or insight and looking at the immediate implications for each one in the room. On day three, I rejoined the group after lunch. Simon (a colleague) had spent the morning working on questions raised by the Myers-Briggs Type Indicator concerning implications for individual behaviours and awareness. I felt a need to reconnect with them so that we could work, to renew our working alliance. On re-entering the room I felt quite distanced from the group.

I asked them straight out how they were feeling. Kevin was feeling uneasy, and others concurred; Tomás felt filled up. I asked what their impulse was: What do you feel like doing right now? Nigel said he wanted to hide; others said they wanted to run away; some said they wanted to do *something*. I then asked them to go away for a few moments alone to write their answers to these questions: What am I learning about myself as a leader? What do I need to do differently to be effective? What am I learning about this group? What do we need to do differently?

On their return Tomás said he felt they were on the edge. Kieran, the new HR director, talked about mutual accountability and recounted an old story about 'your end of the boat seems to be sinking'. Harry talked about lack of openness affecting business performance and how he felt some weight come off his shoulders. Kevin said he did not want to go back to the feelings of isolation. We discussed the relevance of all this for the performance and growth of the business. Brian said he was aware that he was not doing 80 per cent of the job of leadership – communication.

Terence, who had said little up until this point, said he was getting a different view of leadership. Tim, the new head of the US operation, said that if we were looking for the future of the firm, 'don't look outside this room – talk to yourself first'. Tomás offered the view that leadership involves developing other leaders, not just followers. Kevin joined this comment, saying that they had to give everybody the opportunity to be a leader. Nigel said he had been given the space to work and to grow – he wanted to invite others to 'the edge'.

This conversation felt qualitatively different to me from those earlier in the week. It was more optimistic, self-reliant and future-focused than I had experienced. I felt that in the latter conversation the group were exploring their own power.

Mead's theory of symbolic interaction is an important basis of the theory under exploration here. From a perspective of complex responsive processes, communicative interaction, which includes conversation, is a process in which gestures by the leader will call forth, evoke or provoke, responses from other participants in the interaction. These responses are paradoxically evoked by the gesture and simultaneously selected by the responder. This selection depends on the history of the responder. These responses in turn constitute gestures, and what is emerging in the process of interaction is the thematic patterning of that interaction. More skilled participants in the interaction will be adept at noticing what is emerging between them and more skilled and/or powerful participants will have a greater capacity to draw attention to emergent patterning. Hence, more skilful or powerful participants will be able to exert more influence on the other participants, and thereby on the emergent thematic patterning.

Mead speaks of the capacity to direct attention:

> Man is distinguished by that power of analysis of the field of stimulation which enables him to pick out one stimulus rather than another and so to hold on to the response that belongs to that stimulus, picking it out from others, and recombining it with others. . . . Man can combine not only the responses already there, which is the thing an animal lower than man can do, but the human individual can get into his activities and break them up, giving *attention* to combining them to build up another act. *That is what we mean by learning or by teaching a person to do a thing.* You indicate to him certain specific phases or characters of the object which call out certain sorts of responses.
>
> (Mead, 1934, p. 94, emphasis added)

Mead's description of teaching speaks directly to my practice; I am working with meaning which arises from my gestures and their associated responses in the group, and vice versa. I notice the responses of the group and point to aspects of them, and this forms another gesture to which members of the group respond: 'One can say to a person "Look at this, just see this thing" and he can fasten his attention on the specific object. He can direct attention and so isolate the particular response that answers to it. That is the way in which we break up our complex activities and thereby make learning possible' (ibid.). I cannot say what will be significant for anyone in the group, but I can point, using a question or an observation.

Earlier in the week I had introduced the concept of value creation as a measure of strategic effectiveness. Neville, the Chief Financial Officer, was unfamiliar with the concept. This is one of the crucial measures which outside investors would examine; basically, they would want their investment to grow. I had stayed with this theme continually since Monday, often referring to Neville in a complimentary way, while obliquely implying that he had to get on top of this concept and its implications for the firm. Now I had added more demands to the group – the supposed demands of the investors. I asked Neville straight out how the revenue and cost curves of the firm were doing.

To my shock he said that costs were rising faster than revenues and that at current trends they would meet in a few years. Ted had told me nothing of this. This is not an uncommon situation in firms, especially manufacturing firms. All firms are constantly engaged in attempts to widen the revenue/cost gap. The second shock was to observe the impassive response of the group to his words. I asked the group: 'Do you know what he has just said?' There was little response. 'You are going out of business.' There were some questions about details and some about increased sales. I said: 'I wonder if you heard that – you are going out of business.' There was silence. I went on to elaborate why what we were doing was crucial to the firm's future. The group felt a little traumatized; I worried that I may have pushed them too far, but slowly a discussion got underway in which the future of the firm was discussed with a seriousness which I had not seen earlier. I noticed that many of the ideas which had been introduced were being used in the debate. For me there was a sense in which understanding had shifted.

As discussed above, one of the acts of leadership is drawing attention to what may be significant so that new sense may be made of a situation.

Indeed, Mead appears to assert the superiority of the psychology of attention over the psychology of association. In this case in SSL, the tools of analysis were being put to work in a new appreciation of the situation facing the company. Mead taught that meaning is jointly constructed in human interaction in the totality of gesture–response. But responses do not arise entirely anew: history, memory, and, therefore, previous learning, play a role. 'It was not until the psychologist took up the analysis of attention that he was able to deal with such situations, and to realize that voluntary attention is dependent upon indication of some character in the field of stimulation. Such indication makes possible the isolation and recombination of responses' (ibid.). Put simply, he is more convinced by a theoretical explanation which deals with human relatedness than one characterized by introspection. For me this suggests an emphasis in my practice which should understand learning to derive from the *act* of interaction: 'intelligence and knowledge are inside the process of conduct' (ibid., endnotes to section 13).

Several interesting points follow from this for me as a teacher. If meaning is jointly constructed then it follows that I, as one member of the group, cannot simply *choose* what meaning arises from our interaction, although I am free to have intention about it. In systemic theories of organizational learning, the implicit theory of learning is that the meaning of interaction may be chosen (by the teacher), in the same way as it is implied that organizational futures may be chosen (by the manager). Just as a manager has to let go of the idea of control of the organization as an ideology of management, so a teacher has to let go of the idea of the control of meaning as an ideology of learning. The teacher cannot then be a 'manager of meaning', deciding what something means from outside of an interaction of which I am part. This is not to say that the teacher has no influence in the process of meaning-making, just that it is not what systems ideology would imply. As part of the continuing process of gesture–response, the teacher can skilfully notice responses within herself and others to what is going on in the group and gesture towards those which appear most fruitful to pay attention to; this will evoke/provoke responses in others present, potentially transforming the emerging thematic patterning. The teacher, therefore, has the potential to influence the emergence of novel thought as a participant in communicative interaction in the continuing process of gesture–response, paying attention to the constantly emerging patterns of meaning.

It also follows that learning involves the continual production of new meaning. Why is this? For example, if I contribute an idea exactly in a

way that I have done many times before, not only is this new to the
student, but in making meaning of it she is responding from her
own history of relating; the meaning is potentially new to both of us.
The response of the student constitutes a new gesture to which I will
respond, again potentially making new meaning.

Learning about change

From this point on, the workshop group focused almost totally on the
business issues facing the firm. At the beginning of the week, Ted had
mentioned to the group that he and Steve, the Chairman, were in contact
with some sources of venture capital with a view to recapitalizing the
firm to assist its growth. I reminded them of this and offered my opinion
that if the firm was going to go this route the game would change
immeasurably. To explain this point, I offered a view that up until now
the firm had measured its success in largely historical terms, using a
mixture of narrow accounting measures and impressionistic views
of success. The essential difference with the involvement of venture
capitalists would be that the firm would have to appear a good investment
in the future; that is, it would have to be able to demonstrate a plausible
likelihood of a continuing profit stream into the medium-term future.
The measures of performance would focus on the likelihood of success
in the future, rather than success achieved in the past. To use the jargon,
they would use 'leading indicators' in addition to 'lagging indicators'.
These leading indicators would include: market acceptance of current
offering; achievement against milestones in current business plan;
progress in technical development; establishment of key relationships
with customers, industry groups and other elements of the industry value
chain; and the continuous building of talent. I then formed project groups
to develop proposals to strengthen the firm's performance in each of these
areas. They were to present their views on the issue as it related to SSL
and their suggestion for the first practical steps to concrete activity.

There was considerable discussion about the relevance of these topics and
their importance to the future of the firm. The introduction of the likely
demands of the venture capitalists seemed to both threaten and energize
the group. My own view was that the firm was not remotely ready to take
on the demands of venture capital partners; it did not have a clear enough
sense of its proposition to the market, the product/service was not clearly
enough established as a radically different offering, and the standard of

management was not sufficiently sophisticated to cope with the level of complexity they were taking on. This view had been forming since Monday morning and continued to grow stronger. Why, therefore, had I introduced the spectre of the demands of venture capitalists at this time? Since Monday I had worked through most of the standard issues in strategy: value creation, customer value proposition, competitive advantage and its sources, competitive strategies, strategic organizational capabilities and so on. The group had taken up these concepts with various levels of skill and interest. We had worked through many issues concerned with leadership.

In introducing the question of the demands of possible venture capitalists, I was, I believe, attempting to supplant the role of the Scullys as the arbiters of performance, with a harsher and, in my view, more realistic set of demands. I wanted to deny them the comfort of unthinking reassurance that things would be OK, if only they could please me. There had to be only one way out, and that was to work through the strategic issues. The fantasy venture capitalists had to become proxies for the wider capital and customer markets.

On knowledge

For Elias, knowledge arises in the interaction of individuals in a 'figuration', a web of interdependent individuals; it is a social phenomenon. More importantly, knowledge is not seen as having a separate existence; it is an aspect, along with thought and speech, of the same entity, which he calls 'symbol'. The important aspect of his 'symbol theory' for this chapter is the view that knowledge is 'mistakenly broken down into three mutually exclusive functions: there is knowledge (the thing itself), how it is stored (thoughts) and how it is communicated (language)' (Dalal, 1998, p. 96). Thoughts are already contained in language, and are structured by it. Moreover, our psyches are structured by language. The significance of this for the enquiry of this chapter is how language may constrain and enable the development of new knowledge; that is, learning. However, a changed use of language is not simply the use of a different tool; it is a change in thought and in psyche, because they are different aspects of the same thing: 'This basic similarity, perhaps *identity* is . . . at the root of the possibility to convert speech into thought and thought into speech' (Elias, 1991, p. 81, quoted in Dalal, 1998, p. 99). Stacey takes up the theme of identity in the theory of complex responsive processes, saying that 'conversational processes, having transformational potential, by their very nature threaten the continuity of identity' (Stacey, 2001, p. 182). This is because Stacey asserts that identity is, in effect, the characteristic patterning of the knowing of an individual.

Recall also the earlier definition of strategy as concerning the identity of an organization; that is, its characteristic patterning of knowing. In relation to my practice, I take this to mean significant learning (that is, changes in thought processes) may be experienced as significant challenges to identity. My identity had changed over the week as I participated in the changing thinking of the group. I had experienced my self at times as having different levels of competence, as harsh and gentle, intransigent and accommodating.

Elias' principal contribution is in his fundamental re-examination of the nature of knowing, and especially of the assumptions which underlie classical epistemology; that is, the notion of a knowing subject which stands opposed to the world of knowable objects, from which it is separated by a broad divide. The problem was how the subject was to gain 'certain knowledge of objects across this divide' (Elias, 1998, p. 281). His idea that issues of concern in social interaction, like knowledge, are part of a continuous process and do not have a separate existence, places my work in a different conceptual context. As knowledge is, for him, a social phenomenon arising through interaction, this is a much closer description of what I am part of, as opposed to seeing me as someone attempting to 'hand over' knowledge *despite* the 'messy' social context. My practice is intensely interactive and Elias is saying that this is precisely how knowledge (or more accurately, *knowing*) arises. My understanding of my practice is not the transmission of static reified knowledge to individual contained minds; it is the participation in a continuous and active process of knowledge creation. This more accurately describes my practice, and the management practice of my students; that is, it more closely describes lived experience.

On power

As the mood of the group has changed with the growing realization of the seriousness of SSL's situation, Ted's demeanour has also changed, as has his relationship with the group. He has begun to sound more like the CEO than just another member of the group. Some members of the group talk as if the information had been withheld, some acknowledge that they had not really been paying attention to SSL's trading position. The discussion begins to turn to the future and what the group have to do as a result of their meeting. The theme organizing the conversation is to do with survival. The atmosphere is becoming a little more edgy. There is a perceptible deference to Ted and his senior managers. The play of power is now more visible. The principal argument in this chapter is that effective leaders are those who are the more skilful participants in the process of communicative interaction. However, in addition to skill, I also argue that the more powerful will exert more influence on the other participants, and hence on the emergent thematic patterning of the interaction in which they are engaged. Learning about leadership requires learning about power, especially about its influence on knowledge.

Knowledge and the apparent truth it expresses are the outcomes of social processes and reflect another of Elias' great interests in human interaction – power. Elias says that *all* relationships are power relationships where there is interdependence. This aspect of the relationship exercises a kind of constraint on both parties, which, while limiting the relationship in some ways, may also enable it. For example, with my students, I serve a function for them which constrains their freedom of action, but also enables them to engage in a learning process. Simultaneously, they constrain my range of actions, but enable me to discharge my responsibilities, to earn a living, and to learn from them. Elias also points to the relationship between knowledge and power, saying that what is known or not known will also reflect the interests of the power structures of the time; that is, their ideologies, and make it seem natural that it should be so.

Conclusion

The learning process which I have attempted to describe in this chapter develops the capacity of others to engage in meaning-making, attentive, live conversation by doing it. It is characterized by 'giving prominence to distinctions which our ordinary forms of language easily make us overlook' (Shotter, 1996, p. 215). However, Shotter also points out that this must be done in the context of our daily flow of life, 'for only in the stream of thought and life do words have meaning' (ibid.). My practice is intensely involved with the actual lived experience of my students, and I seek to notice with them the very things that do not make sense, which cause anxiety or which may lead them into theoretical ways of classifying their experience without really attempting to 'enter it' or understand it. Moreover, I seek to remain in the paradoxical experience without trying to supply a one-sided idea which will settle the matter. This is, as Shotter calls it, 'joint action'. 'In joint action, the organizing centre, so to speak, of communicative activity is neither in the individual, nor in the linguistic system, but in the momentary *situation*, in the "interactive moment", within which communication is taking place' (ibid.). What is critical to the argument of this chapter: 'And what is especially important about this dialogical form of practical understanding, is that it is not an individual achievement' (ibid.).

Shotter, in his exploration of Wittgenstein essentially adduces a similar argument to Griffin (2002); that is, that what matters, what is real, is what is happening between us, and that this is not being controlled by (reified) external forces:

> as he sees it, it is the very insistence on the classical search for an already existing order hidden behind or beyond appearances, and our belief that we ought to *convince* others of the *truth* of our claims by systematic argument, that deflects of precludes us [from] coming to a grasp of what is utterly unique and novel *in* the moment by moment emergence of appearances (our voicings) as they unfold before our very eyes (or, better, in our ears).
>
> (Shotter, 1996, p. 227)

In the debate on organizations, the management lexicon is laden with concepts (such as 'strategy', 'culture' and 'intellectual capital') which act to propose an already existing hidden order. It is one of the greatest ironies for me as a management teacher to spend so much of my practice attempting to attract attention to managers' actual lived experience, and away from concepts which have come into common use through the efforts of earlier management teachers, and which have become a competing reality.

Stacey views organizations and individual minds not as 'things' with a fixed nature, but as processes which are characterized by unique patterns of interaction which are continually reproduced and simultaneously have the potential to change. Equally, knowledge is not a 'thing', but a pattern of interaction arising from communicative interaction between bodies in the 'living present'. Knowledge and knowing are patterns of coherence which are continually reproduced, and which have the potential to change or remain the same; that is, change or continuity.

How might this change my view of what I am engaged in? In engaging with SSL, I am not trying to change a 'thing' which is outside the room. SSL consists of the pattern of communicative interactions in the room, of which I am, albeit temporarily, a part. Therefore, if I wish to make a difference to this organization it will be as a result of my interaction with the people who are also part of the process. However, because I am only part of the process (however influential) I cannot *choose* the outcome. Equally, if knowledge is a pattern of communicative interaction I can only make a difference to knowledge, that is, to help people to know more or know differently by participating in the process that is knowing and knowledge creation. It also follows that if I am engaged in this process of knowing my own knowing will be changed simultaneously. I may say that I am teaching SSL, but they are also teaching me. There is a further dimension: it also follows that if knowledge is a process, then *what* I want the managers to know is the same as *how* I wish them to know; that is, the process *is* the learning. The one-week workshop is not the 'container' of knowledge – it is the knowledge. Insofar as I wish them to learn about organizations, leadership and strategy, these will be experienced as aspects of the process of continually reproduced coherence of interactive communication with the potential for change that is the organization.

References and further reading

Dalal, F. (1998) *Taking the Group Seriously*, London: Jessica Kingsley.

Elias, N. (1978) *What is Sociology?*, New York: Columbia University Press.

Elias, N. (1991) *The Symbol Theory*, London: Sage.

Elias, N. (1998) *Norbert Elias On Civilization, Power and Knowledge: Selected Writings*, ed. S. Mennel and J. Goudsblom, Chicago and London: The University of Chicago Press.

Elias, N. (2000) *The Civilizing Process*, Oxford: Blackwell.

Elias, N. and Scotson, J. (1994) *The Established and The Outsiders*, London: Sage.

Gergen, K. (2001) *Social Construction in Context*, London: Sage.

Gerstner, L. (2002) *Who Says Elephants Can't Dance?: Inside IBM's Historic Turnaround*, London: HarperCollins.

Goudsblom, J. and Mennell, S. (eds) (1998a) *Norbert Elias on Civilization, Power and Knowledge*, Chicago, IL: The University of Chicago Press.

Goudsblom, J. and Mennell, S. (eds) (1998b) *A Norbert Elias Reader*, Oxford: Blackwell.

Griffin, D. (2002) *The Emergence of Leadership: Linking self-organization and ethics*, London: Routledge.

Mead, G. H. (1934) *Mind, Self and Society from the Standpoint of a Social Behaviorist*, ed. C. W. Morris, Chicago, IL: The University of Chicago Press.

Mintzberg, H. (1994) *The Rise and Fall of Strategic Planning*, Harlow: Prentice-Hall.

Schein, E. H. (1988) *Process Consultation: Its Role in Organization Development*, New York: Addison Wesley.

Schein, E. H. (1993) 'How Can Organizations Learn Faster? The Challenge of Entering the Green Room', *Sloan Management Review*, winter, pp. 85–92.

Schein, E. H. (1995) *Organizational Culture and Leadership*, San Francisco, CA: Jossey-Bass.

Shaw, P. (1997) 'Intervening in the Shadow Systems of Organizations: Consulting from a Complexity Perspective', *Journal of Organizational Change Management*, Vol. 10, No. 3, pp. 235–250.

Shaw, P. (2002) *Changing Conversations in Organizations: A complexity approach to change*, London: Routledge.

Shotter, J. H. (1993) *Conversational Realities: Construction of Life Through Language*, London: Sage.

Shotter, J. H. (1996) 'Articulating a Practice from within the Practice Itself: Establishing Formative Dialogues by the use of a "Social Poetics"', *Concepts and Transformation*, Vol. 1, Nos 2/3, pp. 213–237.

Shotter, J. H. (1997) 'The Social Construction of Our "Inner" Lives', manuscript submitted to the *Journal of Constructivist Psychology*.

Shotter, J. (1999) 'Living Moments in Dialogical Exchanges', *Human Systems*, Vol. 9, pp. 81–93.

Stacey, R. D. (1992) *Managing the Unknowable: Strategic Boundaries Between Order and Chaos in Organizations*, San Francisco, CA: Jossey-Bass.

Stacey, R. D. (1995) 'The Science of Complexity: An Alternative Perspective for Strategic Change Processes', *Strategic Management Journal*, Vol. 16, pp. 477–495.

Stacey, R. (2001) *Complex Responsive Processes in Organizations: Learning and knowledge creation*, London: Routledge.

Stacey, R. D. (2003) *Strategic Management and Organizational Dynamics: The Challenge of Complexity*, London: Prentice-Hall.

Stacey, R.., Griffin, D. and Shaw, P. (2000) *Complexity and Management: Fad or radical challenge to systems thinking?*, London: Routledge.

Streatfield, P. (2001) *The Paradox of Control in Organizations*, London: Routledge.

Wittgenstein, L. (1953) *Philosophical Investigations*, Oxford: Blackwell.

Index

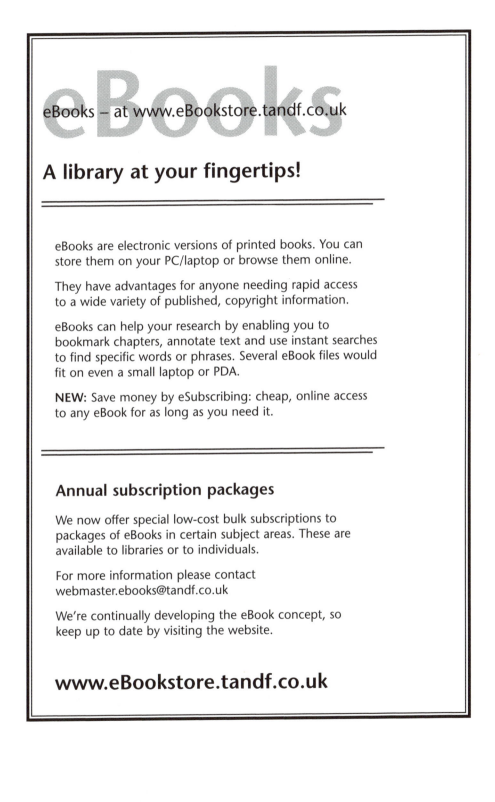